The Best of Frank Deford:

I'm Just Getting Started

Other Books by Frank Deford

FICTION
Love and Infamy
Casey on the Loose
The Spy in the Deuce Court
Everybody's All-American
The Owner
Cut 'n' Run

NONFICTION
The World's Tallest Midget
Alex: The Life of a Child
Big Bill Tilden
There She Is
Five Strides on the Banked Track

The Best of Frank Deford:

I'm Just Getting Started

TRIUMPH
B O O K S
CHICAGO

"Pas de Respect," "The Rabbit Hunter," "Hooked on Golf," "Frank Deford Goes Bowling," "Got to Do Some Coachin'," "B. D.," "Driven Crazy by Baseball Caps," "Kenny, Dying Young," "One of a Kind," "The Team Player: Bill Russell," "A Gentle Goliath," and "When There Were Still Elusive Barriers" were originally published in *Sports Illustrated*. "The Lost Generation," "Lessons From a Friend," "Why Cowboys Became Kings," "How We Lost Our Pastime," and "Coming of Age in America" were originally published in *Newsweek*. "Barkley's Last Shot" was originally published in *Vanity Fair*.

Library of Congress Cataloging-in-Publication Data
Deford, Frank
    The best of Frank Deford : I'm just getting started / by Frank Deford.
        p. cm.
    ISBN 1-57243-360-4
        1. Sports—United States. 2. Sports journalism—United States. 3. Radio broadcasting of sports—United States. I. Title.

GV704 .D44 2000
796—dc21   00-027190

This book is available in quantity at special discounts for your group or organization. For further information, contact:

Triumph Books
601 South LaSalle Street
Suite 500
Chicago, Illinois 60605
(312) 939-3330
Fax (312) 663-3557

Printed in the United States.

ISBN 1-57243-360-4

Book design by Patricia Frey.
Jacket design by Salvatore Concialdi.

Contents

Got to Do Some Coachin': Nolan Richardson

Commentaries

B. D.

Commentaries

Barkley's Last Shot

Commentaries

For Christian and Scarlet,
who have endured,
despite having a writer for a father

Introduction

I suppose that what sets this particular collection apart from other collectanea is that it is bimedia, and devotes about the same amount of space to selections of mine from magazine articles and radio commentaries. There is, however, a certain appropriateness to this mixture, because whereas most of us automatically lump the electronic media—radio and TV—together, I have found from experience that writing for radio is much more like writing for print than it is like writing for television.

In fact, while I started doing commentaries for National Public Radio in 1980—and I'm fast approaching my thousandth—even twenty years on, I still don't quite think of them as *audio*. Instead, to my mind, it's just me reading what I have written, rather than letting someone else read it themselves. And I think that this is the best of radio, still—the writing, incidentally read.

This is not to suggest, of course, that the voice doesn't matter. I have never forgotten what Howard Cosell told me once. Television, Howard said, was obviously the most powerful communications instrument ever invented, but radio offered, in its own one-dimensional way, an even greater potential concentration of authority. He expanded to explain: the person listening to someone on TV cannot help but be distracted some. Even if it is the President of the United States delivering a vital address, your eye may be drawn to the color of his tie. Is a hair out of place? No matter what, television is inescapably visual. Ah, but the radio message does not have to compete with the messenger. The voice alone can command us. In fact, most listeners just assume that everyone on the radio is of perfectly average dimension, one-size-fits-all. It shocks people who meet me to discover that my voice belongs to a body that is six-feet-four. "You don't talk that tall," someone once told me.

Cosell, by the way, generously and specifically cited Paul Harvey as possessing the most masterful radio manner, although he subtly suggested that he, Cosell, might be the runner-up—fair enough. Yet for however much we find ourselves in the thrall of a voice like Harvey's, still, the radio voice is fleeting. If you write something for the printed page, it stares up at the reader, unforgiving, and especially if the words offend you, it sears. On the other hand, no matter how the radio voice may momentarily concentrate the mind, having spoke, it moves on. I'm quite sure that I could say, "I've become a cannibal," and a listener would say to himself: "Did he really just say he's become a cannibal?"—but by then I'd be on to something or other about the NBA playoffs, and my cannibalism would quickly be forgotten. But, of course, we reread written words that matter to us on the printed page and let the smoke come out of our ears.

I find that people who write me letters about my articles address specific points. People who write me about my NPR commentaries deal with them collectively. Well, there is one notable exception. Should I err of pronunciation or grammar, I will hear about it. Oh boy, will I ever hear about it. NPR listeners have extraordinary powers of concentration when it comes to my mistakes. They are defenders of the faith—of the English language. It is very humbling.

I am very fortunate, too, that I've enjoyed the opportunity to speak about sports to such a broad and informed audience as the one that listens to me on *Morning Edition*. Sports is invariably segregated from everything else in the news. It's always been that way, going back to the sports pages that originated in the nineteenth century. Many countries even have whole daily newspapers devoted exclusively to sports, and sports is invariably a ghettoized segment of the local TV and radio news. (It has also somehow been decreed that sports and weather must be of absolute equal weight in our televised world.) Indeed, now that ESPN and other all-sports channels are becoming so popular, some local TV outlets are dropping the sports segment altogether from the news, further removing sports from the flow of the mainstream. Alas, even as much of a quality publication as is the *Sports Illustrated* for which I've written for twenty-nine years, even as much as it celebrates fine writing, even as bright as are many of its readers, I know that that audience is limited, almost exclusively, to sports fans.

But the challenge of NPR is that I know a great many people are listening to me who don't otherwise know much about sports. That's a bit frightening. I know, too, that many of these listeners are women, who are only lately come to sport. I have been advised, by a most distinguished female college president, that she listens to me naked, at her dawn toilette. The First Lady of the land, putative Yankee fan she, has informed me that she first stirs to the sound of my voice Wednesday mornings.

Oh, of course, I know that some listeners who don't care about sports take the opportunity to switch the dial or depart the room when the sports guy comes on. There remain out there plenty of the disciples of Mencken—he who once said: "I hate sports as rabidly as a person who likes sports hates common sense." But I suspect that most of the faithful hold fast to NPR, staying there to suffer me and sports for three minutes—perhaps even to learn a little something about a subject they're not altogether familiar with. That's not bad. Communications have become so fragmented nowadays; we settle so easily into our personal, safe little niches. C. P. Snow's famous dissertation on the sad separation of our two intellectual cultures would now be something like a disassembling of twenty-two cultures (or two hundred and two cultures?). I've often thought that newspapers ought to ape the NPR model and run a sports column once a week—*not* in the sports section, but on the Op-Ed page (perhaps rotating it with a music column, a movie column, a business column, and so forth). That way we each might be more inclined to try reading about subjects outside our comfortable little spheres of interest.

Writing for radio does require some accommodation—inflection, animation. It is not simply words on paper put to tongue (and accordingly I have occasionally made some slight changes in printing my commentaries here, where I have thought that what I originally wrote best for the ear didn't necessarily also best serve the eye). I am lucky, though, in that one of my assets as a writer is that, whereas I am tone deaf and can't carry a tune, I have always had a good ear for literary pace and rhythm. Years ago, one of the disc jockeys who so generously donates his time to read *Sports Illustrated* to the blind told me that my stories read better than the magazine's other writers. (Understand, they weren't necessarily better stories; they just were better for the telling.) So, I was fortunate in that I had some natural facility when I stumbled into radio.

Growing up, I was, in fact, in that vanguard of print journalists who were quite at home with radio and TV. Of course, some newspaper writers—Walter Cronkite and David Brinkley, most famously; Jim

McKay and Brent Musberger, in sports—made the full switch to the air. But I believe that mine was the first generation of writers to dabble in broadcast, keeping a foot in both camps. Especially in sports, when I first broke in in the '60s, the newspaper veterans tended to look down on broadcasters—if not, in fact, despise them.

It was not just a matter of competition either; jealousy was in the air, inasmuch as the glamorous "voices" tended to be better known and better paid than us shabby press box denizens. Then technology heightened the battle. Suddenly, radio reporters were ambulatory, with huge astronaut-like packs on their backs that allowed them to go where only fellows with pencils and pads had previously been able to venture. (Cosell was among the first in these brigades.)

I can still recall standing there open-mouthed in the Yankee locker room as Dick Young, the brilliant and combative columnist for the New York *Daily News*, unleashed a torrent of vulgarity into the microphone of some poor radio reporter, who was trying to record the answer of a Yankee player to a question that Young had asked. Young saw that the ground had shifted; now he was going to be scooped on radio by his own good reporting, for men with portable tape recorders could pirate the answers to *his* questions and play them over the air long before Young's paper hit the streets the next day. (Gamely, the Yankee player answered Young's question, even while Young babbled obscenities into the microphone—yet still managing to jot down the player's words. It was, for me, quite a lesson in journalistic concentration.)

But for younger writers like me, who had not only grown up with radio, but also with TV, there was no inbred antipathy toward the broadcast boys. It was all just reporting; it was all just part of the game. Anyway, I was more interested in writing long magazine feature pieces than I was in breaking hard news. Let radio and TV have the games. The culture of sport interested me more.

As for commentary, I was tremendously influenced by my exposure to the British style of sportswriting, which placed more emphasis on assessing—even, if you will, reviewing—a game or a situation, rather than trying to take you inside and give you the skinny. Especially given television's pervasive presence, wouldn't it be better to comment rather than illustrate? So, the American columnists who most appealed to me were Red Smith, the New York stylist; then Jim Murray and Scot Ostler in California and Tony Kornheiser in

Washington—all who chose to look at sport humorously—and most recently, Rick Reilly of *Sports Illustrated*, who can be marvelously original, and Harvey Araton of the *New York Times*, who has the British critic's eye to him. (Maybe it's the Anglophile in me, but the best sports commentator I've ever read is still Simon Barnes, the current lead sports columnist at *The Times* of London, who is by turns deliciously cynical and vividly insightful.)

But if television first changed the way print covered sport, and if the mobile radio reporters made it even more difficult for writers to do frontline reporting, another internal factor may have changed sportswriting even more. Younger writers find this hard to believe now, but when I came into the profession, sportswriters and their sweaty subjects were really quite congenial—often even good friends. (You'll get some sense of this, I think, if you read my piece on Bill Russell, which begins on page 251.)

Among other things, hardly any of us were making much money. Players enjoyed having a drink with me, not only for my incredibly charming good company, but because I could put our beery tête-à-tête on the expense account. But it's also true that we shared confidences and insecurities, met each other's wives and girlfriends, and generally carried on the most normal of friendships. Then too, in those quaint times, players needed to work in the off-season to make ends meet; getting what they called "ink"—especially "good ink"— might help make them more attractive job prospects. Besides—and maybe most important—back then, players actually read. They read newspapers every day, magazines often, and yes, some of them even read books. So they understood what writers were up to; they appreciated what we had to do, even if they didn't always enjoy what we wrote. The point was that they had us in context.

Now, though, players have too much money to suffer the working-class journalistic stiffs who also are in the employ of sport. Modern athletes are insulated by agents and sycophants. As for dealing with the greater world, they were raised on television, keep earphones or cell phones at their ears at all times, and have had little contact with the written word. A writer covering a sports team today may write effusively about a player for weeks on end without the player being aware of the coverage. Then, one critical article, and a hanger-on might point it out—"did you see what that blankety-blank wrote about you?"—and the athlete has a fit.

Yes, of course, some modern athletes are terrific guys. Some are exceptionally bright. Some of them make an effort to understand what journalists are trying to do. Some (see the Charles Barkley piece, beginning on page 185) simply are social animals; they can't help themselves from slumming with just about anybody, even writers. And yes, even in the halcyon days of yore, there were always crabby athletes who behaved rudely with the press. "He learned to say hello, when it was time to say good-bye," the New York writer Frank Graham once observed wryly about one crosspatch, who suddenly grew agreeable as his career neared its end and he decided he could use some good ink.

Notwithstanding, the ambiance is not nearly so pleasant as it used to be—and this inhibits discourse and makes sportswriting more difficult. I so enjoyed getting to really know athletes, to deal with them as people, to try to figure out what made them tick. It's so hard to get cozy anymore, though; indeed, the locker room can even be flat-out adversarial. I'm not so sure that if I'd come into the profession later on I would've stayed in it. Sportswriting, like every other part of journalism now, is too much about celebrity and not enough about humanity.

Still, writing about sports remains more honorable and more full of talent than most critics would accord it. I think that what the late Bartlett Giamatti—a curious hybrid: academician and sports executive—once wrote, still obtains. Giamatti concluded:

> There are more good writers in the sports section—or more good writing—than in the same proportion in any other section. I believe more beat writers on given sports write well than general assignment reporters write well, and the sports writers have tighter deadlines. More sports columnists write well—logically, clearly, analytically, strongly—than the aggregated national and local columnists elsewhere in the paper write well. There is more sheer talent for writing English well on the sports pages than anywhere in the newspaper.

I'm very blessed that I've had the opportunity to express myself with regard to sports in such varied venues as writing for an intelligent magazine that is strictly about sport and speaking on an intelligent radio program that is about everything. I have two quite distinct audiences and I know, from meeting people and from my correspondence, that the twain doesn't often meet. This collection is, then, something of an opportunity—for the people who read me in *Sports Illustrated* to hear a different voice of mine, and for the people who hear me spouting off opinions on NPR to read me as a writer of stories.

—F.D.
Westport, Connecticut
January 6, 2000

Sports Centered

■   ■   ■

I am informed by the *American Journalism Review* that a survey of almost three hundred broadcast students at three major journalism schools reveals that better than half the males want to go into sports. In particular, among the young American men who aspire to actually be on the air, more than twice as many would rather cover games instead of news.

I suppose I should be delighted at this revelation. After all, as someone who's been a sports journalist for most of my working life, these figures would seem to be affirming of my vocation. But still, proud though I may be of my profession, it never occurred to me that it was meant to be a working *majority*. That more than half of young men in TV would want to cover sports has the same ring to it as if we learned that more than half the males in medical school wanted to concentrate on cosmetic surgery.

The contrary news, by the way, is that only eight percent of the aspiring *female* broadcasters want to go into sports—which also means, by process of elimination, that soon most all the anchors and reporters on television will be women.

More important, this is just another example of the sportification of our society. It indicates how so many more young people—young males—are determined to go into sports, even if they can't *play* sports. For instance, one of the most popular new majors on campus is sports management, wherein you study to be a general manager. Oh my, the nerds are invading sports, too.

But then, it's difficult not to also conclude that as women infiltrate into positions of authority in almost all professions, at least a certain number of frightened and insecure men will turn to sports business as the last mostly-male power refuge.

Another evidence of sportification is that more and more old, terribly rich men seek to cap off their careers by buying sports teams. It's the best way to let people know you're really rich, to buy a team. And for the merely very rich, luxury boxes have become the yachts of the fin de siècle.

Yet still, it never fails to amaze moral custodians that most taxpayers are delighted to pay for stadiums or arenas and donate all sorts of additional financial goodies to the fabulously wealthy men who own the teams. Rationally, of course, it makes no sense that the poorer people in our society will pay for stadiums that benefit the richest people, and newspaper editorialists are always running to professors to absolutely prove how foolish the people are.

But, of course, the voters know very well that they are giving foolishly unto the wealthy owners. They continue to vote that way, though, because that's how the system works—if you want sports in your city. It's very much a medieval arrangement. Back then the serfs contributed crops to the lord of the castle, because he provided protection. Today, the taxpayers contribute to the sports owner, because he provides amusement. It's only a question of what's important in life.

Likewise, why would any American boy want to grow up, to stand in some dangerous war zone, uncomfortable and at risk, shouting news into a microphone over gunfire, when he could be seated comfortably behind home plate at Yankee Stadium or above the 18th green at the U.S. Open, safe and peaceful, telling the guys all about what really concerns them—the fun and games.

What Is a City Worth?

■   ■   ■

The question that is sooner or later asked in every city in the republic is: What does a new stadium cost?

That, of course, is easy to answer. Everybody will give you a construction estimate. Unfortunately, the question nobody does know the answer to is: What is a new stadium *worth*?

Like dueling psychologists at a murder trial, you can find totally opposite responses. For example, in Cincinnati a couple of weeks ago, voters passed a sales-tax resolution to pay for new twin baseball and football stadiums, after they were assured that keeping the Reds and Bengals would bring in a quarter of a billion dollars more to the metropolitan economy every year.

But, just as quickly, you can come up with experts who maintain that this is total hogwash, that stadiums and the teams in them supply only a few jobs to a handful of millionaire ballplayers, and that what money is spent at the game is simply being diverted from the mall or the movie theater. By this judgment, new stadiums are indefensible Taj Mahals, their justification all the more suspect since they are more luxurious all the time, with emphasis placed on paying for ornate, cloistered boxes for the wealthy.

Moreover, multipurpose stadiums are now considered déclassé. Like the Romans, with the Coliseum for the lions and the Christians and the Circus Maximus for chariot races, baseball and football both now demand their own custom amphitheaters. Cities without these gorgeous edifices can no longer compete—either to attract new teams or merely to hold onto their old ones. Arenas for basketball and hockey grow larger by the year, accommodating twenty thousand or more now. Otherwise, franchises depart for larger pastures.

And then, alas, you are no longer a Big. League. City. Oh, the shame of it.

So, it is easy to reject designer stadiums and gargantuan arenas as voluptuous choices that take away from the real urban needs of the poor and the sick and the uneducated.

But what do cities have anymore? What can they offer? How can they entice a retreating suburban mass back to visit? Among the other attractions, the theatre has been reduced to a predictable rota of musical comedies, and the age of classical music fans appears to correlate to the AARP mailing list.

However extravagant stadiums and arenas may be to construct, they do bring anew young life to the cities. And they bring different people together, to congregate—to commune—in a public place . . . no less than what cathedrals used to do in another time.

It may be painful to accept that mere games can mean this much to us. It may be agonizing to understand that the greatest direct beneficiaries of these publicly-funded buildings are the modern robber barons—men named Irsay and Modell and Steinbrenner. But that is simply the price we must pay. How else do we celebrate the city in our society if we don't have cathedrals to share? Where else are we going to come together again?

Ultimately, we must remember not to just ask: What is a stadium worth? But: What is a city worth?

The Bard Goes to the Super Bowl

■   ■   ■

William Shakespeare is enjoying another major revival, and so I think it is time that The Bard go to the Super Bowl. Thus, the curtain opens on Shakespeare's *Super Sabbath, part 31*, with the two star quarterbacks, Bret Favre of the Packers and Drew Bledsoe of the Patriots, encountering each other in the New Orleans French Quarter shortly before the big game.

act 1

FAVRE:	Hail, young Bledsoe. What serendipity joins us quarterbacks Here within the Quarter upon the quarter of the hour?
BLEDSOE:	Beware, noble Favre, for soon enough, by Patriot authority, 'Twill be your Green Bay team that will be drawn and quarter-ed.
FAVRE:	Forsooth, Bledsoe, for the quarterback you may be, You speak with but half a wit and full all of nothing.
BLEDSOE:	Oh, mark me, good Favre, for though have they called you Most Valuable of Players for your autumn grandeur 'Tis winter now, and this January encounter, will send you Out upon your shield, and *me* aloft to Disneyworld.

EXEUNT the two quarterbacks.

act 2, scene 1

ENTER LORD RUPERT OF FOX, who delivers a woeful soliloquy:

LORD
RUPERT: How dismal is this television world,
     That I should come from distant isle,
     To empty all my pretty purse for rights
     To this grossly spangled grid spectacular,
     Yet find upon my field of schemes *no* America's team
     To prance its star-blue rogues before a breathless fandom
     (Nor e'en San Fran's heroes, measuring up two score and nine)
     But, instead, a coupled unknown elevens:
     The underdog, hailing from the Athens of America, so call-ed,
     It's better rival from a frozen crossroads, where, perchance,
     More cheese resides than do viewers for Fox news.
        (Despairing:)
     Oh, what sparse ratings means this ghastly pairing?
     Cowboys, Cowboys! Wherefore art thou, Cowboys?
     But, soft ye now, here comes the rugged Parsells.

EXIT

scene 2

ENTER BILL PARSELLS, THE PATRIOTS COACH.

PARSELLS: Once I brought true Giants to this titled greensward,
     But now, all my pigskin genius must be applied
     Am I to obtain vict'ry for my current yeomen.
     Alas, these Patriots are known, e'en 'mongst friends
     As Patsies!
     Patsies!!

ENTER BLEDSOE AND MANY OTHER PATRIOTS, running cross the stage, exulting.

PARSELLS sees them and raises his arms in hope.

PARSELLS: But hear me from without the sideline stripe:
     With the royal arm of daring Bledsoe, I will make
     The Pack the patsies and my own Patriots super men!

BUT SUDDENLY, there is a forbidding voice, and then a ghost appears before PARSELLS.

GHOST: Beware, rank Parsells.

PARSELLS: Hark! What spectacled spectre appears before me?
               This glinting, gap-toothed apparition
               Who speaks my name with Jersey brogue?

GHOST: You sniveling weak sister, who are you
               But one more doleful denizen of the AFC
               Daring to proclaim an eminence above my Packers?

PARSELLS falls to his knees, crying out.

PARSELLS: Oh, I am lost, a trembling pigskin pretender
               For e'en should I presume to lead yon heroes
               'Gainst the mortal foes who wear the gold and green,
               What chance have we when 'tis a spirit rises
               And that wraith reveal-ed is the sainted Lombardi?

GHOST: Do not mess with my Packers, Parselllllls . . .

act 3

ENTER, FROM ALL SIDES, ALL MANNER OF SUPER BOWL REGULARS—
gamblers and corporate types, scribes (and Pharisees), and two announcers, the ebullient MADDEN and the pithy SUMMERALL.

MADDEN: Good Summerall, now winter's best day approaches, and
               Together we must take to our perch high within the dome
               To give there meaning to those who but
               Cast their mere eyes 'pon the scrimmage scene.

SUMMERALL: Aye, wise John.

MADDEN: So, only give me your accustomed silence,
               Though, betimes, your occasional sweet acclaim
               For my dear profundity—both for how I speaketh in color
               And how I draw the reveal-ed wisdom upon the replay.

SUMMERALL: Aye, sage of the booth.

MADDEN: Now, friend play-by-play, pray let us assume our vantage,
               There above the hash-ed marks, to tell to all, all we know.

SUMMERALL: Well said, cheerful voice.

MADDEN: Our only fear: the game, as usual, from bad to worse'll
               Leave Fox's audience caring but for more commercials.

EXUENT ALL.

Pas de Respect

■　　■　　■

People are always bitching about being stereotyped because of their heritage. But let me tell you: Just wait till you're *not* stereotyped. Then you'll be sorry. Then nobody grants you quaint genetic characteristics that allow you to get away with stuff. Nobody says "Well, no wonder he acts that way. Hey, it's O.K. because he's a _____." No. If you're not stereotyped, then you're just stupid all by yourself, laughed at strictly on your own hook.

How well I know this. Because, unlike most Americans, I've been deprived. Like Peter Pan without his shadow, I have no visible heritage, no direct connection to the land of my forefathers. Instead, I've had to slog through life simply as American. No hyphen before that. No qualifying I.D.

The World Cup made me think about this. You see, I am from a forgotten tribe. Not lost, you understand. That's romantic: lost. My tribe is simply forgotten. I am a Huguenot. A French Huguenot. Who remembers us? But hey, we remember the Incas, and who has even *seen* an Inca? As Tom Brokaw, a lapsed Huguenot, once declared when he attended another ethnic celebration, "There are very few songs that start, 'When Huguenot eyes are smiling.' "

At one time we Huguenots were among the noblest of all immigrants, among the first to come to the colonies in search of religious freedom. Paul Revere was a Huguenot. But as time went on, we were assimilated. My original family name was Dufour, which is so lovely and ethnic, but some damn ancestor anglicized it to bland old Deford. And there's no Huguenot homeland to vacation in. No Huguenot newspapers, no Huguenot food, no Huguenot expressions. Not even any Huguenot jokes. No "There was this atheist, this Jew, and this Huguenot, and . . . "

Hardly anybody can even *spell* Huguenot, and the British pronounce it HYU-ghe-no, as opposed to the way we say it (HYU-ghe-naht). How can you stereotype a people you can't even pronounce? Besides, what red-blooded American believes that Protestants could be discriminated against?

But, you see, we Huguenots were the minority in France, and it was the majority who gave us something of an option: Leave or get burned at the stake. But still: I am (was), French, and—Hallelujah!—here were my people (my bloods) in the World Cup final. At last I knew what it was to feel like an Irishman or an Italian or a Jew or a Puerto Rican! *Ich bin ein* minority!

Of course, there was a certain amount of angst, of conflict. After all, it was the forefathers of Les Bleus who wanted to burn my ancestors at the stake. Besides, nobody likes the French. All my life, because I cleverly, deceitfully pass as non-French, people have dissed the French right in front of me, unaware of my deep, wounded feelings. For everybody who's insecure, the French are fair game to kick around. And I have had to put up with this cruel slander. Of course, I don't much like the French either. But it's the principle of the thing. It's the only heritage I've got, even if they did want to burn me at the stake. Nobody's perfect.

Every now and then I have met another Huguenot—but it's not easy to tell. It doesn't say *Huguenot* on your driver's license. There are no Huguenot bars. But: Frank Perdue, the chicken man, revealed to me that he is a fellow Huguenot. So did Pete Rozelle, the late pro football commissioner. Then there's Brokaw—although he does not seem to have come out as a Huguenot.

Then . . . last week: France *trois*, Brazil *zéro*. At last, my country of origin had won the World Cup. Everybody was trilling, "Vive La France!" The nouveau fans were climbing on the Gallic bandwagon. Now, for the first time in my life, I could be one with my glorious heritage. I could stand on the rooftops and belt out *La Marseillaise*. I could be Dufour again. "Bonjour, mes amis!" I cried down at the Sunoco station.

Moreover, much was made of the French being so heterogeneous, so tolerant. It was Frenchmen of Algerian descent, Frenchmen from Guadeloupe who had won the Cup. The tricolor was, suddenly, a veritable Jesse Jacksonian rainbow.

Of course, for all the patriotic speeches in Paris, all the self-congratulation—nowhere any apologies to the Huguenots. Nowhere even a mention of Huguenots. No room in the rainbow. All my hopes for financial reparations or for being allowed to build a casino on the French land that used to belong to my family—dashed. After a lifetime of waiting to be taken back into the embrace of the land of my fathers, the World Cup had shown me that, alas, Huguenot eyes can never smile. I'll never be stereotyped like all those Americans with another past, an alternative persona. I'll never be a Dufour. I'm stuck as old Deford. Anglicized name, Americanized body. Forever.

Just Like Switzerland

■   ■   ■

We are now about to enter that strange quadrennial phase, when, all of a sudden, the United States of America, the world's only superpower, finds itself on the dark side of the moon . . . while the entire rest of the planet earth goes bonkers over the World Cup.

That's soccer, the bizarre sport you purposely play without the use of your hands—the very devices that raised humankind above lesser beasts. And you wonder why we're the world's only superpower.

Already, the mad disease is sweeping the globe. The usual riots in South America. In England, a poll of young men found that ninety-five percent of them would rather watch a World Cup game—even on television—than make love to "the woman of their dreams." And you thought they were nutty in Green Bay, Wisconsin.

And, as much as all the world points its toes for the Germans and the Brazilians, perennial powers on the soccer pitch, for now all the antipathy has been directed at the French, who are hosting the Cup this time around. Four years ago, in an unsuccessful effort to stir up interest in heathen America, the World Cup was played here, in our huge football stadiums, with minimum domestic interest. But now, in France, the stadiums are petite and the European ticket demand sky-high. When the French finally put some ducats on sale for the rest of the world, it quickly became impossible even to get through to the box office on the telephone.

In fact, it is approximately as difficult to buy a World Cup seat as it is to score a goal in a World Cup game—which, invariably, ends one–nil. Europe went apoplectic, growing even angrier at the French than under normal, everyday circumstances. In typical British tabloid understatement, the *Daily Star* declared: "A good kicking on their Gallic derriere is the only language the greedy frogs understand."

Isn't it wonderful? When the World Cup is on, nobody even thinks to complain about Americans.

You see, I think, in fact, that the best part of the Cup is that, for once, we in the United States are basically out of it. In everything else, we are up to our ears, out front—keeping the peace, threatening war, enforcing agreements, stuffing the UN, financing, pontificating, making movies, winning gold medals. But now, for once we can be just like Sweden or Switzerland. Oh, we do have a team in the World Cup, in a first-round group with Germany, Iran, and Yugoslavia. It sounds like a typical week with Sylvia Pajoli of National Public Radio, doesn't it? But the only people in the U.S. who care about soccer are those odd, disparate extremes of rich suburbanites and newly arrived immigrants. What a wonderful sitcom it would make—maybe it would even replace "Seinfeld"!—as the Junior League blonde just out of Wellesley falls for the uneducated young Caribbean immigrant—at a soccer game. It's the '90s version of *Abie's Irish Rose*.

In the meantime, though, soccer belongs to the rest of the world, and we are the only sane people around, using our hands and our minds together, as God intended, so that we might regain the world again as soon as the madness finally ends in France in July.

Words to Play By

■　　　■　　　■

Many baseball terms have moved into our everyday vernacular. Every Broadway producer wants to hit a home run. A foul ball is the rascal your daughter is in love with. A good salesman takes a lot of orders by throwing a change of pace. And everybody is now on guard in this world when they hear they're going to have to play some hardball.

But overlooked, I think—and much more interesting—is how baseball has taken words from the general lexicon and applied them altogether differently to the game.

For example: *deep* and/or *shallow*. Outfielders are deep when they play back, further from the plate, or shallow when they're closer. So far as I know, this is the only place in our usage in which *deep* and *shallow* are employed in a lateral sense. Everywhere else, *deep* and *shallow* refer to the vertical—as, for example, when a team has a deep pitching staff.

If a batter hits a long ball, he gives it a good ride. I wonder how that developed? Everywhere else, if you provide a ride, you take someone along with you. If baseball patois was like the rest of language, you should *send* a long ball on a trip, rather than give it a ride. In this regard, don't forget that a home run became "a round trip," but a double never is called a one-way trip.

But then, there is no logic to baseball argot.

Why is a slow pitch an off-speed pitch? A slow thoroughbred is not an off-speed runner. Rather, he is a bum, a stiff, or a muskrat. *Off* invariably has a definitive quality to it. The light is off or it is on. *Turn it down* or *turn it up* provide gradations, but on is on and off is off. You are on the bus or you are off. But only in baseball is *off* (and *on*) used in a qualitative sense. He took a little off that pitch. He put something on it.

One of my favorite baseball expressions is *range*—as a verb. A musician has great range. So does a company's product line. So, for that matter, does an outstanding jump shooter in basketball. But only shortstops regularly range deep into the whole. *Range*, as a baseball verb, is employed more than all the other ranges put together. Nobody ever said, for example, that Bill Clinton ranged more to the center. Why is that?

But my favorite baseball verb is *shade*. Damn, but that's beautiful. Wake me up in the middle of the night and tell me the outfield is shaded around to the right, and I can picture exactly what you mean. In fact, is it possible that a lot of this descriptive baseball vocabulary developed on the radio for fans who could not see the game? Or does it date back to antiquity? I can see Spalding or Hanlon or some other nineteenth century manager in my mind's eye now, coming out of the dugout and screaming to the outfielders to shade to the right.

I'm pretty sure a breaking pitch has always been around. Why? If I asked you to describe a curve in the road you would never say it breaks. Possibly *breaking pitch* comes from the ocean, where a curling wave breaks. And yet, we never say that a curve ball explodes, which is, of course, what so often happens when something breaks.

Only a fast ball explodes, even though a fast ball doesn't break.

A batter who hits a ball down the line—that is, a right-handed hitter who slugs the pitch to left field—is said to *pull* the ball. Why? When you pull something in the rest of the world, you bring it to you. Only in baseball do you step into something, swing away, and then have that result identified as a pull.

I also like it when a batter punches the ball the other way (which is a very accurate usage) and it is referred to as *fighting the pitch off*. The reason that fascinates me so is that fighting off is otherwise almost exclusively used in amorous terms. The heroine fights off the cad's advances.

To me, though, perhaps the most intriguing baseball term of all is *take*, as in he takes the pitch. Otherwise, *take* is a very aggressive word. Take a dollar. Take a chance. Take it or leave it. Take a hike. To take a pitch should mean to rip into it and give it a ride . . . excuse me, take it on a trip.

But in baseball, take means not to take.

Take that.

The Lost Generation

■　　■　　■

You're The Second-Best Golfer in the world. You're Faldo or Price or Els or Montgomerie or Lehman or Norman or . . .

Whoever.

Whatshisname.

You're The Second-Best Golfer in the world and you thought you had a really rich contract with Titleist or Callaway or somebody, but now it's chump change compared to what HE's got.

But then, you're The Second-Best Golfer in the world and nobody even cares anymore what ball you're playing.

Or what you're wearing.

Or what you're hitting with.

Or, for that matter: what your name is.

You're The Second-Best Golfer in the world, and when the guy next to you on the airplane finds out what you do for a living, he asks you if you know HIM.

And what's HE really like?

And what's Fluff, HIS caddie, really like?

You're The Second-Best Golfer in the world and when you arrive at the tournament, everybody tells you, isn't it wonderful because HE will actually play here this week.

You're The Second-Best Golfer in the world, and while you're certainly not as stupid as Fuzzy, you are human, you're one of the boys, and did-you-hear-the-one-about, and now, can you believe this, all of a sudden, because of HIM, *you're the minority?*

You're The Second-Best Golfer in the world, and you remember when you made your first thirty-six-hole cut at a tournament, won $640 for finishing tied for 24th place, went out and applied for an American Express card.

Now you've moved up to the Platinum card, but all of a sudden HE *is* the American Express card. And you can't even leave home without HIM.

You're The Second-Best Golfer in the world, and you hit it right on the button, perfect, right down the middle, 270 yards, and that leaves you only 60 yards short of HIM, because he kinda misplayed his drive.

But, anyway, you absolutely are The Second-Best Golfer in the world, and, after all, you're playing a game for mature, thinking men, where physical prowess is only part of the act, and you've miscalculated with the four-iron and put the approach short in the trap, whereas HE faded the eight-iron hole high, two feet straight in for the birdie.

You're The Second-Best Golfer in the world, and HE doesn't even know you're the guy paired with him today, but already you're thinking that maybe, just maybe, HE can't play a Scottish links course all that well the first time, in a few weeks, so there's at least one tournament all year I got an outside chance in.

If the wind really blows like a madman off the Firth of Forth.

And HE doesn't like the food.

You're The Second-Best Golfer in the world, and your agent keeps telling you that if you just put a little snap in your best Arnold Palmer anecdotes, you can maybe get a shot on Leno or Letterman, or, for sure, a pop on Tom Snyder . . . but HE's already done Oprah and Barbara Walters and turned down the president.

You're The Second-Best Golfer in the world, but away from a tournament city, you can't even get a good table at a steakhouse, because nobody knows you from the Culligan Man, but already HIS mother has a Q-rating higher than Téa Leoni or Craig T. Nelson and HIS father just sold his book to Miramax.

Starring Bill Cosby, no doubt. With Wilford Brimley as Fluff.

You're The Second-Best Golfer in the world and you finally got a deal to represent a resort in Florida with a certified PGA course and a mall. Already, though, HE's got a deal representing a whole country.

Thailand.

I forget: Is Asia just a tour or is it a whole continent, too?

You're The Second-Best Golfer in the world, so why are you already looking ahead to the senior tour on ESPN2?

You're The Second-Best Golfer in the world, and you've reached a point where maybe you win a couple more majors, and they mention you in the same breath as Snead or Nelson, but all of a sudden you realize nobody has even heard of Snead or Nelson anymore.

Also, for that matter, nobody has anymore ever heard of Jones or Hogan or Nicklaus.

You're The Second-Best Golfer in the world and nobody even stays still and quiet when you putt out, because they've got to run to get a good spot so they can shout "You The Man" louder than the other butt-kissing, putter-sniffing guys when HE tees off.

You're The Second-Best Golfer in the world, longtime par-busting star of the tour, and suddenly you realize there is no "tour." It is just HIS show.

But then, you're The Second-Best Golfer in the world, and suddenly you understand: there is no second-best golfer in the world.

And you're the second-best golfer in all the world of golf, and then you realize there is no golf anymore. It is just HIM, playing around.

It is just Tiger Woods.

Alone.

And this is the way it's going to be for another twenty years.

Mind if I play through?

What Ever Happened to Frank?

■   ■   ■

Sometimes things creep up on you, and all of a sudden you realize that everything's completely changed while you weren't paying attention. For example, one day, out of the blue, it just occurred to me that they weren't making any more Franks. For someone who was born with a Frank in the White House, and who has himself been a Frank all his life, this was, naturally, quite upsetting.

I first realized the sad truth when I saw a bunch of children's personalized balloons hung up alphabetically in a store. There were Michael balloons and Sean balloons and Kevin balloons, but no Frank balloons. The free market was telling me something. I checked my daughter's school roster. Not a Frank in the whole school. Not even a Francis.

My spirits were briefly revived when, in quick succession, first the New York *Daily News* and then the New York *Post* came out recently with entire front pages saying only: WIN ONE FOR FRANK and PRAYERS FOR FRANK. And not only that, but these were two different Franks.

One was Frank Torre, the brother of the Yankees manager, and the other was Frank Sinatra. On further thought, though, it occurred to me that these were both sick, old Franks, and so I was back in a funk again. It wasn't like some handsome young Frank made the front page for going out with Julia Roberts or staging a rock concert.

Frank used to be such a good, solid name. The mythic, quintessential early American sports figure was named Frank Merriwell. The author could have named him anything. He *chose* Frank. The first great slugger was Frank "Home Run" Baker. But now . . . ? Since Frank Robinson . . . ?

Anyway, like a good reporter, I checked it out. Where exactly did Frank stand? I tabulated the first names from the baseball, football, basketball, tennis, and golf Halls of Fame, and then threw in the heavyweight champions.

As it turns out, Frank is, overall, a very honored sports name. Frank tied for eighth place with Tom. (Dick and Harry, by the way, were far behind.) Frank and Tom were just ahead of Willie, Mike, Sam, Tony, Ernie, and Red, and just a smidgen behind Jack and George.

I was surprised that so many great athletes have been named George. I mean, no offense—the Father of Our Country and all that—but I just don't think of George and sport together.

As a name, too, George stands all by itself. For instance, I lumped the Tonys and Anthonys, the Richards and Dicks, the Franks and Frankies. So plain old-fashioned George was the shock of this extremely sophisticated survey, with a margin of error of plus-or-minus two touchdowns.

There were, however, no real surprises in the top five. Joe was fifth, Jim fourth, Bill third, John second, and—ta-daaa—Bob was first. So, there it is. Bob is the great American sports name. Now you know.

The curious thing to me was how many reasonably common names are only owned by a single Hall of Famer. There is only one Arnold, for example, one Reggie, one Rick, one Ron, one Alan. That quite put me off. Alan seems like such an All-American, sporty name. *Give the ball to Alan. Alan shoots and scores!* Doug, too. *Doug, Doug, he's our man. If Doug can't do it, no one can.* But: only one Doug. And one Terry, one Sid, one Bart, one Wayne, one Greg, one Lee, one Jake—only one Jake?—one Ken, and, can you believe this? Only one Chris. I would have thought there would have been lots and lots of fabulous Chrises. Almost everybody who calls me "Mister Deford" nowadays seems to be named Chris.

Also, just for the information of all of you people naming your boys Justin, Jason, Eric, Noah, and Adam, there has never been one single Hall of Famer with any of those stylish '90s names. In fact, there has *never* been a great Kevin or a great Sean. That made me feel better, to be frank with you.

The Rabbit Hunter: Bobby Knight

Success is feminine and like a woman; if you cringe before her, she will override you. So the way to treat her is to show her the back of your hand. Then maybe she will do the crawling.

—William Faulkner

I. Rabbits

As Bobby Knight is the first to say, a considerable part of his difficulty with the world at large is the simple matter of appearance. "What do we call it?" he wonders. "Countenance. A lot of my problem is just that too many people don't go beyond my countenances."

That's astute—Bobby Knight is an astute man—but it's not so much that his appearance is unappealing. No, like so much of him, his looks are merely at odds. Probably, for example, no matter how well you know Coach Knight, you have never been informed—much less noticed yourself—that he's dimpled. Well, he is, and invariably when anyone else has dimples, a great to-do is made about them. But, in Bobby's case, being dimpled just won't fly.

After all: DIMPLED COACH RAGES AGAIN. No. But then, symbolically, Knight doesn't possess dimples, plural, as one would expect. He has only the prize one, on his left side. Visualize him, standing in line, dressed like the New Year's Baby, when they were handing out dimples. He gets the one on his left side. "What the bleep is this?" says little Bobby, drawing away.

"Wait, wait!" cries the Good Fairy or the Angel Gabriel or whoever's in charge of distributing dimples. But it's too late. Bobby has no time for this extraneous crap with dimples. He's already way down the line, taking extras on bile.

"Countenances," Knight goes on, woefully. "I just don't have the personality that connotes humor. It kills me. I get castigated just for screaming at some official. And the other coach? Oh he's perfect, he's being deified, and I know he's one of the worst cheaters in the country. It's like I tell my players: your biggest opponent isn't the other guy. It's human nature."

Knight happens to be a substance guy in a style world. Hey, he could look very good in polyester and boots and one of those teardrop haircuts that anchormen and male stewardesses wear. Very good: he's tall, 6' 5", and dimpled (as we know) and handsome, and the gray hair and embryonic potbelly that have come to him as he crosses into his 41st winter are pleasant modifying effects.

In the early '60s, when Knight was a big-talking substitute on the famous Jerry Lucas teams at Ohio State, he was known as Dragon. Most people think it was in honor of his fire-snorting mien, with the bright and broken nose that wanders down his face and makes everything he says appear to have an exclamation mark. Only this was not so. He was called Dragon because when he came to Ohio State, he told everybody he was the leader of a motorcycle gang called the Dragons. This was pure fabrication, of course, but all the fresh-scrubbed crew cuts on the team lapped it up. It was easy. People have always been charmed by him; or conned; anyway, he gets in the last word.

It's never neat, of a piece. When Knight stands up, coaching, with his hands in his pockets, he looks like a street-corner guy. But with his tousled hair, the tie forever undone, there's also a childish aspect to his appearance:

Wear your tie, Bobby.

All right, Mom, I'll put it on, but I won't tie it tight.

The boy-coach who got his first major-college head-coaching job at 24 may be middle-aged now, but still, every day, in some way, adolescence must be conquered again. "Listen to me," Woody Hayes pleaded with him once. "Listen to me, Bobby, because I've made a lot of mistakes and you don't have to repeat mine."

The real issue isn't the countenance, anyway. The real issue is the rabbits. And Knight knows that. In the Indiana locker room before a game earlier this season, Knight was telling his players to concentrate on the important things. He said, "How many times I got to tell you? Don't fight the rabbits. Because, boys, if you fight the rabbits, the elephants are going to kill you." But the coach doesn't listen to himself. He's always chasing after the incidental; he's still a prodigy in search of proportion. "There are too many rabbits around," he says. "I know that. But it doesn't do me any good. Instead of fighting the elephants, I just keep going after the rabbits." And it's the rabbits that are doing him in, ruining such a good thing.

Pete Newell, the former Cal coach, a mentor: "There are times Bobby comes so close to self-destructing." Edwin Cady, a Duke University professor, after the Indiana Athletics Committee he chaired recommended Knight's hiring in 1971: "He's in a race now between overcoming immaturity and disaster." And even the warmest, most benign observers of the man offer variations on these themes.

Others are much more critical—especially since the sad events of July 1979 at the Pan American Games in Puerto Rico when Knight, the U.S. basketball coach, was arrested for aggravated assault on a police officer (and subsequently convicted *in absentia* and sentenced to six months in prison). "Bobby's so intelligent, but he has tunnel vision," says another Midwestern coach. "None of that stuff in Puerto Rico had to happen. On the contrary, he could've come out of there a hero. But he's a bully, always having to put people down. Someday, I'm afraid, he's going to be a sad old man." Says an Eastern coach, "He'll get away with the bullying and the vulgarity only so long as he wins. But the shame is, he's so smart, and he's so faithful to his principles, so why can't he understand that other people have principles too?"

Such criticism doesn't necessarily affect Knight in the ways and to the extent that most people imagine. In a sense, he enjoys being misunderstood, so no one can get a fix on him. It's like the effect Indiana's good defense has on the coaches of its opponents: "The average coach wants his team to score points," Knight says. "It's his character, his machismo, whatever you want to call it, that's at stake. So if I make a coach concerned enough about my defense stopping his offense, then he'll forget about *my* offense."

Though Knight may not give a hoot whether most people like him, it genuinely upsets him that anyone might think he's impulsive, much less berserk: "Hey, I'm not dumb and too many people look at our operation as if we're all dumb here," he says. "Only people really involved here know what the hell we're doing. See, I don't think people understand what I can or can't do. They're not cognizant of my situation and *what I know about myself.* I always know what I'm doing."

Yet as intelligent as Knight is about most things, as searching as his mind is, he's also encumbered by a curious parochialism that too often brings him to grief. When all is said and done, his difficulties in Puerto Rico resulted mostly from his inability to concede that San Juan isn't just another Chicago, or that the Pan Am Games aren't another Mideast Regional—and it's their own fault that they're not. Knight's mind is too good to be wasted on a mere game—and he probably recognizes that— but he's personally not comfortable away from the precisely circumscribed environment in which college basketball is played. Therein lies the great conflict in him.

Does anybody else in this universe of shifting sands still have the control of a coach? No wonder it's difficult for a person like Knight, who tends toward prepossession anyway, to be confused about the limits of his dominion. Puerto Rico, women, writers, shoe salesmen, NCAA bigwigs . . . all of them are just more Rubicons to cross. He's in command; an awful lot of what you see is a good act. Says Harold Andreas, the high school coach who first hired Bobby as an assistant, "He can be as charming as anybody in the world or he can be the biggest horse's ass in the world. But *he* makes that decision, and he does it in a split second." Everyone identifies Knight with bad language, but the fact is that he can talk for hours, if he chooses to, using much less profanity than the average Joe. He doesn't have a foul mouth; he simply deploys bad language when it can be a weapon.

Knight is forever putting people back on their heels, testing them, making them uncomfortable in some way. Stop them from scoring points, and they won't be prepared to stop you. Although it's fashionable to say Knight rules by intimidation, he actually rules more by derision. He abuses the people he comes into contact with, taking the license to treat them as he does his players.

"O.K., it's true sometimes I intimidate a kid," Knight says. "Usually when I first get him. That sets up the best conditions for teaching. But that's only true with basketball players, not with anyone else. I don't think I'm overbearing with people, but look, that's an awfully hard thing for a man to judge of himself."

Most find him guilty. But, here, you judge. Here's five minutes of typical Bobby Knight. This isn't extreme Bobby Knight. This isn't Puerto Rico Bobby Knight. This is just some everyday stuff, the way he keeps an edge, even over people he likes.

It's practice time, and two of Knight's acquaintances are sitting at the scorer's table. One is a black man, Joby Wright, who starred on Knight's first Hoosier team in 1971–72. Six years after his athletic eligibility ran out, Wright returned to Indiana to get his degree; now he's going for a master's in counseling and guidance. All along, Knight helped Wright and encouraged him with his academics, as he has many of his players. In Knight's nine years, only one Hoosier among those who have played out their eligibility has failed sooner or later to get a degree.

The other person at the table is a white woman, Maryalyce Jeremiah, the Indiana women's basketball coach. Now it's an accepted fact of life—disputed, perhaps, only by Nancy Knight, Bobby's wife—that Knight is a misogynist, but Jeremiah he at least abides. She's a coach, after all.

Knight advances on Wright, and says, "Hey, Joby. Do me a favor."

"Sure, Coach."

"I want you to get my car and go downtown." Wright nods, taken in. Knight slams the trap: "And I want you to go to a pet shop and buy me a collar and a leash to put on that dog out there." And he points to one of his players, a kid Wright has been working with.

O.K., it's a harmless enough dig, and Wright laughs, easily. But Knight won't quit: "Because if you don't start to shape him up, I'll have to get some white guys working on him. You guys don't show any leadership, you don't show any incentive since you started getting too much welfare."

Wright smiles again, though uneasily. Now, understand, Knight isn't anti-black. Just anti-tact. That's the point. One of his former black stars once recalled a halftime against Michigan when Knight singled out two of his white regulars as gutless, and then went over as they cowered and slapped their cheeks, snarling, "Maybe this'll put some color in your faces." It isn't *racial* prejudice. Still, still . . . .

Knight walks down to the other end of the scorer's table. "Hey, Maryalyce."

Brightly: "Yes, Bobby?"

"You know what a dab is?"

"A what?"

"A dab—D-A-B."

"No, what's that?"

"It's a dumb-assed broad," he says, smirking.

"I don't know any of those," she replies—a pretty quick comeback.

But he won't leave it alone. The edge, again: "Yeah, you know one more than you think you do."

And he moves on. The white woman shrugs. It's just Bobby. The black man shrugs. It's just Bobby. But why is it just Bobby? Why does he do this to himself? He's smart enough to know that, in this instance, he isn't hurting his two friends nearly so much as he hurts himself, cumulatively, by casting this kind of bread upon the waters, day after day. Why? Why, Bobby, why?

What a setup he has. Forty years old, acknowledged to be at the top of his profession. Says the very coach who disparages Knight for being a bully, "Any coach who says Bobby's not the best is just plain jealous." Knight has already won 317 games, and nobody, not even Adolph Rupp, achieved that by his age.

Someday Knight could even surpass Rupp's record 874 wins, a seemingly insurmountable total. Knight has won one NCAA championship, in 1976, and five Big Ten titles in nine seasons; he was twice national coach of the year; he's the only man ever to both play on and coach an NCAA champion. He's the coach at one of America's great basketball schools, one that's also an academic institution of note. The state worships him; Hoosier politicians vie for his benediction. His contemporaries in coaching not only revere him for his professional gifts, but some of his esteemed predecessors—mythic men of basketball lore— see Knight as the very keeper of the game. The torch is in his hands.

He's also a clever man and delightful company when he chooses to be. Beyond all that he has an exemplary character, without any of the vices of the flesh that so often afflict men in his station and at his time of life. He's devoted to his family, Nancy and their two sons, Timothy, 16, and Patrick, 10. His supporters fall over themselves relating tales of his civic and charitable good works, a light that Knight humbly hides under a basket. In this era of athletic corruption Knight stands foursquare for the values of higher education that so many coaches and boot-lickers in the NCAA only pay lip service to. His loyalty is as unquestioned as his integrity. He is the best and brightest . . . and the most honorable, too. He has it all, every bit of it. Just lying there on the table. He has only to lean down, pick it up and let the chip fall off. But he can't. For Knight to succeed at basketball—not only to win, you understand, but to succeed because "That's much harder," he says—all the world must be in the game. All the people are players, for or against, to be scouted, tested, broken down, built back up if they matter. Life isn't lived; it's played. And the rabbits are everywhere.

II: Coaches

Perhaps the most revealing statement that Knight makes about himself is this: "You know why Havlicek became such a great pro? Just because he wanted to beat Lucas, that's why." Yes, of course, Knight hasn't even mentioned himself, but that's the trick. Obviously, if only subconsciously, he's not really talking about John Havlicek superseding Lucas; he's talking about himself superseding Havlicek and Lucas both.

The best thing that ever happened to Knight was that after high school—he's still the greatest star ever to come out of Orrville, Ohio—he didn't amount to a hill of beans as a player. Knight the failed hero has not only served as the challenge for Knight the coach, but also Knight the disappointed hero is the model for the Everyplayer Knight coaches. That boy was limited, self-centered, frustrated, a pouter, then a bitcher, ultimately a back-biter against his coach, Fred Taylor, who once called Knight "the Brat from Orrville."

The one thing Knight could do was shoot, a strange low-trajectory shot that was deadly against zones when he had the time to get it off. To this day, no Knight team has ever set up in a zone defense. It's like Groucho Marx, who once said he didn't want to be part of any club that would have him as a member.

Although Knight only started two games in three years on the Buckeye varsity, he was a major figure on the team, something of a clubhouse lawyer and a practical joker (which he still is). Dragon and a roommate led the Buckeyes in hustling tickets, and he stunned his wide-eyed teammates with his brash high jinks. On a trip to New York he boldly swiped a couple of bottles of wine from Mamma Leone's restaurant, and not only pilfered a few ties from a midtown shop, but with the contraband under his coat, he went over to a cop who entered the store at that moment and started chatting him up.

There is little Knight's players can put over on him because he did just about all of it himself. Taylor wasn't the only coach Knight challenged, either. In his senior year at Orrville, he defied the school's new coach by refusing to leave a game for a substitute and was booted off the squad. Although subsequently reinstated, he found that season so unsatisfying that he gave up his baseball eligibility to barnstorm with an all-star basketball team in the spring. "I regret that more than anything I've ever done," he says, because he could hit a baseball and hit with power. Knight probably would've been better at baseball than he was at basketball.

Knight was also a pretty fair football end, and as he should've been a baseball player, so, by temperament, he would have made a better football coach. Wilkinson, Bryant, Hayes, Schembechler, Parterno and Royal are all friends and/or models of his, and he has a tape of Lombardi exhortations, plus a Lombardi polemic hanging on his office wall. And, like football coaches, Knight devotes himself to studying film, back and forth, over and over, like some Buddhist monk with his prayer wheel.

In the dazzle of the tight arena, basketball coaches tend to be popinjays, ruling by force of personality, glint of teeth, while football coaches are distant, solid sorts, administrators, with scores of lieutenants and troops. Being a basketball coach doesn't seem to prepare you for anything else in life, but even football coaches who can't win get bumped upstairs to assistant athletic director (a football coach who wins becomes athletic director). "I've always thought there's a greater depth to football coaches," Knight says.

But that's subsidiary to the main point: Knight loves all coaches. He will ask people who knew Rupp well to tell him about the old man. What made the Baron tick? Why did he do this? How? He has spent many hours listening to Sparky Anderson. He calls in the old basketball masters and studies at their feet. In his office, the only photographs (apart from those of his teams) are Pete Newell and Clair Bee. Even as a boy, he would go off on scouting trips with coaches. Bill Shunkwiler, his football coach at Orrville, remembers that after school, when other kids were hanging out, chasing, Bobby would come by Shunkwiler's house and the two of them would sit and have milk and cookies and talk coach talk. Knight still keeps in touch with many of his old coaches, still calls them "Mister," and there is, in Coach Knight, almost a tribal sense of heritage and tradition.

"I just love the game of basketball so," he says. "The game! I don't need the 18,000 people screaming and all the peripheral things. To me, what's most enjoyable is the practice and preparation."

The ultimate contradiction is that Bobby Knight, of all people, profane as he is, seeks after purity. What troubles him is that the game must be muddied by outlanders and apostates—the press, for example. In fact, Knight has studied the subject, and he understands the press better than some writers who cover him understand basketball. He even numbers several writers as friends, and sometimes he will actually offer a grudging admiration beyond his famous institutional assessment: "All of us learn to write by the second grade, then most of us go on to other things." But his truest feelings were probably revealed one day recently when he blurted out, "How do they know what it's like if they've never played? How? *How?* Tell me: How can they know?"

At the base of everything, this is it: if you're not part of basketball, you can't really belong, you can only distort. He has taken over the microphone at Assembly Hall, the Hoosier's arena, and told his own fans to back off, be good sports, even to stop using dirty words. Imagine, Knight telling people to improve their language. "It showed no bleeping class," he snapped afterward.

He just always wanted to be Coach Knight, officially expressing this desire in an autobiography he wrote when he was a junior in high school. It was entitled *It's Been A Great Life (So Far)*. Nancy Knight remembers nothing otherwise: "All Bobby ever wanted was to be a coach, in the Big Ten." Even now, when Knight deliberates on the rest of his life, he doesn't go much beyond his one love. "I hope," he says, "that when I retire I'll have enough assistants in head jobs so I can live anywhere I want and still have a place nearby where I can go over and help out and watch some films." As much as there is such a thing, he's a natural-born coach.

III: Older People

Knight's father—his square name was Carroll, but everyone called him Pat—was a railroad man from Oklahoma, who came to Orrville because it was a railroad town, a division point. The main Pennsy line passed through, and the city slickers from Cleveland and Akron had to journey down on a spur to little Orrville to catch the Broadway Limited. So, despite having only 5,000 folks when Bobby was growing up, Orrville was not quite as closed and homogeneous as you would expect of a Midwest coloring-book place, set in a dell, with a water tower.

Knight was born there, one of the last of the Depression Babies, on Oct. 25, 1940, a couple of weeks before FDR won his third term over Wendell Willkie and the objections of the Orrville electorate. He was reared in the '50s. Actually, the '50s were not much different in attitudes and values from the two decades that preceded them, but what sets the '50s apart is that they came right before the upheaval of the '60s. But just as the '60s flowered, Knight went off to coach at West Point, where his '50s just kept on going, even becoming sort of a badge of separation.

The '50s are too often disparaged for being simple, everyone in lock-step. But more accurately, what the '50s offered, in spades, was defini-tion. In analyzing pre-'60s coaches like the unrepentant Knight, observers tend to confuse definition with discipline. Knight most of all wants to know where people stand—and that they do stand for some-thing. Here's an example of how rigidly lines were drawn when Knight was growing up.

Shunkwiler takes out a copy of the 1958 *MemORRies*, the high school yearbook when Knight was a senior, and peruses the photographs of the boys, skipping the ones with pompadours, stopping on the ones who, like Bobby, wore crew cuts. "Athlete . . . athlete . . . athlete . . . ," he says. He comes to yet another boy with short hair. "Not an athlete." And hastily, "But a good kid." It was that easy then. More than one-third of the 200 or so boys were involved in athletics. Many of these were also involved in girls, too, but only *in their place*. If a coach so much as saw one of his players holding hands, he would bark out: "Hey, no skin-to-skin!"

The coach, you see, was a giant of a man in this well-defined culture. Shunkwiler recalls that if a coach was notified by a teacher that one of his players was causing a problem, the coach would take the boy aside and, presto, "That would be the end of the trouble." Jack Graham, another of Knight's Orrville basketball coaches, once kicked Bobby out of practice. Knight didn't head to the locker room, though; he waited patiently in the hallway so he could see Coach as soon as practice ended. "Bobby under-stood," Graham says. "I told him, 'There's only one man who can be the boss out there, and, Bobby, that's the coach.' "

Early this season Knight purposely overreacted one day so that he could boot his star, sophomore Guard Isiah Thomas, out of practice. He needed to show the kid, and the whole team, that there can be no excep-tions. Some things don't change. Coach Knight can throw his star out at

Indiana University as sure as Coach Graham could at Orrville High. On the team, on the court, time is frozen; *it's been a great life (so far)*.

What Knight didn't learn from his coaches came by example from his father, though theirs was an unusual relationship. The father and son weren't buddies, which has led some people to conclude that Knight's deep affection for older coaches is a manifestation of a perpetual search for a father figure. To some extent this analysis may be true, but the relationships in the Knight household were more complex than that analysis suggests.

Bobby was born six years into a marriage that had come late in life. Though he was an only child, he had a companion at home—his maternal grandmother, Sarah Henthorne. "A classy lady—the love of Bobby's life," says Pauline Boop, who was Knight's childhood next-door neighbor and remains his friend. No wonder he gets along so well with older people; he grew up in a house full of them.

Both of Knight's parents worked—Pat on the railroad, Hazel as an elementary school teacher—and although they were loving, they weren't enthusiastic about the thing their only son loved the most, basketball. But at least Knight always had an ally in his grandmother. She was the one who followed his basketball closely. No matter what the hour, when Bobby came home he would go and kiss her good night. "I think he was closer to his grandmother than he ever was to me or his father," says the widowed Hazel Knight, who still lives in the house on North Vine Street, across the field from the high school where Bobby starred for the Orrville Red Riders.

Knight came home for spring vacation of his sophomore year at Ohio State, right after the Buckeyes had won the national championship. One day he returned to the house in the afternoon, and his grandmother was sitting there in her favorite chair. She had gone shopping in the morning and was tired. It took a while before Bobby realized that she wasn't napping, that she was dead. He remembers it very well: "She was just sitting there. Her legs were crossed at the ankles." Knight's grandmother had been sick all winter, and there are those in Orrville who say she willed herself to stay alive until the season was over and her beloved Bobby could come home from his basketball to see her. It was during the next two seasons he had all the trouble with Fred Taylor.

Knight's father died a decade later, when Bobby was 29. In those 29 years, Pat Knight owned only three automobiles. Most places, he walked.

He rarely tipped; "Nobody tips me," he would say. The only thing he ever bought on time was the house on North Vine Street. And he hated to do that. He took out a 20-year mortgage and paid it off in 4-1/2 years. He gave up golf and many other pleasures until he could square accounts. Now, you see, now we are talking about discipline. "My father was the most disciplined man I ever saw," Bobby Knight says. "Most people, they hear the word discipline, and right away they think about a whip and a chair. I've worked up my own definition. And this took a long time. Discipline: doing what you have to do, and doing it as well as you possibly can, and doing it that way all the time."

Pat Knight was very hard-of-hearing, which limited his communications with his son. He would turn off his hearing aid every night and read the evening paper, front to back. "And he believed every word he read," Knight says emphatically, explaining why he becomes so distraught when the press fails to meet his expectations. Pat also introduced his son to hunting and fishing, and to this day that's Bobby's escape. There are no outsiders to louse it up; it's as pure, God willing, as basketball should be.

"People are always surprised when they hear about my fishing," he says. "Everybody thinks I'm going to get so wound up I'm going to have to leave in five minutes. But I don't carry over that stuff you see on the court. There's nothing I enjoy more than winding down some river, floating along, watching for deer, counting the squirrels." A warm smile, a pause, and then: "And nobody knows what you've done that day except you and the guys involved."

IV: Women

This particular day, he had been away, hunting down in southern Indiana with some of the guys. Nancy had a meeting to attend in the evening, but she passed it up, because Bobby was late getting back. She cooked a huge, scrumptious dinner, but apparently that's standard fare at the Knights'.

Whatever other ambiguities Knight has to deal with in these cloudy times, Nancy isn't one of them. "She's just a great coach's wife," he says. She knows her man, too, knows not to intrude on the game. When Indiana won the NCAA in Philadelphia in 1976, Knight and some old friends from basketball and Orrville went out to dinner afterward—the victory celebration, the culmination of his career. Neither Nancy nor any other woman was included.

Says Steve Green, one of Knight's better players, who graduated in 1975, "He feels women are just an obstacle that must be overcome. Players' girl friends didn't really exist for him. Just didn't exist. If he heard me talking to someone about my wedding, he'd be yelling, 'Don't do it! Don't do it!' "

It is instructive that Knight's language seldom goes beyond the anal stage. In the course of a day, he describes an incredible number of things being done to the derriere: it's burned, chewed out, kicked, frosted, blistered, chipped at, etc. Plus, almost every time he loses his temper, there is invariably a literal bottom line, involving the suggestion that the posterior be used as a depot—for money, a whistle, the Time and Life Building, what have you. But, when addressing the fairer sex, Knight has a reputation for purposely expanding his anatomical vocabulary to include graphic references to the male genitalia. This curious proclivity has offended people of both sexes and, perhaps more than anything, has tarnished his personal reputation.

One of Knight's heroes is Harry S. Truman, which is why Give-'em-hell Harry is conspicuously honored by bric-a-brac in Knight's office. But this graphic assessment of another president, Lyndon Johnson, by columnist William S. White, is eerily applicable to Knight: "His shortcomings were not the polite, pleasant little shortcomings, but the big ones—high temper, of course, too driving a personality, both of others and himself, too much of a perfectionist by far . . . Curiously enough I think one of the reasons he didn't go down better . . . was that his faults were highly masculine and that our society is becoming increasingly less masculine; that there's a certain femininity about our society that he didn't fit into."

On the subject of Bobby and women, Nancy Knight demurs: "I certainly couldn't have been married more than 17 years to a man who hates women. But I can understand how Bobby feels about some of them. I believe a woman should try and stay in the home. I've never been anything but very happy and satisfied to spend my life raising a family."

Nancy is, really, the only woman who ever came from the outside into Knight's life. She isn't pretentious, and their sprawling house, hidden in the woods just outside of Bloomington, is warm and comfortable. But those who would deal glibly in harsh housewife stereotypes must be careful. Everyone who knows the Knights well has the same one secret: Nancy influences Bobby *more than you ever would guess.*

Like many coaches, she often speaks for her husband in the first person plural— "We got the job at West Point"—but in neither a proprietary nor insecure way. He has the court, she has the home. It's defined.

Nancy acknowledges that Bobby's disputes with the press may well be exacerbated by her overreaction to criticism of him. "I read about this ogre," she says, "and he's the gentlest, kindest person to his family. He does so much good everywhere, I just can't stand to see the man I love being torn apart."

It would also seem that Bobby is equally protective of Nancy. His seemingly exaggerated responses in two major controversies may be traced in part to the fact that Nancy was involved peripherally in each. His protracted altercation with this magazine [*Sports Illustrated*] centers on disputes he has had with Senior Writer Curry Kirkpatrick, who did a piece on the Hoosiers in 1975. But Nancy was also personally wounded by a throwaway line of Kirkpatrick's, just as she had been by a passing reference another *SI* writer, Barry McDermott, made in an earlier article. In trying to humorously mock Knight's martinetism, McDermott suggested that the Hoosiers players had gone over to the coach's house for a holiday meal of bread and water. Nancy, who prides herself on being a gracious hostess and accomplished cook, took the crack literally. "I cried and cried," she says.

Then there were the 1979 Pan Am Games. Puerto Rico was, in many respects, an accident waiting to happen. Those who know Knight best say the episode traumatized him, and while he's a chatterbox, he talks compulsively on this subject. And he still won't give an inch. "There is no way I was going down there and turn the other cheek," he says. "If there was trouble, I was ready to give it right back to them. The first day we were down there, they burned some American flags. There was tremendous resentment toward the United States, tremendous hostility. Listen, America means a lot to me. If the guy. . . "

What guy?

"The *Guy*. If The Guy says tomorrow, hey, this country is in trouble and it needs you in this position or that one, then I give up coaching tomorrow and go."

So, even before the officious San Juan policeman threatened him—cursing him, poking at him—Knight was simmering. Then he became concerned for the safety of Nancy and his two sons. "It was terrifying," she says. "We had to change apartments. I couldn't sit in my seat at the games. I had to stay at the press table. I feared for my life and my children's."

However Knight behaved in Puerto Rico—"You have no respect for anybody. You treat us like dirt. You are an embarrassment to America, our country. You are an Ugly American," a Puerto Rican sports official snapped at him after the Pan Am basketball final—it must be understood that Knight perceived, correctly or not, that the three things he values most in his life were being menaced—his family, his country and his team.

V: Players

Late in his senior year at Ohio State, Knight considered a job at a high school in Celina, Ohio as the coach of basketball and an assistant in football. He liked the place, but walking back across the school's gridiron, he kicked at the turf and shook his head. "I thought, if I'm going to be a basketball coach, I can't be diverted," he says. "I wanted vertical concentration. That's still the essence of my coaching." So he took a lesser job as a basketball assistant, without any football responsibility, in Cuyahoga Falls, Ohio. In his first game as head coach of the 10th-graders, he broke a clipboard.

Intensity?

A year later, with Taylor's help, the Brat from Orrville got the assistant's post at West Point under Tates Locke, enlisting in the Army to qualify for the job. When Locke left in 1965, the brass stunned everybody by giving Pfc. Knight the job. "I've never had any apologies for being a head coach at 24," he says. "I was making 99 dollars a month then. I have no sympathy for people who don't make progress because they won't accept the pay somewhere."

Money has never motivated Knight. He has turned down raises, preferring that the money go to his assistants, and he professes not even to know what his salary is—except that, relative to what other teachers at Indiana make, it's too much. This is not to say, of course, that Knight wears a hair shirt. He has a television show, a summer basketball camp, the free use of a car, and, he volunteers, Checkers-like, "I did take a fishing rod once." Also, it's an absolute point of pride with him that he must be paid as much as the Hoosier football coach, Lee Corso. But just as pointedly he has advised alumni and the commercial camp-followers who grubstake coaches on the side to take a wide berth. Recently, however, Knight decided he was a fool to look a gift horse in the mouth, so he solicited bids from shoe companies that were willing to pay him in hope that his players would wear their sneakers. Adidas won, but instead of sticking this "pimp money," as he calls it, in his own pocket, Knight turned it over to the university.

This isn't going to endear Knight to the coach who's looking to put a new Florida room on the house, just as a lot of Knight's colleagues weren't thrilled two years ago when he kicked three players off his team for abuses of training rules (drugs, obviously), and then trumpeted that he was the only coach extant with the "guts" to live up to his principles. But his honor even exceeds his smugness. "He just doesn't cheat," says Newell. "Never. Bobby doesn't even rationalize. Instead, what he does do is the single most important thing in coaching: he turns out educated kids who are ready for society."

Now Knight is on an even broader crusade, trying to impose on others, by legislation, his devotion to academics. He would like the NCAA to pass a regulation that would deny a college some of its allotment of athletic scholarships if its players don't graduate within a year after their eligibility ends. That is, if a coach has five so-called student-athletes finishing up on the team in 1981 and only two graduate by 1982, then the coach can only replace the five with two new recruits. "With this, you're making the faculty a police department for the NCAA," Knight says. "Even if you can get a few professors to pimp for a coach, you can't buy a whole damn faculty." He laughs, devilishly. "And how can a coach vote against this plan? How can anyone vote publicly against education?"

Nothing pleases Knight as much as the success his players have had off the court. Indeed, he uses their accomplishments to justify the controversial "way we operate," saying, "Look, if all our players were losing jobs, I'd have to reassess my way. And if I heard some of my old players blistering my ass for the way I run things, I'd have to reassess. But, you see, despite all the crap you read, the only ones who've ever complained are the kids who didn't play, got frustrated and quit."

But, tit for tat, it may also be true that Knight's players have a high success rate because only success-oriented types would select Indiana basketball in the first place. In other words, the twigs only grow as they were bent a long time ago.

Knight's honesty extends to his recruiting. When a recruit is brought to Bloomington, he's introduced to the whole squad, and not merely sequestered with a happy star, a Mr. Personality and a pretty cheerleader. Parents of recruits are encouraged to talk with parents of present squad members. Knight doesn't have a missionary instinct. He isn't, he says, "an animal trainer. Recruit jackasses, they play like jackasses."

Instead: "We've drawn up a personality profile, and you might even say it's a narrow-minded thing."

So, black or white, rich or poor, the neatly groomed Indiana players tend to be well-intentioned young things, upwardly mobile, serious about education and so well adjusted that they can endure Coach Knight's wrath in fair exchange for the bounty of his professional genius. Calculated coach, calculated players.

The hand-picked Hoosiers are expected to speak to the press, even in defeat, the better to mature and cope. They dress in coats and ties on game days, and during the season must wear trim haircuts, without beards or mustaches.

Significantly, things have gone awry only since the national championship season, soon after which a number of players quit, some castigating Knight, and two seasons after that when the coach bounced the three players for disciplinary reasons. "All of a sudden I won, and I thought I could be a social worker, too," he says. "I thought I could take a guy off death row at Sing Sing and turn him into a basketball player." Never again. The prime result of that convulsion has been an even more careful weeding-out process. A single blackball from a team member can eliminate a prospect from consideration, and as a consequence, a sort of natural selection of the species has occurred. The system has become so inbred that, as contradictory as this sounds, rough-tough Knight's team now includes a bunch of nice Nellys. The Hoosier basketball coaches all worried about this even before this rather disappointing season—Indiana was 10–6 at the end of last week—confirmed their fears. Knight himself, like a grizzled old soldier, waxes nostalgic about the single-minded roughnecks who chopped their way to victory for him at the Point.

Had Knight never won a game at Indiana, he would have secured a lasting reputation for his work at Army, where he succeeded with little talent and no height. At Indiana, as well, the mark of Knight as coach goes far beyond his mere W–L totals. When he arrived in Bloomington, the entire Big Ten played run-and-gun, in the image of Indiana, the conference's traditional lodestar: racehorse ball, the Hurryin' Hoosiers. It wasn't just a catchy sports nickname. It was a real statement. The Hurryin' Hoosiers. The Bronx Bombers. The Monsters of the Midway. There aren't many of them. But no matter how much the old alumni whined at the loss of tradition and hittin' a hundred, Knight went his own way. From Knight's arrival through last week, Indiana has gone 215–65, but, more significantly, the average Big Ten score has declined from 74.0 to 67.5 in that span.

His strategic axioms are firm—no zones, disciplined offense—but he exercises latitude year by year, permitting himself to be dictated to by his material and the state of the art. He has such consummate confidence in his ability as a coach that he suffers no insecurity about crediting the sources of his handiwork. It all came from other coaches, didn't it? His defense is based on the old Ohio State pressure game, which Taylor had borrowed from Newell. His offense is an amalgam of the freelancing style used at Princeton in the early '60s, by Butch van Breda Kolff ("The best college coach I ever saw"), intertwined with the passing game that the venerable Hank Iba employed at Oklahoma State.

This season Knight was willing to modify some of his most cherished tenets to permit Isiah Thomas more artistic freedom. But, ultimately, those who would survive at Indiana, much less succeed, must subjugate themselves to the one man and his one way. Incredibly, 10 of Knight's former assistants are head coaches at major colleges, but those who coach under him are strictly that: underlings. Among other things, they aren't allowed to utter so much as a word of profanity before the players. Only Bobby.

He prowls the practice court, slouched, belly out, usually with a sour, disbelieving expression upon his visage. He is dressed in Indiana red and white, but of a different mix-and-match from his assistants'. Except for a few instructions barked out by these subordinates, the place is as silent as a tomb. Only the most privileged visitors are permitted to watch this class.

The chosen few watch on two levels of consciousness: what they see before them, and what they anticipate Coach Knight might do next. If he really contrives to make a point, he will perhaps merely rage, or pick up a chair and slam it against the wall, or dismiss a hopeless athlete. It's like technical fouls—you don't ever get them, you take them. And, like every good coach, Knight knows how to deal with the unexpected. One day a few years ago Knight kicked a ball in anger. He caught it perfectly on his instep and the ball soared toward the very heavens, straight up. More miraculously, when it plummeted back to earth, it fell into a wastebasket, lodging there. It was a million-to-one shot, something from a Road Runner cartoon. But nobody dared change his expression. Finally, Knight began to grin, then to laugh, and only at that point did everyone else break up.

"I've always said, all along, that if I ever get to a point where I can't control myself, I'll quit," Knight says stoutly, though unmindful, perhaps, that he can drive things out of control even as he skirts the edge himself.

VI: More Rabbits

John Havlicek once said, "Bobby was quite a split personality. There were times when we were good friends and, then, like that, times when he wouldn't even talk to me." Knight says, "My manners set me apart in a little cocoon, and that's something that's very beneficial to me." Maybe, but too many people humor Knight instead of responding to him, and that may be the single real deprivation of his life.

The one group of people who can still treat him honestly are the older coaches, Dutch uncles, who have earned his respect. A few years ago he took on as an assistant Harold Andreas, the man who had first hired him as an assistant at Cuyahoga Falls. What a wonderful gesture! Andreas retired from coaching in 1977. And so, in Andreas' place as the father/grandmother figure, Knight hired Roy Bates, who used to coach one of Orrville High's rivals. Bates, who recently took a leave of absence because of poor health, is a no-nonsense fellow with a crippled left arm, whose teams were 441–82 in basketball and 476–52 in baseball. Bates adored Knight, and though Knight had three younger assistants, it was the older man he was closest to, literally and otherwise. Bates always sat next to him on the bench.

Still Bates had to be tested, like everyone else. He has had a radio show in Ohio since 1949, and one time a while ago, when he was staying at the Knight's, he asked Bobby to do a five-minute tape with him. Bobby said sure, but then he put Bates off and put him off. Finally, one day Bates said, "You know, Bobby, I've had that radio show for 30 years without you on it." And with that, he put on his coat and headed for the car. By the time Bates had started up the driveway, Knight was out there, waving for him to come back, and as soon as Bates arrived back at his home in Ohio, Bobby was on the phone to him. Knight was still in control of himself. But not of events.

"Bobby has got so much," Bates says. "And nobody can ever get him. He doesn't cheat. He doesn't drink. He doesn't even chase women. But for some reason he thinks he has been a bad boy, and no matter how successful he becomes, he thinks he must be punished."

This may be the best clue of all. Certainly Knight accepts success defensively, if not suspiciously. His office celebrates underdogs like Truman and Lombardi, who weren't expected to triumph but, given the chance, thrived on their own sweet terms. And Patton is in evidence, as you might expect. A mean-spirited quote of his hangs on the wall, keynoting a display—an anthology—of paranoid sentiments.

Patton warns ominously that if you strive for a goal, "your loyal friends [will do] their hypocritical Goddamndest to trip you, blacken you and break your spirit." A flanking prayer advises, "If man thwart you pay no heed/If man hate you have no care. . . . " And an essay entitled "The Penalty of Leadership" warns, "The reward is widespread recognition, the punishment fierce denial and detraction."

Is it really that lonely at the top?

Knight also passes out copies of *If* to visitors.

And yet, as wary as he is of the hypocritical rabbits all around him, Knight is, in many respects, even more unsparing of himself. The game, we hear so often, has passed so-and-so by. With Knight, it may be the reverse; he may have passed it by. But he loves it so, and therefore he must concoct hurdles so that he can still be challenged by it. He even talks a lot about how nobody is really capable of playing the game well. Ultimately, it may be the final irony that the players themselves must become interlopers, separating him from the game.

Already he has gone so far that at age 40 winning is no longer the goal. "Look, I know this," he says. "If you're going to play the game, you're going to get more out of it winning. I know that, sure. Now, at West Point I made up my mind to win—*gotta win*. Not at all costs. Never that. But winning was the hub of everything I was doing. And understand, I've never gotten over West Point. Winning had to be more important there, and I had a point to prove. I was just coming off a playing career during which I didn't do as well as I'd hoped. I had to win. And so, to some extent, I won't change.

"But somewhere I decided I was wrong. You could win and still not succeed, not achieve what you should. And you can lose without really failing at all. But it's harder to coach this way, with this, uh, approach. I'm sure I'd be easier on myself and on other people if just winning were my ultimate objective." He pauses; he is in his study at home, amid his books, away from all the basketball regalia. "I never said much about this before."

It was a good secret. Now, Bobby Knight is one step closer to utter control of his game. Now all those dim-witted rabbits cannot touch him. They'll be looking at the scoreboard and the AP poll, judging him by those, but they won't have a clue, not the foggiest. Nobody holds a mortgage on him. Now, you see, now we are talking about definition.

Nancy says: "People keep asking me if Bobby is mellowing. We're not mellowing. What we are, we're growing up with the game. You've got to remember that not many people get a chance to start coaching in their 20s. We're not mellowing. Growing up is still more of the word for us."

There is still so much time for the Knights to take what is theirs and enjoy it. It can be a great life (someday).

Pious Hypocrisy

■   ■   ■

Having attained a certain age, here are the four things in life that I positively know will never work:

1) Communism

2) Anything that says "easy-off"—especially if it is spelled "E-Z"

3) Giving a small boy a goldfish to take care of

4) College athletics played by college students

Understand, college students can play sports in college, but it is simply beyond the capacity of avaricious men to create a fair system wherein genuine amateur students play so that they might accumulate great sums of money and prestige for their repositories of higher learning.

The hapless officials can adapt, adjust, mix-and-match, shake it up, correct, and even start over from scratch, but big-time college athletics in America cannot work. The term *student-athlete* is simply an oxymoron, and you can't build a system that is grounded on a basic contradiction.

The NCAA, which was founded by Teddy Roosevelt essentially to keep Ivy Leaguers from maiming each other on the gridiron, ends this century as it began, seeking vainly to keep educators from cheating one another. Currently, the NCAA is striving to change its academic eligibility requirements for athletes and is considering also the possibility of barring freshmen in basketball from playing on the varsity.

The need to amend its current entrance requirements was forced upon the NCAA by the Third Circuit Court of Appeals, which ruled that the minimum of 820 on the SATs was discriminatory to African-American athletes. Obviously, the only other entrance standard you can apply is one involving high-school grades, and that can only result in even greater widespread corruption.

After all, we know that now, even in college, athletes' grades are routinely fictionalized. The current scandal at the University of Minnesota, where it was disclosed that hundreds of learned term papers were churned out for basketball players by a scholarly ghostwriter, is, surely, only Minnesota's bad luck. It is common knowledge that, all over the country, athletes are greased through mock courses by a fifth column of professors who are jock sycophants. Even in the finest colleges, the athletes have grades far below the rest of the student body. Take the SATs out of the equation, and the fraudulent system would only expand in its crookedness, for it is wishful thinking verging on Pollyanna not to believe that high schools would cheat on grade reporting in order to assure a star athlete a college scholarship.

The only way we will ever get an honest collegiate athletic system is to let each college set its own academic standards for athletes. If State U. wants to bring in eighth-grade dropouts to stock its football team, fine, let it. Then, if your school doesn't want to play State U., cross it off your schedule. I'm sorry, but after a century of seeing that the NCAA way simply doesn't work, I have concluded that honest prostitution is vastly preferable to pious hypocrisy.

As for denying freshman basketball players the opportunity to play on the varsity so that they might acclimate themselves better to college life, this is noble do-gooding based on the premise that a young basketball player who goes to college is . . . there to go to college. The point of American big-time college sports is eligibility, not education, and until eligibility is removed as the issue, all the earnest talk is, well—it's just academic.

Bus Protocol

■　　■　　■

One of the most celebrated charms of Spring Training is its time-lessness—or, anyway, its ability to carry you back in time. For example, one thing you always see during Spring Training is buses. Even the world champions take buses during Spring Training.

This is ironic. It used to be that the bus was a sign of the proletariat in sports, just as it is in the rest of society. The minor leagues were actually referred to as the "bus leagues." If a player got cut, he would moan that he was going back to riding the buses.

But buses are much nicer now. They even have air-conditioning and toilets. Buses are not automatically déclassé. And since major leaguers in all sports ride a lot of buses during the regular season—short trips from the hotel to the park and to the airport—there is even a very distinct bus protocol. It is especially fascinating that even though the sports are all different, the same types of people sit in the exact same places on all team buses.

The manager or the head coach always sits in the front seat, on the right hand side, across from the driver. You can tell if a head coach or manager is personally close to an assistant if the assistant sits by the boss on the bus. Where people sit on the bus reveals much more about their relationships than where they sit on the team bench or in the locker room.

Generally, on a bus, the assistant coaches and the other support troops—trainers, PR men, writers, and broadcasters—come next, sitting in the first rows behind the driver and the manager. They may sit with some of the older players, although it is improper for any non-player to appropriate an empty aisle seat next to a player. Only players take the empty aisle seats next to players.

To the far back of the bus are all the noisy types, the wise guys, the "in" crowd. You will recall that Phil Linz played his famous harmonica after the Yankees lost a game . . . from the back of the bus. If there are any card games, they will also take place in the back.

Basketball is the best bus sport because there's just enough guys to justify a bus, but there are still plenty of seats to spread out in. This is particularly important if you are seven feet tall. Football teams need two buses, but then, football teams don't travel all that much. They just fly out, charter, a couple of days before the game and come right back afterwards. John Madden didn't even learn that he had trouble flying until after he stopped coaching. On a chartered flight you can get up and move around as soon as the plane takes off, so Madden didn't even realize that he was claustrophobic until he had to fly commercial flights, like real people.

I've never heard of any player who got claustrophobic on buses. About forty years ago, there was a terrible team bus accident in the state of Washington, and a player who escaped injury named Jack Lohrke was thereafter always known as Lucky Lohrke.

Not long ago, a bus picked up a college basketball team in upstate New York and took it to Colgate instead of Cornell. Or maybe it was Cornell instead of Colgate. Bus drivers rarely screw up that badly, but often, it seems, they really don't know the best route, and then the players will scream at them.

Bus drivers are universally called "Bussy" by athletes. "Hey, Bussy, where ya goin'?" "Yo, Bussy, hurry up." This is interesting. Although all sports team drivers are called "Bussy," I have never heard the term anywhere else.

A Case for Gambling

■   ■   ■

This is what we know. For half a century, college basketball players have been periodically caught point-shaving. Everybody then weeps and wails and gnashes teeth, lamenting the horrors that gambling brings.

But this we know, too. All sorts of other sports are also bet on, and there are never any fixing scandals attributed to them.

So, as inconvenient as this makes it for knee-jerkers and moralists and the NCAA, it is easy to deduce that gambling on college basketball is only an instrument of the fixes, not the base cause.

In fact, while you don't want young children and impressionable adults to hear this, I would suggest that these regular college basketball scandals would be greatly reduced—maybe even virtually eliminated—if betting on sports was made generally legal throughout the republic, as it is in other civilized sporting nations.

Now, empirically, the reason why fixing scandals occur more in basketball is that basketball is the easiest game to fix—except, that is, for contests that don't involve horses or dogs.

Oh, you would ask, then why are there never any professional basketball fixes? Good question—especially since far more money per game is bet on the pros. The answer, of course, is that NBA players make too much money to risk their careers on even a one-time, big-shot jackpot. Likewise, isn't it revealing that it is never the college *stars* who are caught fixing games? Rather, it is only pretty good college players with no significant future in the game.

You see, it is not just that college kids succumb to temptation because they're offered money. Invariably, instead, the argument that turns their heads toward crime is couched in terms of fairness. *Hey, dude, every-*

body else in college basketball is making money—coaches, athletic departments, sponsors, sneakers, bookies, the networks, the airlines, the hotels. Only the people who, incidentally, play college basketball are locked out of the college basketball bonanza. Don't be a sucker.

For an analogy, it's worth recalling the Black Sox baseball scandal of 1919. Most of the Chicago players who dumped the World Series weren't evil. Rather, they were vulnerable for one prime reason: they were grossly underpaid by their owner, Charles Comiskey. The players felt betrayed and used. It's the same in college basketball today.

Besides, all the gum-flapping and hand-wringing about how sinful sports betting is would strike any rational young man as hypocritical, if not farcical. We live in a society in which betting is legal for lotteries, casinos, slot machines, horses, and dogs, but we then draw some transparent line and say it's illegal to bet on games . . . only, of course, everybody does it illegally, in turn profiting gangsters.

Moreover, the college kids all know that legal sports books operate in Nevada, a circumstance which does not appear to be inhibiting the moral health of a state that is growing faster than forty-nine others. People will bet. Everywhere they will bet on games.

Now, if we acknowledged this tenet of human nature and if we legalized sports gambling in the United States, the profits would not just line the pockets of organized crime. Instead, the profits could be used to pay college players a reasonable remuneration. This would be fair, and it would also reduce the temptation for poor young players to listen to fixers.

Or, we can, like the Pharisees, keep on shouting to the heavens about how dreadful gambling is—while the mobsters grow richer off our high moral posturing.

The prohibition against legal sports gambling simply doesn't work. After the breast-beating dies down again, there will, soon enough, be another college basketball scandal. Kids who see that they are being cheated will cheat.

Sick and Tired of Dennis Rodman

■   ■   ■

Ladeez and gentlemen, children of all ages, I am here today to declare: I am sick and tired of Dennis Rodman.

I am tired of his body. I am tired of his body parts—those that are pierced, and those (few) that are not (yet) pierced. I am tired of his tattoos—and understand, I have nothing against tattoos. Truth to tell, I possess a very modest, very tasteful tattoo myself. But I am tired of Dennis Rodman's tattoos.

While we're at it, I'm tired of Dennis Rodman being naked. I am tired of him being with Madonna. For that matter, I am tired of the whole subject of Dennis Rodman and sex.

I am, too, tired of Dennis Rodman cross-dressing. I have nothing against cross-dressing. You want to cross-dress? Fine. I am just tired of Dennis Rodman cross-dressing. Especially the feather boa. Come to think of it, I do prefer Dennis Rodman naked as a man, rather than dressed up as a woman.

And, of course, I am so very tired of Dennis Rodman's hideous hair.

Evidently, though, these attitudes of mine place me in the distinct minority.

Evidently, I am waaay out of step.

Evidently, shock and excess know no boundaries anymore, even in the redblooded world of sport. This week, Mr. Rodman's memoir has jumped to the top of the best-seller list—arbitrarily placed in the non-fiction category.

I know, I know, I sound like a spoilsport—one of those old fogeys who had a fit when Joe Namath first dared wear a mustache. *Oh, what is sport coming to?* I suppose, in fact, we could argue that Rodman is simply the natural extension of everything different in sport that has preceded him, and that, *come on,* Frank, lighten up, sports is entertainment, and that Rodman is no more vulgar in his field of vulgarity than is Jim Carrey serving up Ace Ventura, Pet Detective on the silver screen, or Howard Stern on another part of your radio dial.

Let us be grateful for small favors. Not yet this playoff season has Mr. Rodman taken off his shoes before the game is over, as was his wont last year when he was at San Antonio.

So, perhaps I should just forget all the other stuff that takes place off the court. But no, there is a difference, I think, from Rodman and someone like Namath—or Charles Barkley or Andre Agassi or Deion Sanders today—who ask us to laugh along with them. Rodman knows no subtlety. He is merely outrageous, and, so, after a while, this not only irritates me, but more important, in the vernacular, it disses the sport itself.

But yes, Dennis Rodman has triumphed. He is a household curiosity. He is on *Saturday Night Live*! On *Oprah*! His book is number one on the best-seller list. The color of his hair is an issue in every game. Fine. But I'm sorry—there is a limit. Yes, by God, there is a limit. I'm sick and tired of Dennis Rodman. Have a nice day.

Cheatin' Refs

■   ■   ■

The National Association of Sports Officials has advised its members that their newest benefit will be assault insurance. This unique coverage has been worked up specifically for American referees. The reason is very simple: more and more sports officials are being physically attacked.

What is ironic, too, is that despite all the publicity that attends a nasty major-league incident, most of the increased violence directed at officials nowadays is at the lower, amateur levels of sport, where, of course, sportsmanship is supposed to matter most. Sadly, more often than not, it is *parents* themselves who assault officials at games in which their children are playing.

On the major-league level, instant replay has proved that top officials make the right call an incredible amount of the time. But because replay also shows that sometimes referees are wrong, those few instances stand out and produce more irrational hyper-criticism.

However, at the same time when sports officials across the board have been subjected to this greater condemnation—even to violence—just for allegedly making the odd bad call, ten National Basketball Association referees have been indicted for a real crime—tax fraud. Most have already pleaded guilty and have been sentenced. What these officials did was exchange expense account, first-class airplane tickets for coach seats, and then pocket the money differential without reporting this income to the IRS.

Other officials in all sports are furious at the NBA refs. The guilty parties are, after all, the cream of the crop—and the best paid, too. Barry Mano, himself an official and editor of *Referee* magazine, tells me: "Officials around the country really feel let down by what the NBA referees did."

Yet there is a most curious public response which has quite confounded these same rank-and-file officials. What the NBA refs did—dishonestly, illegally—has created no backlash whatsoever from fans. Not even at NBA games last year did honest officials hear cracks about how they must be untrustworthy, like their cheatin' colleagues.

The officiating association expected, naturally, for their whole noble profession to be castigated. After all, officials are supposed to be Caesar's wife, men of integrity who, by their honor, can maintain the integrity of our games. But paradoxically, American fans seem to have been generally undisturbed by the illegal actions of sports officials as private citizens, even though the trend is to grow angry, even violent toward these same men for making ordinary professional decisions in games. "It's amazing," Barry Mano says. "All anybody seems to care about anymore are Ws and Ls." Wins and losses.

I don't have to belabor the obvious analogy here to the broad national response, which treats President Clinton's private behavior and public actions independently. But the way sports fans have acted toward referees certainly supports that contradiction, indicating again how comfortably do Americans now divide public people into two distinct and unconnected parts.

You know exactly what it's like? It's like the scoring for figure skating, in which the judges give two different scores—one for Technical Performance, the other for Artistic Expression. It would make a great deal more sense to evaluate all our public officials that way in the future. For example, I give President Clinton a 4.2 for Technical Performance, but a 5.8 for Artistic Expression.

In any event, it is said that you can tell a great deal about a whole culture from its behavior toward sports. If so, our attitude toward sports officials suggests that we place little value on the whole of personal character anymore and are only concerned with specific results.

Little Boxes

■ ■ ■

Sometimes things all over the country just seem to happen, as if by constitutional osmosis. For example: receipts. All of a sudden, across the fifty states, contiguous and otherwise, without warning, people at cash registers wanted to give you a receipt. Then they started *forcing* receipts on you.

You could not turn down receipts, even if all you bought was a newspaper or Tic-Tacs. *Here is your receipt, sir—Here is* your *receipt.* Then it got even worse. I started seeing signs that said if I was not given the receipt I didn't want, I would get my purchase for free. I was supposed to tattle on receipt-givers. Never mind; I don't want a damn receipt.

Now, in sports, the newest equivalent of the compulsory receipt is the little box that appears in the upper-left-hand corner of your television screen during a game. It's easy to find. It's catty-cornered from the little symbol in the lower-right-hand corner, which, also like the receipt you do not want, constantly advises you of what network you're watching.

The little upper-left-hand box tells you the score of the game and the time or the inning and other pertinent data. Some channels even add a little animated penalty flag when an infraction in football is signaled. Now, don't get me wrong. I like the little box. Certainly, I like it better than receipts. In fact, as the little box gets more and more comprehensive, it allows me to push the mute button and then just watch the little box instead of the game.

This little box for sporting events arrived about three or four years ago. It was a foreign invasion from soccer games, which is especially interesting, inasmuch as the score in soccer is usually no score at all. Still, network by network, sport by sport, it caught on in America. The penultimate holdout, ABC, added the little box to *Monday Night Football*—much to the disgust of the three announcers, who could see that their vocal responsibility was being usurped by the little box. Three is a lot of announcers even if you don't have a little box.

That left only NBC lacking the little box. Dickie Ebersol, the foxy head of NBC Sports, said he'd be darned if he was going to put the little box in his games, because then, if the score was lopsided, viewers would instantly click on to another channel. Ebersol wanted NBC to keep lopsided scores to themselves—at least until after the new viewer suffered a commercial or two.

But the drumroll in the public and the press encouraging NBC to get with the program and add a little box *like everybody else* reached El Ninô-sized proportions. Everyone was asking: What's the matter with NBC?

And, sure enough, poor Ebersol finally had to cave in for the World Series. Yes, NBC has added a little box, although if you've been watching the Series, you've seen that NBC's little box appears only *before* the pitch and in the lower-right-hand corner. NBC Sports, like all institutions that succumb to public pressure, is doing it incrementally and acting like it was its idea all along. To have the little box on the screen during the pitch would, NBC says, very pretentiously, be . . . well, it would be artistically cruel, like painting a mustache on the Mona Lisa.

Hey, I'll bet you in another year the weather and the Dow Jones averages will be in a little box on Tom Brokaw's NBC news. And then on *Frasier*. Little boxes have won. Thank you, and don't forget your receipt.

Bad Boys

■   ■   ■

Following the accusations of sexual assault against Michael Irvin and Erik Williams, there was raised abroad in the land a great hue and cry that Jerry Jones, the Cowboys' owner, must clean up his Augean stables. Many critics, led by Dave Anderson, the Pulitzer Prize-winning sports columnist at the *New York Times*, demanded that Jones summarily banish the accursed accused.

But then, of course, we found that justice anticipated may be justice denied, and quite possibly Irvin and Williams are altogether innocent. Notwithstanding, it is the reaction to the incident that strikes me as more revealing than the incident itself.

The almost reflexive cry for punishment tells me that whereas we used to be inclined to believe that athletes could be our heroes, so tarred is the reputation of today's athlete—perhaps particularly today's football player—that now we have come almost a hundred and eighty degrees about. Now we are disposed to think that athletes must be the bad guys . . . even creatures of evil, cousins of O. J.

Certainly we feel betrayed by these fellows, and one senses again—with the cries for the heads of Irvin and Williams—a public bitterness that is heightened by frustration and envy. It just does not seem fair that men blessed to make a fortune in sports should not be held more accountable when they abuse what so many of us take as a privilege, rather than a profession.

So often, in fact, when an athlete now misbehaves, the public seems more upset that he is not sufficiently punished—rather than at the offense itself.

Curiously, it used to be exactly the other way around. Historically, athletes had no rights and were dealt with capriciously by star-chamber justice. Basketball players, for example, have gone to their graves, banned from ever playing professionally after being merely *accused* of misdeeds.

Now, though, athletes seem to be afforded a job protection that those of us in more prosaic professions do not enjoy. If the United States Olympic Committee could not dare bump Tonya Harding off the American team, then no mere professional football player is much in jeopardy.

And consider, specifically, the march of NFL justice. Thirty years ago, Paul Hornung, a much bigger star than Irvin, was suspended *indefinitely* from the league for placing a few bets at small change on his own team. The commissioner did allow Hornung back after a season's suspension, but there was initially no limit; his suspension could have been for life. Meanwhile, Irvin, who was accused of a sordid sex-and-drug felony and fined and put on probation by a Dallas criminal court, was given a mere five-game suspension earlier this season. He was even allowed to keep on practicing with the Cowboys.

In college football, at places like Nebraska, players who commit heinous crimes are forgiven by victory-hungry coaches who pose as humanitarians. In baseball, when Roberto Alomar of the Orioles actually spit in an umpire's face, he received a slap on the wrist, and even that penalty was postponed for his and his team's convenience.

So, you may not like it, but do not expect teams or leagues any longer to fire players for the sort of personal misbehavior that would put you or me on the unemployment line.

Here is the irony: years ago, we admired athletes more than they deserved, and, by holding them to a higher standard, felt comfortable in punishing them in draconian terms whenever they let us down.

Today, we pretty much assume athletes are rubbish, and so, since we expect nothing much of them, we excuse them of their crimes.

Either way, we have made a special class with special conditions for those who play games.

Super Bowl Sunday

■   ■   ■

I'm not going to give you that stuff about how, when I was a child, in January I had to walk to school through eight-foot snow drifts after milking the cows. Nevertheless: January has changed.

It used to be that the only two things that distinguished January were the bowl games on the first day of the month and then exams later on. There was nothing else in the vast tundra of the early part of the calendar until we reached Valentine's Day.

But now things have changed, at least for college students, for whom exams have been moved up, to before Christmas. This, by itself, has improved January by 34.7 percent. Also, many more bowl games have been added, to fully anesthetize us on the first day of the new year far more than any liquor we might have ingested the night before. And, in most parts of the country, it doesn't snow anymore in January, so now we have two Marches instead of one January and one March.

Best of all, we have added two holidays to what used to be January. First, there is Martin Luther King Jr. Day, which is a touching new holiday that is proving to be a great boon to the skiing industry. It certainly is a wonderful legacy for Dr. King that, because of what he stood for, many white Americans now get a long weekend of skiing.

Of course, neither Washington nor Lincoln had anything to do with kitchen appliances, which is what their birthdays stand for now, so that is certainly appropriate.

The other new January holiday is Super Bowl Sunday—a special day of fellowship for Americans, a chance to come together with dear friends and family, maybe even your wife, if she promises to keep her mouth shut and not ask any stupid questions when John Madden has his chalkboard out.

Super Bowl Sunday teaches us an important lesson, too, that winning and losing really don't matter. What does matter is beating the point spread.

Lately, too, Super Bowl Sunday has begun to take on even more meaning. It has become an important economic holiday, second only to Christmas. For now, everybody wonders about Super Bowl commercials, which are almost as significant as the game itself. Which old companies will be on? Which new companies will debut? How will Americans take to these commercials? How well will the lucky network do financially?

Now there are more Super Bowl stories on the business pages than on the sports pages. In fact, reading the papers, I get the distinct impression that whatever incidentally happens to the Bills and Redskins Sunday, our free enterprise system is on the line if Bud Bowl IV doesn't play well, if Master Lock's only commercial of the year doesn't click, or if the latest Nike extravaganza doesn't win critical raves.

Clearly, the question before us now isn't whether we should Buy America, but: Should we Buy Super Bowl?

Hoop Geography

■   ■   ■

What I am positing here today, class, is that American college basketball is most reminiscent of European history, intrigue, and warfare. Okay?

To begin in the middle, both Europe and college basketball are anchored by a powerful central force. In Europe, of course, this is Germany. In college basketball, it is the Bloomington-Lexington axis, which was tenuously formed by the ancient marriage of the two royal hoop families of Hoosierana and The House of Blue Grass.

The Kentucky-Indiana alliance seldom wavers in its power. It is invariably run by strong generals who are not to be questioned. Baron Adolph Rupp. Generallissimo Bob Knight. Field Marshals Denny Crum and Rick Pitino.

In fact, of all our basketball duchies, the Kentucky-Indiana empire alone expands, in more rapacious seasons, to embrace, moving east, Cincinnati or Morgantown, or north into Michigan. But the core is ever solid, always the heart in the realm of basketball.

The Appalachians are a channel, making North Carolina England. Just as the British Isles were fed by two strains—the Norman and the Germanic—so too Carolina. The tribe of Everett Case migrated from Indiana, introducing the modern sport to North Carolina State, to be quickly followed by the tribe of Frank McGuire, which invaded from New York.

Basketball New York is France. It amuses itself, eats and drinks with gusto, but seldom wins. Unlike the other great college basketball territories, the northeast boasts no lasting powers, no Kansases or Kentuckys. Rather, it has many nice vineyards—St. John's, Georgetown, La Salle, Villanova, even Princeton—which, however, only occasionally produce a vintage crop.

Rather, what matters most in the northeast, as in France, is the hub— Paris or New York. First, for basketball, it was Madison Square Garden. Then it was the networks. The teams, like good wine, are merely interchangeable.

Kansas is Italy. Ponder that. Yes, it was here that the game put down its cultural roots and spread. Dr. James Naismith, who invented basketball, himself coached at Kansas. Alas, Naismith was a very good inventor, but a very bad coach. More important, a Kansan named Phog Allen succeeded him and became Caesar, eventually sending out his lieutenants, Baron Rupp and Dean Smith, to rule other parts of the continent.

It was also Kansas that inspired the renaissance of college basketball, bringing Wilt Chamberlain out from the wine country, thereby making the sport truly continental.

In Europe, barbarians regularly sweep out of the East—from the time of Attila to the Soviets. In college basketball, the only difference is they come from the West. Occasionally, when Kansas, Carolina, Indiana, and Kentucky interbreed too much and weary momentarily of their hegemony, savage tribes, led by brilliant warlords, pour out of California. They conquer all in their path, but grow exhausted and eventually die out, leaving no discernible traces behind. It is easier for archeologists to uncover Etruscan villages from twenty-five hundred years ago than to unearth any evidence that UCLA only recently scorched arenas across basketball land.

And finally, in keeping with Nevada's status as a neutral free state, the University of Nevada–Las Vegas is Switzerland. Believe me, as in Europe, nothing ever really changes in college basketball.

Hooked on Golf

If I had my way, no man guilty of golf would be eligible to hold any office of trust or profit under these United States.

—H. L. Mencken

Of course, it was many decades ago that the Sage of Baltimore wrote these audacious words. So, good grief, what would poor Mencken say now on the subject? Back then, three quarters of a century ago, when he was so exercised, golf had hardly intruded on the body politic; it was but a country club game, played by the elite. People then actually used *golf*, the noun, as a verb. They *golfed* (as they yachted and summered).

Today, surely, Mencken would be apoplectic, besieged as we all are by golf. Everybody, including a lot of rude, déclassé people, plays golf. Moreover, I've suspected for a long time that although there are more of them now, golfers remain a people apart—that, as Fitzgerald said about the very rich, golfers are different from you and me. Well, anyway, from me.

Golf has become an utter phenomenon, ubiquitous upon the earth (especially the United States division), a dominant cultural force that has replaced most sensible, traditional American activities such as reading, the cocktail hour, sunbathing, worship of the Almighty, bridge and matinees.

Worse (better?), if Mencken's proposed antigolf statute were enforced, the entire government and much of Wall Street would be disenfranchised. The *New York Times* has even reported, with a straight face, that a survey showed that the lower an executive's handicap, the more successful he is as a businessman. It tells us a great deal that the pollsters, apparently assuming that all execs play golf, didn't even bother to check out the possibility that not playing golf would make an executive even better at business. But then, few bona fide serious Americans can, any longer, plead not guilty to golf.

How well I know. Occasionally, I am invited to play in some charity tournament. (Perhaps you weren't aware that, nowadays, the entire eleemosynary structure in the U.S. rests on charity golf tournaments; giving in America today is on the Golf Standard.) When I reply that I am sorry, but I do not happen to play golf, the response is incredulity. It's as if I have said that I am sorry, but I do not choose to have indoor plumbing in my house; or I am sorry, but my hobby is flag burning.

It's not that I have anything against golf, you understand. I have written, and still passionately believe, that a golf course is the most glorious thing that man and God have ever made together. Ah, you see, precisely because I don't play, I don't notice the rough. And I possess an actual golfing history: I caddied as a boy. I also have friends and family members who play golf, and at least a significant minority of them seem perfectly well-adjusted. I'm not one of those angry triathlon or body-building fanatics who put golf down as a travesty of exercise, a pseudo sport. No, I just choose not to play.

There's a whole other world out there. Golfers find this notion unacceptable. In the U.S. today, if you don't play golf, you must explain yourself.

This has all happened fairly quickly. Why, I can remember when all the beautiful people only skied. Now, in the manner of strip-mining, golf courses are being built on the fanciest mountains in Colorado, even if that means you have to play your short irons rather like a side-hill badger. For a long time, too, I thought that the cathedrals of fin de siècle America were our sports arenas. However, I have come to believe otherwise: The monuments that will be remembered most from this time will be our golf courses, delicately carved out of the most prized earth even as the suburban citizen fights in vain for a small plot, in hopes there to raise a family,

But: priorities. Be honest—does America want houses or fairways in the 21st century? There are now something like 100 golf courses that have been retrieved out of the desert around Palm Springs, almost 200 around Phoenix, all using enough water every day to keep the Brazilian rain forest from burning for another 37 years.

But all that seems to matter is that more land is gobbled up for golf courses so that more real estate agents can sell more condos overlooking more water holes to those flourishing new ethnics, the Golfer-Americans. No one—especially, it seems, those low-handicap executives—heeds the cautionary tale that comes from Japan, where huge numbers of the 1,500 or so courses built in the last few years have gone belly-up. In Connecticut it took the charisma of Paul Newman and $500,000 in seed money from him to save 740 acres of open space from being imprisoned as yet another golf development. Of course, rarely does golf have to contend with such a tasteful and resolute eminence as Mr. Newman.

Rather, even as we have become more egalitarian as a society, the institution of golf has been awarded a free pass, been allotted a privileged place in our culture. Doesn't anybody worry that the President of these United States spends obsessive hours on golf courses (even in the depths of winter) when he should be leading the free world? You think Saddam Hussein is out practicing chip shots?

Perhaps this merely tells us that we don't really need a full-time president anymore. Just a First Golfer. Or maybe good golf is simply a symbol of what leadership requires today. It wasn't that long ago that our chiefs had to be able to ride a horse well, wielding a fancy saber at the gallop. No doubt the Clinton Memorial will show him slugging a fairway wood, eyes boldly fixed on the distant green.

Or isn't it interesting that at a time when America is so manic on the subject of fitness, our business and political leaders exercise by riding golf carts—notwithstanding that it has been documented that the calories burned up by playing 18 holes while using a cart can be replaced by consuming one (1) chicken McNugget dipped in barbecue sauce?

But the fitness nuts are silent on the subject. I can only imagine that's because they're all up jogging in place and doing sit-ups at 4 A.M. as they wait in line to sign up for a late-afternoon tee time.

In fact, as near as I can tell, golf has risen above criticism. Even for those pledged to document it, golf isn't a sport so much as it is a sacred way of life. Why, even your hard-boiled, tough-guy sports columnists, including my colleague whose writing is located in the fairway on the back page of this magazine [*Sports Illustrated*], will rag on just about every sport, but they're all like li'l puppy dogs, whimpering verse, when it comes to the links. Just once before I die, I want to read one sportswriter with the courage to write, "F- - - Amen Corner."

You see, golf is what the range used to be, a homey place where never is heard a discouraging word. In fact, by law, there are only three things in golf that anyone is allowed to criticize: 1) the pin placements at the U.S. Open, 2) the rough at the U.S. Open, 3) Colin Montgomerie.

Sometimes, when I lie awake at night, all I can think is: What did poor Colin Montgomerie do to deserve this? Oh, well.

But if there's no criticism allowed in golf, there is this compensatory sociological curiosity: all—*all*—sports jokes are about golf. A friend of mine, a celebrated comedy writer named Jack Winter, first pointed this out to me. Have you ever once heard a tennis joke? he asked. A bowling joke? A football joke? In the entire history of comedy, there has never been a single hockey joke. Yet there are always golf jokes. A veritable plethora thereof.

I have given this a great deal of thought. There used to be many stupid jokes about fishermen. There are still a few hilarious fishing bumper stickers, such as I'D RATHER BE FISHING. But no more fishing jokes. Golf jokes have overwhelmed them. Not only that, but now most of the hilarious sports bumper stickers are also about golf, like MY OTHER CAR IS A GOLF CART.

Even more bizarre, the law about golf jokes is that even though there are thousands of them, they can fall into one of only two categories. First are the magic golf jokes, wherein God, Moses, Saint Peter, et al. are playing together and all making miraculous shots (*har-de-har-har*). Second are the side-splitting husband-plays-too-much-golf jokes. Golf jokes have no other roots, but the variations on the same two tired punch lines just go on and on. Maybe it's because golf is becoming a form of religion, with its own liturgy.

What tells me that golfers are truly a different race, though, is the way they feel about golf balls. Golfer-Americans worship these inanimate objects quite unashamedly. By contrast, have you ever seen, for example, a bunch of normal American tennis players at the start of a match? Balls? Everybody says, "Who brought the balls? Can we use this old can? They're still kinda fuzzy." But Golfer-Americans are absolutely maniacal about their balls. They even attribute human qualities to them, in the same way that Disney anthropomorphizes animals. When a golfer hits a ball awry, he says, "My ball found a bunker," as if this unhappy turn of events had nothing to do with who hit the ball, as if the ball sought out the bunker of its own free will. You ever hear a quarterback say, "My pass found the cornerback"? Of course not.

Golf operates differently. It's like one of those parallel universes that the starship *Enterprise* was always stumbling onto. Where's Spock when we need him? "Captain, huge numbers of chubby, oddly dressed humanoids seem to spend an excessive amount of time at massive out-door temples where they speak to a small, pockmarked sphere. It is most peculiar for what seems to be, otherwise, such an advanced race."

Oh, sometimes I have wondered how my life would have been if I, too, had played golf. I would have spent thousands of hours, hundreds of days, on the course instead of in the world. Nassaus, better balls, mixed foursomes, the driving range, the putting green. And gaily reliv-ing it all at the 19th hole: male bonding. My vacations would have been planned around golf. My testicles would have grown demonstrably larger and more metallic. I would have talked about Big Bertha as the only woman in my life. I would have found just the right ball for me. I would have addressed it. And I would have found all new friends. Joined select Golfer-American clubs, of course. Made blockbuster insider business deals in the locker room after a member-guest.

But probably, too, my life would have been much less productive. Let's face it, the American Dream of most young men, circa 2000, is to rush through life so they can retire and resettle in Dixie or in Irrigationiana, where they can play golf all year round, to the exclusion of all other pursuits. Really, now, is that the freedom that Sergeant York, John Wayne and Tom Hanks fought for? Or as Don Hewitt, my hero and the creator of *60 Minutes*, replied without shame when someone asked him why he, at age 75, and Mike Wallace, a certified octogenarian, still labor every day to create something: "Mike and I don't play golf."

Maybe, I began to think, we are breeding two entirely different races in America. Coexisting, yes, side by side, pretending to get along. Really, though: different beings, different souls, thinking differently, acting differently, treating women and animals and God differently, inexorably heading in different directions—us to the City on the Hill (or, anyway, to the multiplex theater at the mall), they to the gated condo community overlooking the prettiest water hole.

Frank Deford Goes Bowling

I'm sorry to have to be the one to tell you this, but bowling may have an image problem. Why is this, and why should we, as citizens, care? It's not good for America for bowling to fret. Bowling is too ubiquitous.

People I know (or, anyway, overhear) are forever talking about bowling nights. I drive past bowling alleys, and I'm positive that something wonderful (even awesome and mysterious) must be going on in there now, although that was never the case whenever I was there. And I see bowling everywhere on television. Yet bowling isn't in the newspaper, and nobody ever *analyzes* bowling.

By, God, is it ever there, is it ever around. Of all the things in sports (assuming, in the first place that bowling is in sports) bowling is most like senior prom and the church fair and trick or treat and buying a new bathing suit and Jujyfruits.

In the end, here is what I finally decided: Bowling is a lot like a half-time ceremony, *only you are in it.*

You haven't the foggiest idea who made me think these thoughts. If I gave you a million guesses, you'd never guess right. You would guess Rumpelstiltskin before you guessed the right answer.

And the right answer is, Richard Nixon.

Yes, of the Whittier Nixons. Several years ago I was interviewing him about Washington, D.C., but he kept bringing up the subject of bowling. Nixon, you'll recall, put bowling lanes in the White House. Jimmy Carter had them yanked out. Harry Truman put bowling lanes in the White House, too, although then they were bowling alleys. Dwight D. Eisenhower removed them, whatever they were called.

Bowling cuts across political lines. Anyway, Mr. Nixon kept haranguing me, saying there were so-and-so many bowlers in the U.S., but the press didn't write enough about bowling. *Sports Illustrated* didn't write near enough about bowling! He didn't come right out and say it, but I got the drift: If Woodward and Bernstein had only been good American boys, writing about bowling or, even better rolling a few lines themselves, then. . . .

Finally, I assured him that someday I would do my best to right this wrong to bowling. If Paul Harvey were telling this story, he would say that I am keeping a promise to a president, or, as Dr. George R. Allen (whom you'll meet later) would have it, I am keeping a PROMISE to a PRESIDENT.

Now please understand, I'm not altogether a bowling innocent. As a child I was a pinboy. I have met both Don Carter and Chris Schenkel. But you would certainly not consider me a pin pal or a student of keglermania. No, I set out to examine bowling academically, not unlike the way the intrepid Margaret Mead ventured off to Samoa. I even had this magazine [*Sports Illustrated*] issue me a small Japanese camera, so that I might also record my impressions on film, to provide a full sensory experience.

(I encountered one major problem as a photographer. I was often too shy to take strange bowlers' pictures from the front, where they could see me taking their pictures, so many of my shots of bowlers are from the rear. Felicitously, this is how we normally see bowlers—their posteriors, not their faces—so you're being treated to some cinema verité here in my debut as a lensman.)

In my study of bowling, here are the 10 things I found most interesting:

1) Nobody really knows who invented bowling, though it almost surely wasn't Abner Doubleday.

2) People involved with bowling have a wonderful sense of humor except when they are talking about bowling. Then they are grim.

3) A study funded by the sporting goods industry shows that the average bowler is wealthier and better educated than the average golfer.

4) Despite the fact that most bowling leagues go for 30 to 35 weeks a year and that a pair of bowling shoes sells for only around $20 to $40, an inordinately high number of bowlers spend a buck or so every time they visit the lanes to rent those funny shoes that look like part of a jester's outfit. This happily amazes bowling proprietors but

is one of the main reasons nobody with any sense believes that No. 3 above is correct.

5) The Bowling Hall of Fame, in St. Louis, is only three years old, but it is one neat Hall of Fame, really dandy. Its centerpiece is a swell bowling shirt display.

6) Bowling clobbers almost every other sport thrown up against it on television: college basketball, tennis, skiing, the Masters golf tournament.

7) The dumbest thing in all of bowling is the authorities' decree that everybody has to say "channel" instead of "gutter." First of all, it didn't work. Everybody still says gutter. I even heard Earl Anthony say it on television. (If you don't know who Earl Anthony is, that proves what President Nixon was saying about how the press isn't doing its job, bowling-wise.) Second, what's the matter with gutter? Like alley, it's a good, honest word.

8) By far the biggest issue in bowling is oil. On the alleys. How much? Spread evenly? All the way down? And so forth. Talk about boring big issues.

9) Nowadays more women bowl than men, and the balance is tilting more toward the females all the time. Better than two thirds of all U.S. leagues are now coed. Dr. George R. Allen says bowling had better watch it or real men are going to start thinking it's a sissy game.

10) Bowling doesn't just have an image problem. No. What it really has is a complex. Boy, does it have a complex.

Bowling headquarters, bowling central, bowling America is located in a Milwaukee suburb named Greendale. The first thing to understand about bowling (not necessarily the most interesting thing, which I have already told you, but the first thing) is that bowling is still Midwest. Very Midwest. Michigan boasts more bowlers than any other state. A large building in Greendale houses, under one roof, the American Bowling Congress (the largest all-male sports organization in the world), the Women's International Bowling Congress (the largest all-female sports etc.) and the Young American Bowling Alliance, which sounds like a 1950s communist front but which merely aims to introduce young bowlers to the joys of the lanes—and future membership in the ABC or WIBC.

The executive secretary of the ABC is Roger Tessman, who is also president of the Federation Internationale des Quilleurs (the last word in that name being a strange, foreign one for keglers). Snipers claim that Tessman spends too much of his time worrying about bowling outside the U.S. of A. And, after all, by any measure—the number of bowlers, alleys, gutters, leagues—about three fourths of the bowling on this planet is American.

My meeting with Tessman was necessarily very brief, because he had just arrived back in the Midwest from Seoul and was making the next connection out to Havana. Besides being an exhibition sport at the Summer Olympics this year, bowling may actually be a medal sport at the 1991 Pan Am Games. This excites many people in bowling. There's a widespread belief that this internationalism will help correct bowling's unfortunate "image" in boardrooms, on Rodeo Drive and over at *GQ*.

Generally, in fact, the two matters they devote their attention to at bowling headquarters are 1) oil and 2) convincing everyone that the typical bowler is a rocket scientist who earns $800,000 a year and wears designer clock socks.

The ABC/WIBC combo may be described as a benign cartel. Together, the two organizations collect $14 million a year in fees from the 6.7 million who belong to sanctioned leagues (out of 67 million bowlers in all). "We're a protection agency, in a way," says Dave DeLorenzo, the ABC p.r. manager, and if that doesn't sound quite right, well, what the ABC (and the WIBC) try to do is protect bowling from itself.

More than any other sport, bowling is a microcosm of life, an ongoing daily battle of greed versus generosity, knowledge versus ignorance, promiscuity versus moderation, darkness versus light, hard versus easy, evil versus good.

At regular intervals, going back to medieval times, bowling has been denounced as scummy; also at regular intervals—though verging on the constant—it has waged a fight against being too easy. Bowling, for example, had a great decline in the U.S. in the *1850s* because scores had become so ridiculously high, and it may have been saved only because the great German immigration to the U.S. that began at about that time added a new crop of bowlers to the population.

Now this easiness business has gotten downright ridiculous. Unfortunately, it goes far beyond bowling. It has to do with human nature. Uh-oh. People like to get rewarded and (though they won't admit it) all the more so if they don't have to work for it. Everybody can't be born with a silver spoon in his mouth, but everybody can get terrific bowling scores, and just as there are unscrupulous folks in this world who will help satisfy your dark desires for pleasures of the flesh; so are there bowling-house managers who will wantonly assist you in rolling strikes. (Bowling house, by the way, is another term the ABC says you're not supposed to use.)

This is done, quite effortlessly, with dressing oil, which, if spread the right (wrong?) way on a lane, will "block" it so that any modestly capable kegler can groove in. Mark Baker, one of the better young pros, says, "In an hour, you can turn any lanes in the country into a place where we can all shoot 250's every game." In the first half-century of the ABC's existence, a perfect game was rolled every two days. Now there are six or seven each and every day, and the ABC spends much of its energy dashing about, measuring oil, fingering the blocked houses and denying the high scores made in those wicked halls.

The challenge of the game also appears to be losing the battle to technology. It wasn't but a few years ago that the best bowlers in the world carried only a couple of old rubber balls around with them. Now the pros might tote a dozen urethane models to each stop and have 100 or 150 drilled to their specifications on tour—largely to deal with the oil. These space-age balls are designed to "grab" oiled lanes better so they'll hit the pocket harder, yielding more pin action and more strikes. A pleasant young man named Bill Hall follows the pro tour around and devotes almost all of his time to drilling holes in the balls in his trailer workshop. While I was in the trailer, Wayne Webb, Professional Bowlers Association Player of the Year in 1980, came in and reminded Hall that a few weeks before he'd gotten a ball slightly different than he'd requested. "Wayne didn't get through eighth grade," a kibitzer says, "but he can tell when his ball is a quarter ounce off."

Small differences like that really matter, too. "The ball is much better than the bowler now," says Dave Husted, one of the up-and-coming young pros. Remember last year when all everybody in baseball yakked about was how the ball was juiced up? Well, bowling is like that—only all the time. Imagine if you were there when Robin Hood split the other guy's arrow, but then all anybody talked about was the type of arrow Robin used, and the consistency of the wood, and how much deer grease he used, and scintillating stuff like that. Are you listening to me, Mr. Nixon? Are you beginning to understand why nobody wants to write about bowling when they can write about people?

But I sympathize with the bowling pooh-bahs. The double bind gets tighter all the time. Anybody who can plunk a buck down for a pair of jester's shoes can score. So nobody ever practices, and still expectations are so high that, even at reasonably modest levels, it becomes more a game of disappointment for failing to be perfect than a celebration for achieving, improving. As Peggy Lee sang, "Is that all there is?"

In fact, the most honest bowling in America is at Koz's Mini-Bowl in Milwaukee, because there the alleys are just 16 feet long. That way, even with little duckpin balls, almost anybody can bowl a 300. (They average five or six each week at Koz's, where they post scores *under* 140.) Many folks in the area do their bowling only at Koz's, because the company is good, the beer is cold, and there's hard truth enough in the rest of the world.

One day, in my journeys throughout bowleriana, I paused to watch a little girl's birthday party at the Bowlmor. It's down in Greenwich Village, up an old elevator, one of only four houses left in Manhattan. I was standing there with a Hispanic guy who was garbed in intercentury attire: a Union Army cap, an earring and Nikes. The first four little girls threw gutter balls. The Hispanic guy and I shrugged. The balls were in the gutter eight feet from the foul line. But then the fifth little girl stepped up. She acted exactly like the others, shoved the ball, and it rolled over and over, and about a half hour later it nudged into the 1–3 pocket, and all the pins tumbled down l i k e   t h i s, and she had a strike, the same as Mark Roth. (Roth is the leading money winner in the history of bowling, whom you also probably never heard of because that kind of stuff is seldom in the newspaper.) The Hispanic guy and I shrugged again.

I finally concluded that the reason bowling always does so well on television is because (there, anyway) it is less like a sport and more like a game show, in which everybody has a pretty equal chance, no matter what. *Pat, Pat, I wanna solve the puzzle, Pat! Vanna, Vanna, I just bowled 298, Vanna!* This drives the pros up the wall. And when the lanes are rigged to make it interesting so the bowlers don't get strikes with every ball, then every Cholly and Bunky down at Happy Time Bowl floods the Pro Bowlers Association with applications on Monday morning. "Hey, anybody can beat a pro on his own lanes," says Baker. "The game's too easy, and the balls are weapons now."

No wonder the pros have little self-regard. Often, when they're required to list their occupation, they write down "self-employed" instead of "pro bowler." Baker's girlfriend told him once, "Why don't you tell people you're a drug dealer and get some respectability?"

When the tour came to Columbus, Ohio, during Thanksgiving week, to the sumptuous Columbus Square Bowling Palace, the lanes were greased to make them as difficult as possible, and as a consequence the scores were the lowest of the year. As NBC prepared to televise the finals on Saturday (TV is so crucial to bowling, with its lack of an appreciable live gate or print coverage, that the players don't refer to qualifying for the finals; instead they talk of "making the show"), the producer, Glenn Adamo; the announcers, Jay Randolph and Bowling Hall of Famer Earl Anthony; and other principals met in the center's nursery to go over the telecast. As soon as Adamo mentioned that Randolph and Anthony would discuss the low scores—how Guppy Troup bowled a 92 one game; how Marshall Holman, the high-average pro for 1987, grew so frustrated over how the lanes were oiled that he threw his ball up against a wall; how the pros were generally threatening to eviscerate the PBA lane maintenance director—Kevin Shippy, who's head of public relations for the PBA, went bananas. "You're not going to say that, are you?" he asked.

"Kevin, that's the story of this tournament," Adamo replied.

Shippy pleaded that the reality of the low scores be glossed over. If not, viewers would be applying for the PBA tour left and right. "But, Kevin, it's been in the local papers," Adamo explained.

Finally, it was agreed that whereas Troup's 92 was a number of record, Holman's temper tantrum didn't have to be discussed on the air. It didn't really matter what the announcers said, because right there on their screens the viewers saw a ruffled journeyman named Leroy Bornhop win his first national tournament by rolling 179 and 169, respectively, in the semis and finals. His scores were barely above the national male average. "Oh, my God," Shippy moaned, only partly in mock despair, "the mailgrams are already piling up on my desk." This is what happens when bowling keeps advertising that anybody can bowl. Anybody believes it, and then anybody wants high scores, like anybody else. Or he quits.

Dr. George R. Allen nods knowingly at this development. Allen is also an erstwhile pinboy, but thereafter he went straight, earned a Ph.D. in marketing, management and finance, became a tenured professor at American University, and then published books on golf, blackjack and craps before circling back in on bowling. Allen then spent three months at the Library of Congress reading about nothing but bowling (this is believed to be a world record), and he's convinced that the end of the bowling world as we know it is nigh. He's like the lousy spoilsport on the *Titanic* who kept saying that they really should get some binoculars up on the bridge. But, of course, nobody listened to him, as nobody listens to Allen. "There's a conspiracy of silence at the top of the industry," he says.

Bowling people watched warily (and from some distance) as they saw me listening to Allen and *taking notes*. Allen told me he wasn't the least bit surprised that (as I bitchily revealed to him) Tessman, the ABC boss-man, was jetting all over the world, hardly pausing to stop in the Midwest. But, like many iconoclasts, Allen always speaks in placid, reasoned tones. He wears heavy horned rims and professorial corduroy coats and ties in subdued earth tones. His only immoderation appears to be his love for bowling and his profligate employment, when he writes, of words in capital letters. An example: "I am able to look at the COMMERCIAL or BUSINESS side of bowling with some degree of expertise. . . . Over the past seven years I have PERSONALLY ATTENDED most of the major bowling activities." And he remains convinced that bowling is going to hell in a handbasket and that it peaked around 1980, when there were 8,867,000 sanctioned league bowlers—three out of every eight folks in the country. By the year 2000, Allen says, there will be barely half that many, with only one in six citizens going to the alleys.

Naturally, nobody who makes his living from bowling wants to hear such sacrilege. Instead, the approved dogma is that because America is aging, all those baby-boomers who jogged and surfed will turn to bowling, and the graying of the republic will be celebrated on crammed Sunbelt lanes.

But Allen asserts that other developments were set in motion long ago that must doom bowling unless it radically changes its ways. He contends that the sport's three commercial "integers"—the Bowling Proprietors Association of America, along with Brunswick and AMF, the firms that manufacture the automatic pinsetters that the BPAA members buy—led the ABC and WIBC astray in the 1960s, changing the very nature of the game for their own self-interest: promoting bowling as recreation and, in the process, transforming it from a sport to an evening out. "Until then the bowler was perceived as an athlete and sportsman competing in a game that took some skill," Allen says, ruefully shaking his head, "but there's been a structural shift, a permanent change." He writes what he believes it has become: "The image of bowling is that of a NOTHING activity . . . RECREATIONAL BOWLERS ARE NOT GOING BOWLING, they are going recreating."

What's happening, Allen says, is that because fewer people who bowl have any real commitment to the sport, they'll drop out—there's now an almost 18% annual turnover in league bowlers—and find another way to spend Tuesday nights, until no one is left bowling but a hard core of the industrial working class in a society with a service economy.

But then, bowling appears to have always been recreathletics. A century ago, when the sport enjoyed its first great boom in America, the accepted procedure was for three teams to roll in each match so that one team could always be up at the bar having a few beers. Nowadays, bowlers appear to want the lanes greased right and the balls turned into bombs so they can all shoot 300's—and have more time to have a draft, flirt with teammates (that's what "mixed" league means) or play video games. What the hell, apart from sex and fishing, Americans appear to bowl more than they do anything else, and look at it this way: Present company excepted, who's ever perfect at sex or fishing?

More and more these days, bowlers go to huge suburban alcazars—48, 64, even more (!) shiny lanes—with baby-sitters, waitresses in little miniskirts, pro shops, video games, the works. These amusement cathedrals are owned and run by sharp businessmen like Jaime Carrion of Sarasota, Fla., whose other commercial interests include things like airlines, real estate, orange groves, and horse and cattle breeding. Carrion's five Florida centers are managed by his nephew, Rafi Carrion, who's typical of the new bowling entrepreneur. He went to prep school in New England and then to the University of Pennsylvania. "Before I got into bowling with my uncle, the only people I ever knew who bowled were Archie Bunker, Fred Flintstone and Ralph Kramden," Rafi says.

I visited Rafi at a state-of-the-art bowling emporium, the Galaxy Lanes, featuring Rafi's Bar & Grille, in Fort Myers, Fla. The place is splendiferous, with all the colors of the . . . galaxy. The bathrooms are tiled and spotless, the air in the building is changed every 20 minutes, there's a TV above each lane so that bored bowlers can watch soap operas between frames, the balls whip back at 60 mph to keep the keglers from lollygagging, and all the scoring is computerized, which is a special blessing, inasmuch as more bowlers than you would imagine never learn how to score.

The Galaxy Lanes came in at almost $5 million, the place is an absolute showcase, and everyone in bowling is convinced that the sport's future lies entirely with such edifices. Rafi knocks on wood, which he does quite a bit. He, too, believes that bowlers will only patronize magnificent buildings like the Galaxy Lanes, that the malling of America is complete.

And then I visited the Holler House, which boasts the two oldest sanctioned alleys in the U.S. The Holler House really is a house, as well as a bar and bowling alley. It's on the south side of Milwaukee, and even people from the ABC sneak down from Greendale to toss down a beer or two and roll a couple lines on alleys that were sanctioned in 1910.

When bowling spread out of the Northeast, it largely followed the pattern of German migration, and so the early bowling concentrations were in "Dutch" towns like Milwaukee, Chicago, Cincinnati and St. Louis. It also drifted south, down to another big German-American city, Baltimore, where a couple of the old Orioles—the Little Napoleon, John McGraw, and Uncle Robbie, Wilbert Robinson—opened a combination alleys-saloon with, as Lola used to sing, the emphasis on the latter. But McGraw was worried about his pitchers' arms when they bowled, and so one spring day in 1901 he commissioned a woodturner named John Dittmar to fashion a miniature ball and pins. They were quickly christened duckpins because, when squarely hit, they flew (a local romantic decided) like little ducks in flight.

Similarly, a bit earlier, up in Worcester, Mass., Justin (Pop) White created skinny little candlepins. And so, until very recently, some parts of New England and the Baltimore-Washington-Tidewater arc had next to nothing to do with tenpins—everybody rolled candles or ducks. However, knocking down the smaller pins is hard, and, as we know, nobody wants any truck with doing anything difficult in bowling, so the 16-pound ball and the 15-inch pins took over the rest of the country. Now they've even moved into candle and duck territory.

Even though the Holler House is in Milwaukee, Marcy Skowronski says, "I got some ducks up in the attic. But then, I got everything up in the attic. I got enough bowling balls up there people left behind to make a rosary out of them."

Marcy slides me a shorty beer, 60 cents. She runs the Holler House along with her husband, Gene. They raised their family there, living in the other part of the Holler House, the house part. It has been in Gene's family for three generations, counting his and Marcy's four daughters. For a long time, Gene's father, Iron Mike Skowronski, who was born in Poland, was the boss. As a matter of fact, the place was just called Mike's Tap until one morning some 30 years ago when a guy came in early, after a fight with his old lady. Marcy was working the bar. The guy didn't want to bowl. He wasn't interested in the alleys at all. Instead, he asked Marcy, "Would you care to get bombed with me?"

What the hell. Marcy said, "Yeah, sure, why not?" and poured a shot and a beer for herself, too.

After a while, as is normally the case, Mike's Tap got real noisy, and when the guy's better half finally found him, she was taken aback some. "She didn't know whether to spit or go blind," Marcy explains. When the wife finally got the guy home, she told everybody she had rescued him from "that holler house." It stuck. Nobody has ever forgotten Iron Mike, though. He was quite a guy. Seventy-nine years old, and he was still smoking 10 cigars a day, drinking copious quantities of Old Fitz— Iron Mike could take a shot of the Old Fitz, hold it in his mouth, take a shot of water and then spit out the water without losing a drop of Old Fitz—and beating most of the younger guys at Indian wrestling.

Iron Mike's picture is still up on the wall. Other accoutrements include a bat used by Harvey Kuenn, an exceptionally large pair of women's white drawers, a big jigsaw puzzle on one of the tables. Sometimes it takes two, three months, but the Holler House crowd finally gets the puzzle done, and then they start a new one. Also, one of those bowling games where you shove a little metal disk and the pins go *up*. A dart board. An old icebox.

And there's an ancient beer pail. In the old days the men in that area worked at big manufacturing plants, Allis Chalmers mostly, and after the whistle blew, the men would bring their beer pails to Mike's Tap to get them filled up for home. Most of the fellows would be sure to put butter on the inside of their pails to cut down on the foam, so they would get more beer. Also: the Holler House jukebox. It has everything from Sinatra to hard rock, plus six dirty songs if you know the right buttons to push, and, of course, it has *Back in the Saddle Again*, by Gene Autry.

The Holler House loves Gene Autry. The regulars celebrate his birthday every Sept. 29. The Holler House also has an annual banquet for the people who play in the disk bowling league, and in February there's a beach night. This is in Milwaukee, remember. Everybody comes in shorts and T-shirts. Sometimes strangers walk in off the street for a beer that night. "They don't know whether to spit or go blind," Marcy says.

About half of the Holler House regulars bowl. Marcy poured me another shorty, and I asked her how much it cost to roll a line, but she couldn't remember. So she asked her daughter Cathy, who was also behind the bar, what the going price was, but Cathy wasn't sure either. And neither was a son-in-law. Evidently, it's 85 or 95 cents, maybe a buck, depending on whatever occurs to whoever is running the joint at the time. There are also shoes available, if you need them. This is the way that's handled at the Holler House: Marcy goes through all the absent regulars' bowling bags until she comes across a pair that fits the customer.

There's a lot of league action at the Holler House. The night I was there, it was mostly ladies. They play a little side deal, too. One of the women brings a deck of cards with photographs of naked men on them. I tell you, after I saw this deck, I didn't know whether to spit or go blind. The way it works is, everyone antes 50 cents, and if you make a strike or convert a tough split, you get to draw a card. The best poker hand of naked men at the end of the night wins the pot.

There are still pinboys at the Holler House. Three games for a buck, plus tips. Pinboys pretty much disappeared in the 1950s when the automatic pinsetters came in. Just in time. The National Child Labor Committee was on the warpath, claiming that pinboys (the ones who really were boys and not the old rummies) were getting only 11 cents a line, staying out too late, getting clobbered by flying wood and associating with undesirables (i.e., bowlers). It was assumed then that once pinboys were eliminated and the beautiful new centers with automatic lanes were constructed, bowling's image problem would be solved. But, of course, it didn't work out that way. Evidently, bowling is just destined never to be respectable.

Only, thankfully, at the Holler House, bowling never changes. Two guys were talking at the bar. The one with his hat on said, "I seen a guy come on TV Saturday with 23 balls that he used."

The other guy said, "Yeah, he's got one for this alley, one for that alley, one for splits, one for—"

"That ain't *bowling*."

"Yeah, bowling is one ball, you and the alley."

At the Holler House, they haven't had but two 300 games in 80 years, and the last one was in 1934. What would you give somebody if he bowled a perfect game at the Holler House? Marcy slid me another shorty and said, "I'd give 'em Gene."

Gene, you will recall, is Marcy's husband.

Gene had a stroke a couple of years ago, and he'd already gone up to bed. He's back to bowling once a month with the boys, though. Still, it made Gene and Marcy think, and so they bought a condo in Arizona. It hasn't what you would call taken, though. "We got furniture and everything," Marcy says. "You'd think we were newlyweds or somethin'. But the last time I was down there, all I wanted was to get back to Milwaukee. I says to myself, 'Marcy, you are not ready for this.' Gene too. He's not ready to leave the Holler House."

Their grandson Michael, age 10, the fourth generation at the Holler House, is already learning to oil the alleys. "Friday nights now is the young people, and as loud as they play the music on the alleys then, I won't even go down there," Marcy says. "But, oh God, I could never give up this place. I could never give up the bar or the alleys."

As we've seen, bowling is many things. Bruce Pluckhahn, who's the curator at the Hall of Fame, says, "You travel the back roads of France, and they're playing types of bowling you can't imagine." And the bowlers. Often in the past, bowlers were above the salt, clearly upper-crust. Or ecclesiastical. Martin Luther, for one, was an avid kegler. In some bishoprics it was believed that the Devil himself bowled, using a human skull for a ball, rolling it down Christ's cross. And priests who sinned were supposed to have to spend all eternity bowling.

But inevitably the lower classes would appropriate the sport, drink and gamble while enjoying it, and so the hypocritical upper crust would get together with the men of the cloth and decree bowling sinful and/or illegal. That was the pattern in Europe and the U.S. alike.

It probably didn't help bowling's reputation when, as early as 1839 in Hartford, Conn., it moved inside (before, it usually had been played outdoors on grass). Generally speaking, Americans look down their noses at indoor exercise. When people play sports outside, it is referred to as "working up a good sweat," and it's approved as healthy. But indoor exercise has always been put down as sweaty, déclassé. Basketball was accepted in American culture only when it moved into huge, plush buildings with cathedral ceilings that gave the spacious feeling of all outdoors. Then basketball players weren't grubby lower-class types anymore—they became "glistening bodies." But no bodies shine in bowling. It's still just indoorsy and sweaty.

Also, most bowling alleys had posts, and everybody hates posts, not only because all they can do is get in your way, but also because posts just seem proletariat. I'm convinced that posts have been very bad for bowling.

Moreover, curiously, no romantic notions ever grew up around bowling, as they did, say, around pool, bowling's companion smoky, indoor, boozing-and-betting game. There have probably been as many bowling cons as there've been pool hustlers, but bowling is terribly self-conscious about its charming rogues. Troup, a former machinist, always appears in garish trousers, his upper limbs weighted down by diamonds and gold, but he's about the only pro bowler these days with a flamboyant public persona. Most PBAers barely crack a smile. Bowling has just never understood that you can profit from being seedy-chic, the way pool has.

Possibly as a consequence of bowling pretentiousness, there's no movie with Paul Newman about bowling. David Letterman wanted to get a bowler on his show, to yuk it up, a la baseball's Buddy Biancalana a while back, but bowling takes itself too seriously to permit such whimsy.

It's wonderfully ironic that the only brush bowling has had with literature was in the story about Rip Van Winkle, and, of course, Washington Irving's tale, published in 1819, involves bowling *and* drinking. If bowling's tradition was already fatefully intertwined with social drinking, it became all the more so in America after the German immigration swelled the sport's ranks in the latter part of the 19th century. German culture was never more prominent in America, and the Teutonic spirit of camaraderie, gemütlichkeit, was a natural for the bowling alley. Significantly and symbolically, the ABC was founded in 1895 at Beethoven Hall in New York City by a group of men who consumed six ponies (half-kegs) of beer. Just as saloons offered free lunches—until we learned there's no such thing—so too did establishments allow keglers to bowl on the cuff so long as they bellied up to the bar between frames. Even today, at fancy places like the Galaxy Lanes, a full 30% of the income derives from "ancillary" sources, mostly food and drink, and many bowling houses depend on the bar for their very existence. At a time when national beer sales are flat and driving home from drinking anywhere is under heavy criticism, this doesn't bode well for suburban recreating.

But bowling's alliance with beer has never flagged. From the 1930s until about 1960, almost all of the top bowling competition involved the legendary beer teams—first, the white-clad Stroh's keglers, then the teams sponsored by Pfeiffer's and Falstaff, finally the fabled Budweiser teams of the fifties, featuring Don Carter, Dick Weber and Ray Bluth. In 1961 there was a brief and expensive disaster with a conventional professional association known as the National Bowling League. (No doubt you recall all the teams in the NBL, but just in case they've slipped your mind: Detroit Thunderbirds, Twin City Skippers, Omaha Packers, Dallas Broncos, Fort Worth Panthers, San Antonio Cavaliers, Kansas City Stars, Fresno Bombers, Los Angeles Toros and New York Gladiators, who actually played in Totowa, N.J.). The collapse of the NBL, which just happened to coincide with the demise of the beer-team era, marked the end of big-time team bowling.

After that, because of the demands of television, bowling was transformed from a team to an individual sport, with the beer companies sponsoring, even producing, most of the TV tournaments. In what may have been sport's hottest free-agent action of 1987, Coors (in a major upset) beat Miller in the battle to sign Leila Wagner, a woman bowler, to an endorsement contract. As a kegler, Wagner ranked a modest 19th in earnings on the women's tour, but she's blonde and built, a former Miss Washington State in the Miss Universe pageant.

Such occasional forays into sexiness aside, women's bowling is even more self-conscious about its image, if that is possible, than men's bowling is. Women bowlers still grit their teeth when they recall the scene from the movie *Arthur* wherein the stuffy valet, played by John Gielgud, seeking to put down a pushy, tacky woman in the most complete way he could, uttered, "Usually, one has to go to a bowling alley to meet a woman of your stature."

As bowling becomes more of a women's sport, the pro "bowlerettes" (as they used to be called) are chafing at the fact that they competed for only $854,000 last year—less than 6% of what was at stake in women's tennis. It has even come to a civil war, with a splinter tour. TURMOIL AMONG WOMEN KEGLERS, cried *The Sporting News*. And Miller and Coors fight hammer and tong over the 19th-best bowler because she's blonde and stacked. Priorities.

Says Bucky Woy, a baseball agent who once ran the women's bowling tour, "Hey, by and large they were pretty attractive. I'll tell you—nicer looking than the golfers and tennis players. But it didn't matter. Image. The image. They change the words, alleys to lanes and gutters to . . . whatever they changed gutters to. But it didn't matter. That was all smoke and mirrors. Even when the numbers were supposed to be good, all you could get for sponsors was Midas Muffler—and Budweiser. It doesn't matter how attractive they are. It never will. Image. The image."

John Falzone, the current president of the LPBT and the manager of a bowling center in Cherry Valley, Ill., expresses the industry's endemic frustration. "The numbers are so outstanding that people have trouble believing them," he says. "A bowler has a higher income than a golfer. *That's proved.* But it doesn't compute."

And so it goes. Everybody in bowling believes the sacred bowling demographics that have been uncovered and issued by the National Bowling Council, while nobody outside bowling believes them at all. Whom do *you* believe? You think Cadillac would sponsor the Masters instead of some café-society bowling tournament if it believed? America's largest bowling emporium is at the Showboat Hotel in Las Vegas. Recently, when the Atlantic City Showboat opened, the hotel-casino complex included some lanes, specifically to attract blue-collar patrons to the slots, according to Frank A. Modica, president of Showboat. Presumably, the Showboat has some idea who bowls.

People in bowling explain away the discrepancy between demographics and public perception by invoking the ever-popular CEO conspiracy theory. According to that theory, all CEOs play golf and tennis—probably, in fact, all CEOs get to be CEOs only because they play golf and tennis—and so they refuse to act on the dispassionate, unbiased figures put out by the National Bowling Council because *the CEOs are protecting golf and tennis.*

Allen's opinion is that the figures the bowling establishment touts are, in a word, hooey. We were talking in a bowling center, and the bowling people were still keeping a careful eye on me. "But that would be . . . fraud," I whispered.

Allen's expression remained unchanged. "I don't use that word," he said. "I might call it hyperbole or public relations or bureaucratic fog."

"I'm glad to hear that," I said, "because I thought I was going crazy. The thing is, people in bowling alleys look exactly the way I imagined they would look, just like they looked the last time I was hanging around bowling alleys. They don't look at all like what I'm told they should look like."

"You're not crazy," Allen said reassuringly. "No one is being fooled by those figures. They're misleading at best, and highly suspect. And I guarantee you there's only one Ph.D. in this building, and you're looking at him."

This set me back a little, as Allen didn't know I wasn't a Ph.D., and I always thought maybe I looked like one. But I let it pass. He went on:

"Of course the numbers don't add up. It's unusual to find anybody from college in a bowling center, because there aren't many of them that go there. And there will probably be fewer in the future, because well-educated people have the kind of schedules that simply won't allow them to bowl the same night of the week, 35 weeks in a row. It's not just that leagues are losing 18% of their members every year, it's that the system repels the most affluent. Besides, who with any intelligence wants to go to a cocktail party with the same people 35 weeks a year?"

Allen shook his head woefully. "No, what you see adds up. Bowling's still very much what it used to be. And, not to be cruel, but as you can see, they're not very good-looking people. They're not well dressed, and they're not in great shape." Allen paused. "But they're good people. They're very good people."

I surely don't know what the future holds for bowling. But I know that the one thing that bothered me on my visit to this peculiar little universe was that bowling seems to be so very embarrassed about itself. In many respects it denies the very people who constitute the heart of bowling, who love bowling, who support bowling, who are bowling. I think bowling will prosper in the long run only if it just lets itself be bowling. We don't need another pseudo-golf or -tennis. We already have golf and tennis for that.

The single most jarring thing I experienced in bowling was when watching Husted, the aforementioned up-and-coming pro, bowl. He's a very good-looking and bright young man, from an upper-middle-class family that happened to own two bowling centers. He had a four handicap in golf, but after high school he went right out on the PBA tour. And this is what Husted wears when he bowls: a snappy red Nike sport shirt, tan pleated khaki pants with a brown leather belt, a wristwatch with a brown leather strap and argyle socks with Nike bowling shoes that look exactly like tennis shoes. *This is not proper bowling attire!* This is like wearing a three-piece suit, a fedora and wing tips to play second base for the White Sox. Bowlers don't even wear their names on the back of their shirts anymore when they're on TV. Bowling changed things for the benefit of stiffs who don't like bowling. Now to see real bowling shirts you have to go to a museum. "I genuinely lament the passing of the bowling shirt," says Pluckhahn. "Tell me, what exactly have we gained now that our bowlers wear golf knitwear?"

Sometimes I thought that, of all the people in bowling, Pluckhahn, the one who is paid to live in the past, enjoyed the finest sense of what the game truly is. Then, too, everybody I met who isn't in bowling but deals with the bowling industry adored the people in bowling. This included folks in television, in the beer business, in the sporting goods industry. Compared with people in other sports, bowling types were everybody's favorite. And it was easy for me to see why. To quote Dr. George R. Allen, "They're good people."

"They're so enjoyable, so down-to-earth, so unpretentious," says Jeff Kramer, a Nike marketing manager. "And you know what I can't understand? Why do the people who run bowling want to appeal to yuppies? Nobody ever liked yuppies. But here bowling already has the best people in the world, and they keep pushing to replace them with yuppies."

The funny thing is, too, that in much of the sports world these days, everybody lauds everything blue-collar. In fact, the only place where you even hear the term white-collar anymore is in the context of white-collar crime. An athlete would probably quit the team if he heard his coach say that he was "a real white-collar player." But the best thing you can say about an athlete is that he's a real blue-collar player. Today, blue-collar means a day's work for a day's pay. It means hustling, dependable, devoted, honest as the day is long. It means: America. Or anyway, the way America was supposed to be when we were taught about America. All the phonies who own or coach or watch in other sports, all the nouveaux and the yuppies, all the white-collar guys who have not quite yet been convicted of white-collar crime, all of them are searching high and low for genuine blue-collar types, and here bowling has all the blue-collar, and all it wants is to be identified with the service economy. Can you believe the irony in that?

The next time I chat with President Nixon, I'm going to ask him what he thinks about that. It's a fine how-do-you-do.

Set 'em up.

The Sports Curmudgeon

■   ■   ■

Watch out! The Sports Curmudgeon is here, and he is angry. He has been locked up in a sports bar all year, reading the agate in the *USA Today* sports section and listening to sports talk radio, until this past week, when, for four days running, he had to hear television announcers refer to The Augusta National Golf Course in the sacred tones usually reserved for Bethlehem, Mecca, the Wailing Wall and the Tomb of the Unknown Soldier.

So, The Sports Curmudgeon has had it up to here, and therefore now releases his Top Eleven list of things he can simply no longer abide in sport. (The reason it is a Top Eleven is because The Sports Curmudgeon is overflowing with so much bile that he can't restrict it to a Top Ten.) Herewith, then, from The Sports Curmudgeon:

Number 1 INTERMINABLE LASER INTRODUCTIONS AT NBA GAMES

The Sports Curmudgeon asks: Has anybody but me noticed that the more the NBA devotes its energy to laser introductions, the more boring are the post-introductions . . . or "games," as we used to call them.

Number 2 VICTORIOUS FOOTBALL TEAMS WHO POUR GATORADE ON THEIR COACHES

The Sports Curmudgeon says, okay, maybe it was funny the first time a dozen years ago. *Maybe*. Once. Maybe. Besides, how stupid are the coaches now not to expect being doused?

Number 3 ANNOUNCERS IN ANY SPORT WHO SAY THAT THE—CHOOSE ONE: SHOOTER, QUARTERBACK, HITTER—HAD "A GOOD LOOK"

Fine women have good looks. The Sports Curmudgeon says: Keep good looks out of sports.

Number 4 BASEBALL SCHEDULING GAMES EARLY IN APRIL IN PLACES LIKE MILWAUKEE AND DENVER

The Sports Curmudgeon says that baseball needs two things: a commissioner and a calendar. Or, a commissioner who can read a calendar. Okay, just a calendar.

Number 5 MALE TENNIS PLAYERS WHO STICK THE SECOND SERVICE BALL IN THEIR POCKETS

"Where has style in sports gone to?" cries The Sports Curmudgeon, bemoaning lumpiness.

Number 6 FEMALE TENNIS PLAYERS WHO STICK THE SECOND SERVICE BALL IN THEIR PANTIES

See same Sports Curmudgeon response, number 5. Only more virulently. Would Kathryn Hepburn stick a tennis ball in her panties? Would Emily Post?

Number 7 AMERICAN SPORTS FANS WHO SCREAM "U!S!A! U!S!A!" WHEN WE ARE BEATING PARAGUAY OR SRI LANKA 75-3

The Sports Curmudgeon says that patriotism is the last refuge of a rotten sports fan.

Number 8 HOCKEY GOALIES WHO LEAVE THEIR LITTLE WATER BOTTLES ON TOP OF THEIR NETS

The Sports Curmudgeon says: We do not need littering on the field of play. What's next? Picnic lunches for the right fielder? A bad precedent.

Number 9 MIKE TYSON

Only The Sports Curmudgeon can't decide whether he disliked Iron Mike more when he was a bully, or now, when he is scared to death of old Evander Holyfield.

Number 10 "SHOW ME THE MONEY"

Next would-be funny guy who says "show me the money," The Sports Curmudgeon says: Show him the door.

Number 11 PRESIDENTS OF THE UNITED STATES OF AMERICA WHO INVITE ALL WINNING TEAMS TO THE WHITE HOUSE

The Sports Curmudgeon says: Go back to number 7. Presidents who do this are only looking for the votes of those jackasses. Hey, why not invite some good losers to the White House?

Now, The Sports Curmudgeon is off to see the new Dennis Rodman movie, so he can start getting his blood boiling again.

And to you and yours, he says: Have a good look!

All I Know about Cars

■   ■   ■

I know very little about automobile racing, except that it is terribly loud and I can never tell who is ahead. But, in honor of the upcoming Indianapolis 500, I would like to share with you the ten things I do know about cars:

1) No matter what I am driving, your windshield wipers will work better than mine.

2) Bumper stickers have never helped a thing.

3) A major reason why Americans drive around in cars is so they can drive around and listen to the car radio. It is a truism that Americans are crazy about cars—maybe. In fact, I think many more Americans are crazy about car radios. Therefore, if radios and other audio devices were banned, untold numbers of Americans would not take to the roads, we would immediately save 2.4 million barrels of oil a day, and we would never have to worry again about the Persian Gulf.

4) If Chrysler still made convertibles, more people would care about what happened to Chrysler.

5) If I were General Motors or Ford, I would pay special attention to number four.

6) The most exhilarating feeling I ever had was when I learned I could actually hold a car suspended on a hill, in gear, playing off the clutch with my left foot and the accelerator with my right. Now that gearshift cars are disappearing, young people will lose something dear about growing up. Of course, car radios are getting better all the time.

7) It is a base canard that women are worse drivers than men. On the other hand, seldom, if ever, will you find a woman who can park very well.

8) Year in and year out, the tackiest license plates in the United States are Indiana's, but they are no match for the Northwest Territory plates in Canada, which are made in the shape of a bear. I'll bet you didn't know that.

9) In the back seat, children like the middle best. You would think they would like a window, but they don't.

10) No matter what I am driving, your defroster will work better than mine.

Vroom, vroom.

Own, Owner, Own!

■   ■   ■

I'm not so sure that Jerry Jones, the owner of the Dallas Cowboys, understands how awful the word "owner" sounds in modern Americanese. It's worse even than such other prime antidemocratic words like "boss" and "landlord" or "tax." But Jerry actually has the word OWNER (in capitals) inscribed on his Super Bowl ring.

Help me out. Do we ever even use the word "owner" outside of sports anymore? Even if you are, in fact, the one hundred percent owner of something, you're more likely to call yourself something amorphous like CEO. It's more workplace correct, less threatening.

There's a story, probably apocryphal, but what the heck, apocryphal is just a fancy word for gossip, about the young Edward McCaskey, the owner of the Chicago Bears. He went to Jim Finks, then his general manager but now deceased, and volunteered that he'd like to do more for the team. "You're an owner, Ed," Finks is supposed to have said. "So own, Ed, own."

But, of course, that's the point. Who wants to just own? Especially if you're already a rich man and already own a whole lot of stuff, what's the sense of owning a sports franchise—a team !—if you're just going to *own* it?

In fact, most of the rich men, like Jerry Jones, who do own teams now, made their money because they were smarter than other people. Now that they've reached the top, having bought the ultimate twentieth-century-capitalist dream, a sports franchise, they're supposed to stop being smart? Jerry Jones wants some credit, too. He wants to be appreciated and not just rich—no less than the rest of us who want to be appreciated and not just poor.

Unfortunately, what Jerry doesn't quite see—or maybe he does, but he just doesn't care—is that sports fans take it as an article of faith that owners are dumb when it comes to sports. In fact, all sports fans know for a fact that only two types of human beings can be smart about sports: ex-players and current fans. Owners might have made hundreds of millions of dollars wildcatting natural gas or inventing software or manipulating real estate deals or selling refrigerators to Eskimos, but intelligence is not transferable *into* sports. Oh no, sports is much too sophisticated for self-made billionaires.

The ideal owners are those, who, like children, are seen but not heard. The ne plus ultra of owners was Tom Yawkey, who owned the Boston Red Sox, but spent most of his waking hours in South Carolina and never got involved with the club he owned. Bostonians complained about everything else *vis-à-vis* the BoSox—they bitched eternally about Ted Williams, the last of Homo sapiens to hit .400—but they never had a bad word for Mister Yawkey. No sirree, now there was an owner. He owned. The team always lost, but he always just . . . owned.

And of course, the worst owner type is George Steinbrenner, but that's fair. He really doesn't know anything.

So, as a consequence of this prejudice, owners are supposed to anoint general managers (we call them GMs, since it sounds better) to run the show, because owners are too stupid themselves. Unfortunately, where this fan philosophy breaks down is that fish rots from the head. If owners are too stupid to run a team themselves, why shouldn't they be too stupid to pick somebody else to run a team?

Well, every now and then somebody like Jerry Jones figures this out and decides to run things himself, and thereby save a salary.

The only trouble is that then there is nobody for the fans to demand be fired when things go sour—and the whole point of being a fan is to call for organizational executions. It's worth recalling that sports fans in America were originally called "cranks." Honestly. And, essentially, they still are. Cranks. Cranky. But here are the poor Cowboys cranks: they're lost souls, disoriented. Jerry Jones is an owner who dares to think he knows about sports—as much, if not more, than sports fans. Jerry Jones actually tells coaches what to do. But—and here's the rub—he has built the Cowboys fans the winner their hearts desired.

What's a poor Cowboys fan to do? If the team loses, it's terrible. But, if the team wins, the owner is vindicated, proven smart. And that's terrible. Jerry Jones has made America's Team so un-American. The owner dares to do more than own. The owner just doesn't know his place.

Golf v. Tennis

■   ■   ■

These are the differences between tennis players and golfers:

Golfers actually love to brag, masochistically, about how much time and effort they must commit merely to get on the course. "Me and Chuck got up at 3:30 just to be able to get to Pine Crest to sign up at 4:30, so we could play at 10. We didn't get home till four."

Tennis players, in contrast, boast how easy it is to play quickly. "I skipped lunch with Howie yesterday and we squeezed in two sets, but were back in time for the budget session."

*   *   *

Professional golf is played by middle-aged men and old men.

Professional tennis is played by young men and baby girls. Go on, name one female golfer . . .

*   *   *

Golf fans are unbelievably positive. They cheer every shot. Even when they can't see where a drive is going, their instinct is to cheer. "Oooohhhh! Aaahhhh. You de man!"

Tennis fans assume that every break of serve is a choke. Nobody ever wins. It's just: the other guy chokes. Greg Norman couldn't have lasted five minutes in tennis.

*   *   *

Golfers are consumers.

Tennis players are skinflints.

*　　*　　*

Golfers study golf magazines, which are the size of encyclopedias, and every month pick out new thousand-dollar kryptonite irons and helium balls, which are guaranteed to add a hundred yards to their shots and hone in on the hole.

Tennis players skim over the rare advertisements in their slim tennis magazines and then go play with their trusty twenty-seven-year-old Head racket, which has (at least) five more good years on it.

*　　*　　*

Golfers remember—and discuss—every shot they ever made. "On sixteen, I took a seven when I shoulda used a six, so it found the trap and then . . .

Tennis players think in the aggregate: "My backhand sucks . . ."

*　　*　　*

Golf pros are more sportsmanlike than the average golfers, while:

Tennis pros are less sportsmanlike than the average tennis players.

*　　*　　*

Golf pros are all married to anonymous brunettes, who suddenly appear, carrying a baby, at the 72nd hole to kiss their victorious husbands.

Tennis pros are all accompanied by a bizarre retinue who helps them live spectacularly embroidered private lives that exceed the saga of any ordinary nineteenth-century Russian novel.

*　　*　　*

Golfers never talk about their spikes.

Tennis players are, on the other hand, very sneaker conscious. But:

*　　*　　*

Golfers absolutely believe in golf balls. They talk as if these balls have independent control over them. If a golfer hits a bad shot, he always says that the ball—not the shot, but the *ball—found* the rough. Or *found* the trap. Golf balls somehow always find places to go all on their own.

Tennis players say: Hey, who brought the balls?

*   *   *

Golf journalists want desperately to themselves play on the course where the pros are playing.

Tennis journalists want to find out with whom the pros are sleeping.

*   *   *

Golfers who hit long are exciting.

Tennis players who hit hard are boring. Pete Sampras was born to be a golfer.

*   *   *

Golfers look good in golf clothes, so long as they carry a club. Very imposing.

Tennis players manage to look bad in tennis clothes because they stick the extra balls in their pockets or their underwear and look all lumpy.

*   *   *

Basically, people play golf so they can bet during a round and drink afterwards, while:

People play tennis so they can tell you that they're in better shape than are the people who play golf.

Worth

■　　　■　　　■

I ronically, even as Michael Jordan's agent asks for the kind of money that *Twister* has been taking in at the box office, money really doesn't matter anymore in sport. Oh, sure, to the players and their agents and the owners, it's still a way of doing business. It's another stat. But while the fans may still think professional athletes are unworthy lucky devils, the money players are paid now is so incredible that, for fans, it's become meaningless.

On the other hand, when players were making salaries that could be related to what the average working stiff made, fans had very strong opinions on salaries, and could, often as not, be very unforgiving, even of their own players' salaries.

Some player would ask for a five-thousand-dollar raise to thirty-five thousand dollars a year, and fans would say: Whoa, he only hit .293, and he only drove in eighty-three runs, and look at other third basemen in the league—so where does he come off thinking he's due thirty-five? Thirty-two five will be just fine, thank you.

When Sandy Koufax and Don Drysdale banded together thirty years ago to try and break through the one-hundred-thousand-dollar glass ceiling, fans everywhere—prominently including Dodgers fans—were . . . well, they were *offended*. There prevailed the view then that we were all sort of in this together—player, team, league, fan, sport—and that if somebody made too much it would somehow throw this whole delicate mechanism off balance.

Besides, in the matter of player salaries, we average Joes could relate to them. If you were making $18,200 yourself, then you had a great sense of what $35,000 a year meant to a player. At a time when I was earning about ten thousand, I can vividly recall going into the Yankees' clubhouse after the 1963 World Series and passing on the news to a couple of friends of mine on the team that their losing World Series share might very well come in at eighty-five hundred dollars per man. I was as thrilled for them as I was envious. We all understood exactly what eighty-five hundred dollars meant.

But now, today, when somebody asks me if I think Alonzo Mourning is worth seventeen million dollars a year, I have no more response than if somebody requested my views on whether or not they should raise import taxes in Luxembourg a quarter of a percent.

What is Michael Jordan worth? What is a breeze worth on a hot summer's day? What is a smile worth? Who knows? Jordan is worth so much to the Bulls as a player, so much at the box office. He is worth so much to the other teams when he comes to town. He is worth something in the NBA's television contract to the Philippines. How much? Who knows?

Never mind Jordan. For *any* player, with salary caps, balloon payments, deferred payments, bonuses—who knows? At a certain point, fans simply stopped being involved, emotionally, in how much any player made, and as the numbers grew it became more and more difficult to even understand the figures, academically. In an odd way, some kind of visceral connection was lost between the fan and the player when money no longer became a personal issue.

Today, basically, the fans just want their owner to pay whatever it takes to get a player or to keep him—while, at the same time, they will rail on about how everybody else's players are overpaid. But it's hollow carping. Our hearts aren't in it anymore. Neither, even, is our bile. We don't know if Alonzo Mourning is worth seventeen million dollars, and frankly, my dear, we don't give a damn.

Walking in a Winter Wonderland

■   ■   ■

L et's hear it for the winter Olympics, which are the sweetest things in sport. Nobody ever protests at the winter Olympics. Nobody boycotts. All the competitors wear the most adorable clothes, either streamlined Starlight Express outfits or sequins. Beautiful music is played in the background. The scenery is darling. If the winter Olympics were a poem they would be Joyce Kilmer, if they were a symphony they'd be Strauss, if they were food they'd be chocolate éclair.

The only thing you ever had to fret about in the winter Olympics was whether there would be enough snow. But now you don't have to worry anymore, because if there isn't enough of nature's own, man can make the stuff.

Once, many years ago, there was a dispute about skiers not really being amateurs. And, oh yes, occasionally hockey players draw blood, as that breed is wont to do on any rink. Outside of that, nobody has frowned, let alone uttered a disagreeable word, since the winter Olympics were started in 1924. As a prime case in point, when the 1936 winter Olympics were also held in Germany, not even Hitler could soil them. In fact, the 1936 winter Olympics were so lovely that the 1940 Games were scheduled for Germany before that stinky old World War II got in the way.

The winter Olympics have branched out in recent years, locating in such exotic places as Japan and Yugoslavia, but except for the odd competitor from Senegal, almost all of the rosy-cheeked athletes come from a handful of nations that are northern in geography, western in culture. Besides, even if dissidents managed somehow to get to the faraway locales, it's much too cold to riot. So, we go along, singing a song, walking in a winter wonderland.

The tenor for the winter games was set by one single athlete—Sonja Henie of Norway. As a twelve-year-old—yes, a preteen—she skated in the first winter games, in '24, and then won the Gold medal in '28, '32, and '36. Sonja was beautiful and graceful and, withal, something of a precursor to the big-time modern athlete, because she was schooled in the sport almost from the moment she could strap on skates by her father, a prominent Norwegian businessman.

It is still possible to argue, I think, that Sonja Henie was the single most popular female athlete of all time, and, as well, the single most dominant Olympian—male or female, summer or winter. She was called the greatest box-office draw in the history of sport, and after taking her third Gold, she went to Hollywood where, at her peak, only Clark Gable and Shirley Temple were more bankable. She also conducted an affair with Joe Louis, heavyweight champion of the world.

To this day, the connection between skating and show business is the most intimate one in sport, and the lovely shadow that Sonja Henie cast will still cover the whole scene in Calgary. Put another log on the fire, press your nose against the windowpane, and enjoy the beauty and the fantasy. We get so little of it—in sport or anything else.

Down in Front

■   ■   ■

One of the earliest stupid jokes I remember is: Why do they call it a grand*stand* if everybody there sits? Well, yeah, but this really isn't true anymore. There's more and more stand-up guys in our stadiums.

I mean, the best rude request in America was always "Down in front!" Even in a more civil society, that was all right, because whoever was standing up and blocking everybody else's view deserved such coarse censure. Nowadays, though, if one person stands up thoughtlessly at a ball game, nobody screams, "Down in front!" Instead, everybody else just stands up, too. They think it must be stylish.

The end result of this dreadful trend is that now, at baseball games, there's a tendency for the whole stadium to stand up when some pitcher merely gets two strikes on a batter. This completely devalues the principle of standing up, which should be reserved only for the most unique accomplishments. (And by the way, I've begun to observe this same sort of cheapening of acclaim in the theatre now, too. Patrons give standing ovations at any ordinary curtain call.)

I think this promiscuous laud-and-honor may be on account of tickets being so expensive now that anybody who goes to an arena or a theater wants to convince themselves that they've been rewarded with something very special—when, in fact, it's just another everyday strike-out or some run-of-the-mill acting.

But worse is that the standing-up is not just in the stands. Football substitutes never sit down anymore. They roam the sidelines aimlessly, like mobs of refugees. Even when they're on the field nowadays, football players don't sit down for a time-out. In fact, nobody calls time-outs anymore just to give everybody . . . well, time out. No, time-outs now are just longer strategic planning sessions. Is it macho for football players to stay on their feet?

Hey, baseball and basketball players—even rough, tough hockey players—use the bench for what God intended—to sit on. I do have one objection, though. When hockey players go to the penalty box, they sit there, too. I think these offenders should be obliged to remain on their feet, like bad little schoolchildren who have been ordered to go *stand* in the corner. Then there wouldn't be as many hockey penalties.

Professional golfers, of course, never get to take a load off their feet—which was why the hardcore purists were so upset when Casey Martin petitioned to ride in his cart. But tennis players take a sit-down break every two games, and boxers plop down on their personal stools after each and every round. Boxers never sit down at the end of a fight, though, because they want to make the judges think that they haven't been the least bit hurt . . . or even winded. After the bell, they idiotically bounce all around and keep shadowboxing, like a chicken that still flops about with its head cut off.

I say: Hey, stay on your stool. I believe that it's perfectly manly and tasteful to sit when you are not playing in the game, and to keep your seat when you are watching the game—raising up off your derriere only when you are presented with the most extraordinary achievement. Otherwise, will you all join with me now in a rousing shout of: DOWN IN FRONT!

Logos

■   ■   ■

The crocodile was first, and by the late '50s, it was already the universal sign for preppies. Of course, early on in America, which knows not crocodiles except in *Peter Pan*, it became the alligator.

But the reason it was supposed to be—and technically remains—a crocodile is because the man who made the shirts was Rene Lacoste, who had gained the agnomen back in the '20s when he and the other Musketeers took the Davis Cup from America to the Bois de Boulogne. Still, one would have never picked Lacoste to be an eventual fashion arbiter. Most old photographs of him show him dressed—when not in tennis garb—in a long overcoat, even in the heat of a Philadelphia summer. This is because Lacoste is a hypochondriac who, indeed, gave up tennis more than half a century ago because he was convinced that his death was imminent. The Crocodile is still alive today, and in his eighties.

After the war, to distinguish his new tennis shirts, Lacoste added the little crocodile emblem over the left breast. And think about it now: in the entire twentieth century, what in fashion has been so significant and lasting as the little logos over the left breast in sports clothes? Why, it's as prominent a factor as the zippered fly.

Now, at the time Lacoste got into the business, sports shirts didn't really exist. I don't even know if people called them "sports shirts" then. Tennis players, for example, either wore white dress shirts with the sleeves rolled up or army-surplus T-shirts. Golfers even still wore ties. The Crocodile moved into a vacuum. Then, après him, the deluge.

Fred Perry, the old English champion, brought out the next distinct line. His emblem was a very correct laurel wreath. Most imitators preferred to ape the alligator, though, and go with animal life. I remember for a long time there was a prominent penguin line. Regardless, if you made sports shirts, you had to have a left-breast logo—the word *logo* began to replace *emblem* and *symbol* somewhere along the way—and so we had birds, a mustache, various initials, motorcars. When Adidas put its fancy three-piece flower-type symbol on its new clothing line, many people thought it was a rendering of a marijuana leaf.

But now, what have we come to? The ultimate left-breast symbol—excuse me, *logo*. You know: think, now say it. That's right. A guy on a horse, playing . . . polo.

In all this Jeffersonian republic, this Jacksonian democracy, there is just no place for polo. I mean, even if tennis and golf and figure skating may be perceived as rich men's games, it's understood that a few common folk can infiltrate them. But the American dream simply doesn't embrace polo. With polo, you can't just sort of break in. You not only have to have your own horses, but you have to stable them and feed them and feed the people who stable them and feed them.

Wouldn't you think Americans—especially Americans in this year of Miss Liberty's centennial—would be turning their backs on polo? But no, here we are, beating down the doors, overrunning the malls, paying small fortunes to buy shirts with a guy playing polo over the left breast.

What with the stock market and all, some people have said it's like 1929 all over again. Gee, I don't know, but if we do crash, I'll say, yeah, we should have known—1986 was the year everybody wanted to wear a guy playing polo on his or her left breast. Don't say I didn't warn you.

The Not-So-Sweet Science

■   ■   ■

It is my own foolish, benighted opinion that, say, fifty years from now we will look back on the sport of boxing in 1980 as we now look back upon such cruel medieval institutions as segregation and child labor. If boxing were anything but a sport, so-called, it would be outlawed by the Supreme Court as cruel and unusual punishment. Alas, in the name of entertainment, we countenance levels of brutality that we would never tolerate in our workaday lives. And boxing is actually enjoying, it seems, something of a revival—witness the four prime-time fights run on ABC last Monday.

About twenty years ago the sport was nearly done in by overexposure on television, and there was also a certain hue and cry raised about its brutal ways—especially after Emile Griffith pummeled Benny Paret to death in a title fight. But then the appealing young Cassius Clay appeared on the scene, a divine intervention, and the barbarism of boxing was saved for humankind for another day.

The sport is helped in that it has always enjoyed a good press in the right places. It has charmed macho novelists. In its base simplicity, it is regularly a vehicle for movies, far beyond its comparative popularity.

Moreover, boxing manages to deflect criticism by arguing that to oppose it is to be against minorities. By this convoluted reasoning, it is maintained that the poor devils ought to be allowed to make a living maiming each other in public.

I think it is worth quoting, then, this simple account from Michael Katz, the boxing writer of the *New York Times*, of a knockout in one of those championship bouts last week (which were, by the by, held on a holy day—Passover). Mr. Katz wrote: "Tate was stunned by the hook, which had been set up by a right to the champion's aching body. His eyes rolled back, and he started to pitch forward from the ropes that Weaver had him pinned against. Weaver tossed in a short, hard right hand for added affect, as Tate slowly fell forward and rolled over on his left shoulder, his face against the canvas. He remained motionless, blood leaving his ear, for minutes."

Ah, sport. Ah, "the sweet science."

Three American boxers have been killed in the ring in recent months, but television has been unlucky, and has not brought any of these slaughters, live, into your living room.

But if there is any solace, boxing has traditionally been as mismanaged as it is cruel. I notice that already, to satisfy the insatiable television monster, everyone who fights on TV must be designated as some kind of champion. Every fight must be a title fight. Boxing champions are becoming like beauty queens, parodies of themselves. Miss Federated Muenster Cheese of 1980. The WBA Junior Lightweight Champion.

And now the middle-aged Clay—Muhammad Ali—is assaying a comeback, even though he is, whisper his friends, also showing the first signs of punch drunkenness.

Must even this fascinating man's great body or mind be sacrificed in the name of ratings? Well, defenders of the sport assure us that there is a reason for Ali's disability—if, in fact, he has begun to stroll down Queer Street. Ali was too good. Do you understand? Because he was good, he earned the right to fight more. Had only he been a bum, he would have been pounded out of the sport before his faculties were rattled. On top of everything else, you see, boxing destroys its best.

It is worth noting, too, that the humanitarians who were so passionate on Ali's behalf when he refused to go into the army are silent now, when he would go into another battle, looking for one more payday between the ropes. Unarmed.

The horrible thing is that the opposition to boxing will surely only be galvanized by one dreadful, fatal bout involving a well-known champion. Pray that it not be Ali. Pray that we can abolish boxing without a televised murder.

Got to Do Some Coachin': Nolan Richardson

A Play in Four Acts

Cast
(in order of appearance)

NOLAN RICHARDSON JR.

OLD MOMMA
Nolan's grandmother

RON HUERY
ANDREW LANG
ALLIE FREEMAN
MARIO CREDIT
CANNON WHITBY
Arkansas basketball players

ANDY STOGLIN
Nolan's assistant

YVONNE RICHARDSON
Nolan's daughter

FRANK POLLITT
Bowie High principal

NEMO HERRERA
CLAY COX
AL FRANCO
Bowie coaches

ROSE DAVILA RICHARDSON
Nolan's wife

DON HASKINS
Texas Western coach

MR. DAVILA
Rose's father

FRANK BROYLES
Arkansas athletic director

DANIEL PLUNKETT
Yvonne's doctor

RAY THORNTON
Arkansas president

DANIEL FERRITOR
Arkansas chancellor

TIME: 1958 to the present

Act I: *Old Momma*

(The curtain opens; the stage is dark. We hear only the sounds of basketball: fans cheering, a ball bouncing, sneakers scuffling, a player shouting to his teammates. A spotlight comes up on Arkansas coach Nolan Richardson, seated on the Razorback bench. He is wearing an open double-breasted white blazer, red polka-dot shirt, rusk slacks, reptile-skin boots and a gold watch. He is an imposing man—6' 2", more than 200 pounds of muscle—dark, the color of mahogany. He is leaning forward and watching the action intently, his big legs spread far apart, his hands clasped together. A whistle blows, and, furious, he springs to his feet, paces a step left, hitches up his pants and then paces right and makes the hand signal for a T: timeout. He freezes in this position; a spotlight remains on him.

Across the stage, another spotlight comes up on his grandmother, Rose Richardson—Old Momma. She is carrying a paper bag, which she puts down on a table. She begins to remove pieces of fried chicken from the bag and arrange them on a plate. In a heavy Southern black accent, she speaks to the audience.)

OLD MOMMA: There was always something so very special about Nolan. I'm not surprised he'd turn out to be the *first* so many times. Why, soon as they desegregated, he was the first Negro to go to Bowie High—that's here in El Paso, and that was 1955, when Nolan was only 13. Then he was one of the first, uh, black players at Texas Western University, and then Nolan came back to Bowie and was the first black man to coach at a desegregated school in Texas. And *then* he went over yonder to Snyder, Texas—to Western Texas J.C.—and he was the first black coach at a desegregated junior college in Texas. And *then* he went to Tulsa, and he was the first black coach at a major college in Oklahoma. And now he's at Arkansas—the first black man to be a head coach in the whole Southwest Conference. And still the only one. *(She grins.)* I always knew that boy was gonna *be* somethin'.

(Old Momma sits at the table and pours from a pitcher. She looks across stage; Nolan comes back to life. He whips off his blazer, and his players begin to gather about him. Andy Stoglin, a huge man with a big mustache and mutton-chop sideburns, joins the group. He is Richardson's longtime friend and assistant. Richardson berates Ron Huery.)

NOLAN: That's just a dumb, freshman thing to do, Huery, and you're not a freshman anymore. *(He whirls toward Andrew Lang.)* And if *you* can't keep your man off the boards, then. . . .

(Nolan stops cold. A beautiful 15-year-old, his daughter Yvonne, wearing a red sweatshirt that reads HAWGBALL, emerges from the dark and stands behind the huddle. Because she is an apparition, none of the others can see her; they freeze.)

NOLAN: Yvonne! What in the world are you doing here? We're in the middle of a game. *(He steps through the huddle to Yvonne.)*

YVONNE: You always said I'd be a part of every team of yours, Daddy.

NOLAN: Yes, but. . . .

YVONNE *(smiling, fingering Nolan's shirt)*: Even if I'm gone, I got you back in polka dots again.

NOLAN: Yeah, I look like a clown again.

YVONNE: Yeah, *my* clown. *(From her neck she takes a chain with a gold cross and puts it around her father's neck.)*

NOLAN: But, baby, that's your cross.

YVONNE: I want you to have it, Papito. *(She kisses him and begins to skip off; then she stops and turns back, smiling broadly. She calls to him.)* Now *you* got to do some *coachin'.*

(The light goes out on Yvonne. The players turn to their coach. After a moment, Stoglin steps over and touches Richardson.)

STOGLIN: Time's back in, Coach.

(Lights fade on Richardson and his players. Across stage, Old Momma rises.)

OLD MOMMA: Nolan and his sisters lived with me ever since his poor momma died when he was only three. And his daddy died when Nolan was 12. We lived here in this old shotgun house—just this room and the two more, straight back. But we got ourselves an indoor toilet this time. And usually there's enough to eat. I work at a place makes fried chicken, and sometimes I can bring these leftovers home.

We're the only black family around here. The rest is all Mexican. When Nolan first went to school, main problem he had was that he didn't speak English good enough. Even grown up, he still speaks perfect Spanish, but I expect nobody down in Arkansas knows that. Who's Nolan gonna talk it to down there?

(Young Nolan enters, wearing his Bowie High baseball uniform. He goes to the table, kisses Old Momma and sits down.)

OLD MOMMA: I don't know why you got that uniform on, since I hear you're not goin' with the team to the Districts.

YOUNG NOLAN: Old Momma, you hear everything. But it's just not fair. I'm the best player, and I can't stay with the team. The rest of 'em'll be staying in a motel, swimming, eating chicken-fried steak—and they're putting me up on the other side of town, staying with some old Negro lady. So I just told Coach Herrera I'm not goin'. That's my decision.

OLD MOMMA: Oh? Well, let me tell you something, Nolan Richardson Junior, maybe you're just not old enough to *make* those kind of decisions. Yes, I know it's not fair, but at least now you're goin' to school with white folks. If you don't go on the trip with the team, fine for you, but maybe you'll just be giving them an excuse not to open any more doors for your own children. Now, make up your own mind.

YOUNG NOLAN: Yes, ma'am.

(Lights fade on Old Momma. Young Nolan steps forward and picks up a baseball bat. A few feet away, the adult Nolan steps into the light and smiles as Young Nolan takes a few practice cuts.)

NOLAN: I wasn't afraid of anyone. I was always big and strong, matured early. But it was some tough neighborhood we lived in. Gangs on either side of me. Drugs. I had a cousin, best young football player I ever saw. OD'd when he was 16. The other kids would say I was afraid of the cops. But I wasn't. No, the only thing I was afraid of was hurting my grandmother, because she put so much trust in me.

(Mr. Pollitt, the principal, appears; he slaps Young Nolan on the back.)

MR. POLLITT: Hey, Nolan, great game in Abilene!

YOUNG NOLAN: Thanks, Mr. Pollitt. I think it was my best game ever.

MR. POLLITT: Should be. Two home runs, couple more hits, stolen bases—and you're the winning pitcher. Baseball your favorite?

YOUNG NOLAN: I don't know, sir. It's my first love, and I like football, too. But basketball is so exciting, and you're right down there *with* the crowd. I love that. Anyway, I've already made up my mind. I'm going to junior college, so I can get into the University of Arizona and play college baseball. *(He waves and runs off.)*

MR. POLLITT: That kid is really something. Football, baseball, basketball—all-district, all three. Runs and jumps for the track team in his spare time. The coaches think so much of him they've all chipped in and bought him a suit for graduation.

(Spotlight downstage. Young Nolan is helped into a suit jacket—over his baseball uniform—by his three coaches: Nemo Herrera, Clay Cox and Al Franco.)

YOUNG NOLAN: Thank you all. First new clothes I ever had. First new anything I ever had.

(Old Momma stands up and steps toward Young Nolan.)

OLD MOMMA: Come on, Nolan. You don't wanna be late to college.

P.A. VOICE: Bus to Tucson. . . .

(Young Nolan runs over and picks up a cardboard box, which serves as his suitcase and holds all of his belongings. He walks to Old Momma and puts down the box; they embrace. The adult Nolan shakes his head.)

NOLAN: The whole way to Arizona, I kept thinking I must be crazy to leave. In all my life I never cried so much leaving a woman as I did when I left Old Momma.

(Old Momma gives a last hug to Young Nolan and then steps back. Young Nolan picks up his box. Darkness.)

Act II: *Rose*

(Spotlight on Rose Davila. She is a small woman, ever smiling. She speaks with a slight Hispanic accent.)

Rosa: Nolan didn't know me at all in high school. He was good friends with my older brother, Mañuel. But he didn't know that Mañuel even had a little sister. And, of course, everybody at Bowie High knew Nolan Richardson. Everybody.

(Lights dim on Rose. Spotlight up on Nolan, wearing Texas Western sweats.)

NOLAN: In 1960, I came back from junior college in Arizona to get married. Married a girl named Helen, a school sweetheart. We had a baby and then another—three before I got out of college. In Arizona, I'd been a J.C. All-America first baseman, and later on the Houston Astros even offered me a $9,000 bonus. But they wanted to send me to Class C ball, and I had a family by then. I enrolled at Texas Western—you know it now as Texas-El Paso, UTEP. They didn't even have a baseball team then, so I played basketball. Averaged nearly 20 a game as a sophomore. I figured I was gonna set a lot of scoring records before I was through.

(A burly white man, carrying suitcases, enters.)

NOLAN: Give ya a hand?

HASKINS: Thanks. My wife and I are moving into the dormitory. Say, I'm lookin' for Richardson. Know him?

NOLAN: *I'm* Nolan Richardson.

HASKINS: Well, I'm Don Haskins.

NOLAN: The new basketball coach.

HASKINS: Right. And you're 20 points a game, huh? *(Nolan puffs up.)* Yeah, and they also tell me you can't guard a telephone pole. *(Nolan looks shocked.)* They say you're pretty good at baseball and football, too. Well, make up your mind, son. If you're not gonna play defense for me, then you better concentrate on one of them. If you wanna play on my team, you'll need this.

(Haskins chucks him an orange shirt and steps away to darkness. Richardson examines it and, resignedly, puts it on.)

NOLAN: I never took this off for two years in practice. I just played defense. Coach Haskins turned me from 20 points a game into 10 a game—but he taught me defense. And that's what I am today: a defensive coach.

(He jumps into a defender's stance and freezes; lights fade on Nolan. Stoglin enters and stands with Haskins.)

STOGLIN: Nolan guarded the best player on the other team, no matter how big the guy was.

HASKINS: Six foot 2-1/2, played like six-eight.

STOGLIN: He'd get so low he'd bang his hands on the court while he guarded a guy. He'd psych his opponent, always talkin' to him. . . .

(Spotlight back up on Nolan. The red shirt is off; he is now carrying a San Diego Chargers helmet.)

NOLAN: I graduated from Texas Western, but there wasn't a spot for me in the NBA. Even though I hadn't played football since high school, the Chargers gave me $500 to come to a tryout camp. Maybe I should have concentrated on one sport, the way kids do now. But I always just *played.* All the Richardsons were always good athletes. My father was a pretty fair boxer—till he started drinking, and that finally killed him. *(He pauses, turning the helmet in his hands.)* Anyway, I had the Chargers made, then I busted a hamstring. . . .

(Another light comes up on Mr. Pollitt, sitting at his desk having a conversation with Coach Cox, who stands there.)

MR. POLLITT: You really think so, Clay?

COX: You won't find a young man in the state of Texas more capable than Nolan.

(Nolan approaches; Mr. Pollitt beckons him to sit in the chair by his desk.)

MR. POLLITT: So, Nolan, you're agreeable? Besides teaching, you'll help with the baseball, football and basketball teams—and the golf. And the salary is $4,500 a year.

NOLAN: Yes, sir. *(He rises, shakes hands, and turns to leave. Cox taps Mr. Pollitt on the shoulder.)*

MR. POLLITT: Nolan . . . Nolan, sometime you'll be ready to be a head coach yourself here.

NOLAN: Me? A Negro?

MR. POLLITT: It's coming, it's coming. What sport you think you'd like?

NOLAN: Football, like Mr. Cox.

MR. POLLITT: No, I don't think so. I think you'd have your best shot in baseball.

NOLAN: What about basketball?

MR. POLLITT: Well, that's the other possibility. You think about that, and don't worry—I'll remember.

(Lights fade. Light comes up on Rose standing in a kitchen, preparing food.)

ROSE: I got married myself, had a daughter. But the marriage fell apart, and I took my little girl and moved back in here with my parents. Nolan got divorced too. His wife got their daughter, but he kept the two boys. It was really a struggle for him.

(Light dims. Another light comes up on Nolan. He has a red, white, and blue basketball. He shoots at a basket offstage. The ball comes back. He shoots again as he talks.)

NOLAN: Last chance. The ABA, a new league. A team named the Dallas Chaparrals offered to match my high school salary—and I was making big money by now. Seventy-five hundred. Had the team made, too—and then *(grabs his leg in pain)* the damn hamstring. That was the one time I was really disappointed. Really. I knew then that it was completely over.

(The light comes back up on Mr. Pollitt at his desk. Nolan approaches.)

NOLAN: I'm sorry, sir; I had to try. I know there were no promises, but. . . .

MR. POLLITT: I know, Nolan. And your old position here—I can't give that back to you.

NOLAN *(hangs his head)*: Yes, sir, I understand.

MR. POLLITT *(rising)*: But the basketball coach quit, and I'd like to give you *that* position.

(Mr. Pollitt extends his hand, and Nolan shakes it vigorously. Across stage, the light comes up on Rose in her kitchen.)

ROSE: Those first few years, all Nolan had was a bunch of Mexican kids—none of them much bigger than me.

(Lights dim on Mr. Pollitt. Nolan puts a whistle around his neck and steps forward.)

NOLAN: Not a one over six feet. But they were great kids, and I taught 'em the same defense Coach Haskins had taught me. And then we started to get more black kids into Bowie, and. . . .

ROSE: Coach of the Year three times in 10 years.

NOLAN: But it was still hard. Summers I'd work for a boys' baseball program. Up at dawn, fix the field, line the diamond. *(He takes off his shirt and wipes his brow.)*

ROSE: My parents' house was right across from that field, and I'd see Nolan out there, working. Oh, that build. It's embarrassing to say, but . . . I loved it.

NOLAN: And one morning, it was so hot, and I remembered that my old buddy Mañuel lived just over across the road there. *(Mr. Davila, fanning himself, comes out and sits down on his front steps. Nolan approaches.)*

MR. DAVILA: Nolan! *¿Que pasa?*

NOLAN *(in Spanish)*: Señor Davila, I'd about kill for a glass of water.

MR. DAVILA: I think we can manage that. Rose!

(She has been peeking out the window, nervously drying her hands on her apron. Now she comes to the door.)

MR. DAVILA: Remember the little sister?

NOLAN *(turning to Rose)*: Well, I can't say that I do, but I still hope I can get some water.

ROSE: The great Nolan Richardson can get a whole pitcher every day.

NOLAN: I may take you up on that.

(Mr. Davila looks at them, smiles and nods knowingly.)

MR. DAVILA: I'll get the water for Nolan. *(He rises and exits.)*

(Nolan and Rose look at each other fondly for a moment. Then she reaches up and puts a flower in her hair; she takes off her apron. Nolan slips on a dressy sport shirt. The lights dim, and the porch light goes on. It is evening.)

ROSE: Well, I hope you didn't just come for some water this time.

NOLAN *(laughing and taking her hand)*: You know, you're amazing, Rose. You always have a smile for everybody; you talk to everybody. I'm such a private person, yet ever since I started talking to you, I've begun to think you're about the best friend I've got.

ROSE: Oh, come on, Nolan. Everybody in El Paso loves you.

NOLAN: I don't mean that. Besides, there are so many contradictions here. This is my hometown, but when I went to school here, I couldn't even go into the restaurants and movies.

ROSE: Will you leave?

NOLAN: Sometimes now I do wonder how much longer I can stay at Bowie. But I won't let myself say, If I were white. No. I've seen too many black kids with burning hate, and I won't let myself get to hating. My grandmother taught me that. We all belong to God, and we're all going to the same place when it's over. And I believe if I go to any other place before that, destiny will take me.

ROSE: You're the best friend I've got, too. Nolan. The best friend I ever had.

NOLAN: I think we've become more than friends. *(He pulls her to him as the lights fade.)*

MR. POLLITT'S VOICE: Nolan, Nolan!

(The lights come up across stage, where Mr. Pollitt is sitting in an easy chair. Nolan and Rose hurry to him, with Little Yvonne.)

NOLAN: We all came to say goodbye.

MR. POLLITT: This old man—with cataracts, too. But I'm not so old or so blind that I can't still make out beauty. Yvonne, you get prettier every time I see you. *(He kisses her and then embraces Rose and shakes Nolan's hand.)* How old are you now?

LITTLE YVONNE: I'm six, Mr. Pollitt.

MR. POLLITT: And you're all ready to go to Snyder? It's just an itty-bitty place, you know.

ROSE: For a chance for Nolan to coach junior college, we'd go anywhere.

MR. POLLITT: Nolan, you should have had that chance long ago. . . . Will you ladies excuse us for a second? *(They nod and move aside.)* Nolan, I've got one favor to ask of you.

NOLAN: Anything, sir.

MR. POLLITT: When I die, will you . . . will you come back and be one of my pallbearers?

NOLAN: Come on, Mr. Pollitt, I don't even want to talk about such things.

MR. POLLITT: Just tell me.

NOLAN: I promise you, sir. Wherever I am, whatever I'm doing, I'll come back here for you.

(Lights go out on the two men. Rose and Yvonne step forward under lights.)

ROSE: And so we went to Snyder, Texas—population 12,000. Western Texas Junior College. And the very first year, Nolan took the team to the national junior college championship tournament. Then Nolan got his best player, Paul Pressey, and we won the national title in 1980.

(Stoglin and Haskins step into the light.)

STOGLIN: A hundred and one wins and only 13 losses in three years.

HASKINS: Western Texas would score all these points, and people would see all these black juco kids fast-breakin', and they'd call it undisciplined.

STOGLIN: No way. The key was Nolan's matchup zone.

HASKINS: It was the defense that made the scoring possible—a lot like the old Celtics or UCLA.

STOGLIN: But it wasn't just that Nolan had winning teams.

ROSE: He'd only bring in good kids.

LITTLE YVONNE: Every team—my 15 big brothers.

STOGLIN: Every coach preaches that his team is family. But Nolan lives that. Rose would cook meals for the players. Didn't seem like there was ever a time I visited when one of the players wasn't spending the night at their house.

ROSE: And when we left Snyder, the whole town gave Nolan a day.

(Across the stage, lights come up on Nolan, who stands under a banner that reads: NOLAN RICHARDSON DAY.)

NOLAN: God, I loved that little town. We still keep a house there, and it's been eight years since we left.

(Lights fade out on Nolan. Stoglin and Haskins exit.)

ROSE: But it was just the same when we got to Tulsa. Nolan was just as popular, and the team kept winning.

LITTLE YVONNE: Daddy won the NIT the first year we were there.

ROSE: The only thing that changed was that Yvonne was growing up.

(Little Yvonne runs off past the teenage Yvonne, who enters wearing a Tulsa blue and gold sweatshirt.)

YVONNE: Daddy's teams were 119–37 and made a tournament every year.

ROSE: But more important, Nolan meant so much to the city.

YVONNE *(giggling)*: And he started wearing polka dots.

(The light comes up across stage on Nolan, resplendent in a blue shirt with gold polka dots.)

NOLAN: I've always believed that a person in my position should be more than just a basketball coach. With my visibility, I can help bring the community together. And especially as a black man, I can show people how to respect one another better.

(Lights down. Across stage, lights come up on Frank Broyles, the athletic director at Arkansas. He is reading a clipping as his secretary comes in with some mail. Broyles shakes his head.)

BROYLES: You know, Donita, we get Tulsa on the TV cable now, and, I swear, all I hear about is this Nolan Richardson. And everybody who knows him tells me he's not just a big-time coach; he's a big-time person. Look at this clipping from the Tulsa paper—calls him "a community treasure, the most popular sports figure ever in Tulsa." I tell ya, Eddie Sutton made basketball in Arkansas, but if Coach Sutton ever leaves, the first guy I'm callin' is Coach Richardson.

(Lights go down on Broyles; lights go up center stage, where Nolan, with an overcoat on, leans down to Yvonne. Rose stands next to him.)

NOLAN: O.K., now, baby, by the time I get back from recruiting in Baltimore, I want you feeling all well again. You get rid of this old bug. (He hugs her, hugs Rose, picks up a suitcase and exits. Lights down. We hear a telephone ring, and when the lights come up, Nolan rushes in, puts down the suitcase and grabs the phone off a night table.)

NOLAN: Hello . . . Yes, this is Nolan Richardson . . . Oh, my . . . When's the funeral? . . . You tell Mr. Pollitt's children I'm leaving Baltimore right away. I'll be there.

(He hangs up the phone and bows his head. The lights fade. Across stage, lights come up on Rose, who is sitting in a chair. We hear a minister speaking.)

MINISTER'S VOICE: Oh, God, accept our prayers on behalf of the soul of Frank Pollitt, thy servant departed. . . .

(Nolan enters, puts down his suitcase and overcoat. He has on a jacket and tie. Rose barely looks up.)

NOLAN: Well, I kept my promise. I was there to help lay him to rest. It wasn't easy. I only made the procession by an hour. I got a flight out of Baltimore all right, but there wasn't a seat out of Dallas for El Paso. I finally . . . Rose, did you hear me? Rose?

ROSE: *(slowly raising her head)*: I took Yvonne to the doctor today, and . . . *(She lowers her head in her hands. Nolan rushes to her as she begins to sob.)*

NOLAN: Rose? Rose!

(The stage goes dark.)

Act III: *Yvonne*

(Yvonne, now 13, steps forward in a spotlight.)

YVONNE: My father got offered the job as head coach over at Arkansas, but I don't think he's going to take it. You see, they diagnosed me with leukemia.

(Rose steps into another spotlight. She looks toward Yvonne.)

ROSE: I call her love child. Only love could make anyone so beautiful.

(Nolan steps up in his spotlight. He looks toward Yvonne.)

NOLAN: Yvonne is so special. My three older kids understand how I feel about her. When they were young, I was struggling, just trying to make a living. Like a lot of young fathers, I didn't have the time for them, the way I do for Yvonne. Besides, we're so much alike.

(Rose crosses to Nolan in front of Yvonne, who watches her parents with a little smile, shaking her head fondly at them.)

ROSE *(crossing to Nolan)*: Nolan, sometimes I just don't understand Yvonne. I know she loves me, but then all of a sudden she'll go for hours and won't say one word.

NOLAN: Rose, won't you ever understand? That's the part of her that's all me. Hell, you know how much I love you, and sometimes *I* don't talk to you. *(He wraps an arm around her, laughing. Their lights fade.)*

YVONNE: I know he's not going to take that Arkansas job, and that's just not fair.

(Lights up across stage. Three Tulsa assistant coaches are standing there. Nolan comes over, and one of them bounces him a ball. As Yvonne turns to watch, her mother steps up behind her.)

NOLAN: Well, you guys can sleep easy tonight. I made up my mind. I'm telling Arkansas no. We'll all be coaching right here again in Tulsa next year.

(They let out a cheer and exit. Nolan turns around. Yvonne has her arms folded.)

YVONNE: No.

NOLAN: Now wait a minute, Yvonne. I've got to have an interview with you.

YVONNE: No.

NOLAN: Listen to me. The doctors here at St. Francis are doing a good job with you. It's best that we stay here in Tulsa until you're well. Then. . . .

YVONNE: Then you might miss the chance, Daddy. You've worked too hard for this. We all love Tulsa, but you don't even have your own gym here. In Fayetteville you'd have a whole state. Please, Daddy. It wouldn't be *fair* if you didn't take the job. Please, Papito.

NOLAN: Well, all right, but. . . .

YVONNE: Yeahhh!

NOLAN: But no more polka dots. New job, new clothes.

(Yvonne kisses him. The lights come up on Broyles at his desk. Nolan steps toward him and meets Stoglin along the way.)

NOLAN: Fourteen years old, she's got leukemia, and she's worried about what's fair for me.

STOGLIN *(to audience)*: Nolan brought me to Arkansas with him as an assistant, but it was a nightmare from the start.

BROYLES: The team Coach Sutton left behind was supposed to be the best in the Southwest Conference. But it wasn't—not by a long shot.

STOGLIN: And there was a lot of drug use on the team.

NOLAN: I lost my best two players to drugs, but I helped save two more that I didn't tell anybody about.

BROYLES: And Coach Richardson's style of play was completely different from Coach Sutton's deliberate style. So when the team lost, some people were even more critical.

STOGLIN: Nolan was ashamed of some of the ugly things they printed in the newspapers.

BROYLES (*holding up a copy of the* Arkansas Democrat): The *Democrat*—in Little Rock—has been opposed to me for 15 years, but to go after Nolan at a time when his daughter was. . . .

NOLAN (*taking the copy, slapping it*): The sports editor wrote that it was "rumored" that they'd burned crosses on my lawn. I didn't even have a lawn. Rose and Yvonne were still back in Tulsa to be near her doctors, and I was living in a condo. (*Throws paper aside. Lights come up on Rose across stage.*)

ROSE: But he'd never bring any of it home. And there I was in this beautiful house in Tulsa, my beautiful baby getting sicker and sicker. We had to start taking her to Minnesota for treatment, and sometimes I just couldn't hold back anymore. (*She begins to cry. The lights come up on Yvonne in her hospital bed. Standing beside it is Dr. Plunkett. Rose moves to her. From the other side of the stage, Nolan looks over. There is pain on his face.*)

BROYLES: Go to Yvonne, Nolan. Anytime. (*Nolan rushes across to her bed; she brightens as soon as she sees him.*)

YVONNE: Papito! (*They hug. Then she feigns irritation.*) Now, *Nolan*, I need an interview with *you*. What's the matter with the Hogs? You got to start doin' some coachin'. (*Laughter. Lights dim.*)

STOGLIN: But it only got worse. That first season at Arkansas, 1985–86, we finished 12–16. And last year, even though Nolan got some new players in, he was away with Yvonne so much—back and forth. I think the guys played better when Nolan wasn't here. When he was here, just seeing him, that hurt too much.

(*The sounds of basketball practice are heard offstage. Stoglin looks in that direction. Nolan appears beside him; his face grows angry.*)

NOLAN: No! No! Stop 'em, Coach. (*Stoglin blows whistle.*) All right, get over here. (*The players move onstage.*) You know, I just got back from a children's hospital. You think you guys got it tough playing basketball? I met a terrific little boy the other day, and the next morning I came back, and he was gone. Gone. He died in the night. You understand? And you're all healthy, and here on a free ticket. Now get out there . . . and . . . do . . . it . . . right!

(The players run off. Lights dim and then come up across stage at Yvonne's bed. Rose nods mournfully to Dr. Plunkett, and they step over to Yvonne.)

ROSE: Dr. Plunkett thinks if you go back up to Minnesota and have a bone marrow operation, it may . . .

DR. PLUNKETT: But it will be very painful, Yvonne.

YVONNE: If I got a chance, let's go.

(Suddenly, the Razorback team rushes onstage to her bedside.)

HUERY: Hey, little sister.

WHITBY: I got those tapes you wanted to trade.

YVONNE: *You* guys make me sick. If you don't start playin' better ball, I'm not so sure I want to be around you.

(She winks; they laugh and kid. The lights come up on Nolan, alone, center stage. He watches his daughter and his players as the scene fades to dark. He shakes his head.)

NOLAN: Nothing worked. Chemotherapy. Bone marrow. At one point the doctors had to break a rib to get at some fungus in Yvonne's lung. She hurt so much. So much morphine. But she never complained. Never said, "Why me, Papito?" Little Daddy. In all my life no one else ever called me little. But she had become bigger and braver than I could ever be.

(The lights come back up dimly on the bed. Only Rose is with Yvonne, Nolan walks over.)

ROSE: We're gonna do the X-rays now, baby.

YVONNE: Oh, Momma. Maybe you ought to just let go. I'm so tired.

NOLAN: They can give you a transfusion, baby. Clean out your blood.

(He sits on the bed and takes her hands. Lights fade. Across stage the lights come up on Stoglin talking to the players.)

STOGLIN: We can't let up. It's only January, and we've already won almost as many games as we did all last season. Coach has so much to worry about—he doesn't need to worry about you.

HUERY: I tell the guys I knew Coach Richardson before Yvonne got sick. A lot of people in Arkansas have never seen that man. The real coach.

STOGLIN: I don't understand how he's gotten through these last couple years. Except that everything in his life prepared him for this. Remember that. Even now, when I talk to him on the phone, when he's with Yvonne, I can tell he's about to explode, but all he'll talk about is you: How's the team doing? How are my players?

(Stoglin's eyes go around the circle. The players reach in and clasp hands, they freeze. Across stage, Dr. Plunkett is walking with Nolan.)

DR. PLUNKETT: I'm sorry, Coach. It didn't work. The bad cells are already back.

NOLAN: Is there anything . . .

DR. PLUNKETT: We could try, but the odds are . . .

NOLAN: No. No more. I won't have my baby mutilated anymore.

DR. PLUNKETT: She could come home with you. I'm sorry, Coach. *(He turns away, pounds the wall, and exits.)*

NOLAN: Yvonne was only home for a day and a half. That one night, we all three slept together, but in the morning she began hemorrhaging, and we had to put her right back in the hospital.

(He turns. Lights up on Yvonne, in her bed. Rose stands there. Nolan steps up to the bed, bends down and kisses her.)

NOLAN: My baby.

YVONNE: Oh, Papito.

(She can barely get the words out. He turns away. Across the stage the team is still frozen in its huddle. Nolan starts toward them, but stops, center stage. Rose sits down on the bed.)

ROSE: We can let you go now, baby. *(Yvonne looks up at her mother for a moment, and then her eyes close. Rose gasps, reaches down and touches her child's left cheek. We can barely hear her.)* One last tear.

(Nolan looks up to the heavens. The players and Stoglin, hands still clasped, sink to their knees. The stage goes dark.)

Act IV: *Arkansas*

(Nolan, in another, more subdued polka-dot shirt, steps forward, center stage. He puts a foot up on a wooden chair.)

NOLAN: It's been over a year now. Yvonne died January 22, 1987. I'm a stronger person today—strictly because of her. But I'm human. Sometimes I ask God, Why? On the other hand, whenever I catch Rose saying that, I say, "Come on, we have to accept it. God just chose to pick from our garden." *(Rose steps out next to him. He puts an arm around her.)* Rose was hospitalized for 12 days this summer—exhaustion, depression. . . .

ROSE: Does it ever get any easier? Sometimes I think I can't function without you, Nolan.

(Stoglin moves onto the stage, and Nolan hugs him with his other arm.)

NOLAN: I knew the people who really cared. There were some who'd say, "Oh, I'm so truly sorry, Coach," and I knew they'd go right around the corner and say, "I'll be glad when this Yvonne *thing* gets settled so he can get back to coaching." But then there were the others who were genuine. Like Ray Thornton, the president of the university. When he talked to me about Yvonne, I could see that he hurt for me.

(Nolan shakes Stoglin's hand and then steps to where Broyles, Thornton and Chancellor Ferritor have entered. He shakes their hands.)

NOLAN: President Thornton, Dr. Ferritor. Hello, Frank.

BROYLES: Nolan, you had a five-year contract with us when you first came to Arkansas. I want you to know that all of us believe that the first two years didn't count. So as far as we're concerned, beginning right now, with the 1987–88 season, you're starting the first year of your five-year contract with the University of Arkansas.

THORNTON: You can stay here for the rest of your life, Nolan. Or anyway, as long as I'm the president here.

(Lights fade on the three men. Nolan turns to Stoglin.)

NOLAN: So, how we doin' now, Coach?

STOGLIN: Well, we're 19–6 so far, Nolan.

(The players run onstage.)

LANG: Just off the conference lead.

CREDIT: We're gonna win it, Coach.

NOLAN: Oh, we are, are we?

STOGLIN: And we've already got two of the top 20 high school prospects in America signed for next year.

NOLAN: Whoa, slow down, Coach. First, we gotta get it done today. Live for today, men. God has really blessed you guys—you're big and strong and healthy. Today! Where I come from, there was too much *mañana.* Today! *(He smiles and taps his own shoulder.)* Course, I got someone who makes sure I keep after you clowns.

HUERY: Don't worry, Coach. Yvonne was our little angel too, and she never leaves my mind.

FREEMAN: Coach, whatever happens to me—and I hope I do make something out of myself—I want you to know I'm always living for two people.

NOLAN: Thanks. Thanks to all you guys. You were all I had to help me try and forget. Thank you for suffering with me. *(He pauses and suddenly barks.)* Now, get the hell out on that court and do some *work.*

(They exit noisily; Nolan moves downstage and addresses the audience.)

NOLAN: I learned one thing above all: Never doubt yourself about what you think needs to be done. I started second-guessing myself and I've had to get back to doing things my way. I've got to be my own judge, jury and executioner. As Yvonne told me, "Nolan, you have *got* to do some coachin'." *(He glances up.)* Right, baby.

(Rose has moved onstage. Offstage, the sounds of basketball begin.)

ROSE: I see him coming back to his old self now.

NOLAN *(looking offstage)*: Come on, you can move faster than that. Come on, come on.

ROSE: It's good to see him fussing at the players. And it's even better to see him get a technical. Nolan even got thrown out of the Texas game a few weeks ago after a couple of technicals—and there he was shaking hands with the Texas team on his way off the court. Now, that's the old Nolan.

(Nolan looks at her and smiles.)

NOLAN: There are no assurances. I tell the players that. No promises. I've got to get it done now. *(He sits down on the wooden chair and looks offstage. He reaches inside his shirt, grabs Yvonne's gold cross and holds it in his fist.)* I am living in history. Right now. At this moment. I am living in blazing history in Arkansas.

(The sounds of basketball get louder and louder. Nolan looks off-stage, his legs are spread, hands clasped. Rose stands behind him, hands on his shoulders.)

ROSE: Nothing good has happened here since we came, but he's back now. The real Nolan. You'll see. *(Out of the shadows behind them come Old Momma and Yvonne.)* They'll all see. Nolan's going to leave some beautiful moments for the state of Arkansas. He will.

(The three women watch the action with Nolan. The noise of the crowd and the game grows louder and louder. There is a whistle. Nolan jumps up, and then silence, darkness.)

CURTAIN

Tough Love

■　■　　■

If you speak to American males of a certain age about the major influences in their lives, a large number of them will cite, foremost, an athletic coach.

And the prototype of that coach-who-made-a-difference-in-my-life is a man who was such a strong disciplinarian that the boys invariably hated him at first. But then, over time, they came to understand that he was putting steel in their backbones . . . and, eventually, they actually came to love old Coach.

Horace Heidt, the bandleader, used to close his radio show by saying: "And remember: It is better to build boys than to mend men." It was trite, but it was true, and nobody performed that job of constructing American boys better than the tough coach with a heart as big as all outdoors. That mythic image has not, either, really been diminished.

Consider the two college basketball coaches who went into the Hall of Fame this year: Don Haskins from Texas-El Paso and Pete Carril from Princeton. One was a big bear of a guy, the other a pip-squeak; one had spent his career guiding, for the most part, disadvantaged minority kids, the other privileged white suburbanites. But go to a Haskins practice or a Carril practice, and it was so much the same. Oh, sure, at either there was a certain amount of cajoling and congratulating and even a little tenderness, but mostly there was caustic criticism loudly ladled out.

Well, mostly, that's how coaches have coached, and that's what boys who have been coached come to love their coaches for. After all, the beau ideal was Vince Lombardi, of whom it was said, affectionately, by one of his players: "He treated us all the same—like dogs."

P. J. Carlesimo has coached very much like Lombardi . . . and Carril and Haskins. His father was a coach who coached that way. That's the way coaches coached, with what the rehabilitation people call "tough love."

Only now, this has all been called to question. You have your pick of reasons. Either society has changed and no one respects authority anymore. Or the players have changed because they get too much adulation and then too much money, so they are too important to be ordered about by anybody.

Probably the answers are yes . . . and yes.

Either way, it is clear that what many boys and young men used to accept as fair discipline they now reject as harsh disrespect. Certainly, this reaction is tied to the fact that so many players—like, yes, Latrell Sprewell—grow up in broken homes, where there is no father to encourage the son, to tell him to tough it out and endure the coach's passing insults and fulmination. Instead, the star player has only his friends, and then his entourage, to indulge him his every complaint.

In this century, too, for a long time, boys anticipated going into the military, where they *really* were going to learn about what it is like to be treated as a dog. Coaches were patty-cake next to what awaited you at basic training.

But now, the ideals of family and service have grown unfashionable, and so the American coach has a more difficult role. Now, of course, Sprewell's attack is extreme both in its brutal passion and that it occurred at the highest end of sport's spectrum. But what it reveals speaks to coaches and players, everyday, at all levels.

Coaches will never again mean quite what they did. Whether they can still matter so much—ah, that answer must await us.

A Man for His Times

■   ■   ■

I t was really quite extraordinary, wasn't it, how much attention was paid to the old man as he lay dying a few months ago? As if he were some great head of state, bulletins were issued, regularly, as he came in and out of coma, on and off life support, as the priests and the relatives arrived to bid him good-bye.

Blessedly, he's out of the hospital now, but especially as we look ahead to a new baseball season, his close call still begs the question: Why does Joe DiMaggio merit so much of our regard? Why do we care so?

Oh, no doubt, he was a superb ballplayer, one of the best. But just in his own era, most experts rank Ted Williams before him; some Stan Musial, too. Willie Mays invariably surpasses DiMaggio as the best center fielder ever. No, great a talent as he was, DiMaggio is more cultural a figure than he is merely athletic.

He represents very well, I think, a place and a moment—the fabled New York City of the middle of this century. The only time we ever had an Oz in America. We can still see young Mr. DiMaggio in one of his rich, sleek suits, with a cigarette and a martini at a supper club, just as well as we remember him in his pinstripes, elegantly patrolling— *patrolling*, that wonderful outfield word—the great green expanse of Yankee Stadium. Indeed, as bizarre a pair that it is, the only two men of our times whom I picture as always wearing a suit—always—are Joe DiMaggio and Richard Nixon. The Yankee Clipper wore his somewhat better.

The Yankee Clipper. Not a nickname. Oh, God no. More a title. DiMaggio was *the* Yankee in those last years when the Bronx Bombers absolutely ruled baseball, and when baseball was still, undisputed, the National Pastime. So, not only does DiMaggio evoke the New York of a certain postwar time, when there were no chain stores, no malls, no suburbs, no rock 'n' roll, he also best represents those last years when baseball ruled supreme.

Ironically, while Paul Simon used DiMaggio's name as an afterthought, simply because it scanned so much better for his song lyric than did "Mickey Mantle," Simon stumbled upon the truth. DiMaggio was the symbol of an era; Mantle wasn't. *Where have you gone, Joe DiMaggio?* asks where has the past gone. Where have *we* gone?

But, curiously, DiMaggio's been forgotten for what matters most in his legend—that he was a significant ethnic figure. Not quite as Jackie Robinson was, nor as Roberto Clemente, but as the first great American star of Italian heritage. Twenty-five thousand Italian-Americans came out to Yankee Stadium that day in 1936 when DiMaggio debuted.

Maybe because DiMaggio was a high school dropout, originally called, simply, "Dago" by his teammates, maybe for that he was always insecure in the larger world—so retiring and distant, mysterious even. And maybe because Italians in America are no longer systematically discriminated against, as they were then, it's easy to forget what DiMaggio endured and how he mattered most under pressure. But long ago we stopped asking: *Where have you come from, Joe DiMaggio?* And that's good.

Finally, too, I think it counted less that he married Marilyn Monroe than that their marriage didn't last. The most beautiful movie star in the world and the most graceful athlete—the perfect physical union for our age, the best since Venus and Adonis—but even they couldn't make it work.

We, as imperfect human beings, took some naturally mean-spirited comfort that even gods and goddesses can fail, too. It is that tragedy of the hero that yet enthralls us as much as the glamour ever did.

How Sports Works

■　　■　　■

This is how sports works in America today:

First, University takes alumni contributions to build new arena instead of buying computers for students, in order to get a better basketball team in order to attract more contributions from concerned alumni.

Next, concerned alumnus pays high school player under the table so that he might keep university in mind.

Alumnus also pays smart friend of high school player to take SAT exams for him.

Smart friend of high school player cannot go to college because all scholarship money goes to athletes, so smart friend becomes drug runner, and Japan makes better appliances.

Player, accustomed to taking money under the table so that he will go to college, takes money under the table from smarmy agent so that he will leave college and go into pros.

Player volunteers for draft, leaves college after sophomore season.

Pro team makes multimillion-dollar offer to draft choice. Smarmy agent rejects, says player is insulted, will go play in Canada or Italy instead.

Pro team capitulates, pays insulted player multimillions. So all other teams must pay their insulted draft choices more multimillions.

All pro teams raise concession prices to pay for draft choices.

After mediocre rookie season, player demands renegotiation since he doesn't have sneaker commercial.

Pro team capitulates. All other teams renegotiate with their mediocre rookies who lack sneaker commercials.

All teams raise ticket prices to pay for renegotiation.

University finishes building new arena, convinces pro team coach to break his contract and come to academia with better contract paid for by alumni contributions.

Still no scholarships for bright students, since alumni contributions are needed for coach's slush fund. So, more bright students become drug runners. American drug trade improves. Dollar loses value.

Pro team hires super coach from other pro team, demands city build luxury boxes to pay for his lifetime contract.

City refuses. Pro team threatens to move to Nashville.

City asks: Why Nashville? Nashville replies: Because Jacksonville and St. Petersburg already have their big-league franchises.

Player becomes free agent, signs for more with new pro team that needs "role player" to become a champion.

Old pro team offers to sign other free agent for even more, but it will have to move to Nashville to pay for this.

So, city agrees to build luxury boxes, team signs free agent to be "role player."

Television network pays owners a billion dollars. Players demand fair share of that—precisely, a billion-two. Owners refuse.

Players threaten to go on strike, in court.

Owners threaten to lock them out, in court.

Fans threaten to boycott, on talk radio.

Other franchise in town tells city: You built first pro team luxury boxes. Now, we want a whole new domed stadium or we will take our franchise to Nashville.

City asks: Why Nashville? Nashville replies: Because Charlotte and Ottawa already have their big-league franchises.

City raises taxes to pay for luxury boxes for one team and domed stadium for other franchise. City then broke, closes high schools. More bright students sell drugs. Germany buys Nashville, moves it to Bavaria.

Strike is called off. All players get raises.

To pay for raises, all teams require ticket holders to put up bonds or they will lose costs to companies, who can put seats down as a business expense.

Fans threaten to boycott, on talk radio.

University takes alumni contributions to build a new stadium, to go with new arena and expensive new coach, in order to attract more contributions from concerned alumni.

Concerned alumnus comes to his luxury box, paid for as a business expense, bringing new high school star, paying him there under the table so that he might soon keep university in mind . . . and on and on and on. Hello, frustrated fan, you're on the air.

Gamesmanship

■   ■   ■

T he shoot-out in the women's World Cup final. The Chinese player stepped up, fired—and the shot was blocked beautifully by Brianna Scurry, the U.S. goalie. The difference between championship or defeat, between going to the White House or going home, between being on the Wheaties box or being toast.

Only it turned out that Scurry had clearly broken the rules, moving forward to cut off the shooter's angle before the shot.

This sort of example occurs often in big-time sport. This one World Cup incident only happened to be the most egregious—and the most publicized.

But there certainly are other cases. For instance, the final seconds of a big NFL game last December. New York Jets near the Seattle goal line. The quarterback, Vinny Testaverde, is stopped just short of the end zone. After the whistle, he nudges the ball forward. Touchdown Jets. Jets win. Bye-bye, Seattle.

The issue, of course, is ethical. Does this sort of activity constitute cheating? On the surface, yes. But, to many people, how can it be cheating if you do something brazen right in front of an official? No, goes the alibi chorus, the only thing these two athletes did was simply exhibit quick thinking. They weren't beating the opposition. They were beating the referees. But: same thing. Hey, it's all part of the game.

And morally, this is pretty much how we look at sports nowadays. Where once we valued sportsmanship, now we prize what we have come to call . . . gamesmanship.

The rationale invariably offered is that we Americans want to win more than anybody else; that there is no substitute for victory; show me a good loser, I'll show you a loser, etc., etc.

But I think values *have* changed. Look, we've always wanted to win. It's just that now we're much more accepting—forgiving even—about the means to victory. And, as is so often the case with our sport, this pretty much reflects the attitude we possess about other elements of our whole broad society. Nowadays, we seem to be a much more divided culture of winners and losers, and once that dichotomy is accepted, then we really don't care *more* about winning; we simply care *less* about the niceties of how the winners won.

Edge has become a much more important word in our language. Everybody is looking for an edge.

It would be sappy then, even old-fashioned, to immediately conclude that we are less honest than we used to be—on the field, in life. I don't know. I do think that whereas it used to be cagey to stretch the rules, to see how close you could come to skirting the line, now we feel less compunction about stepping over the line. So, at least in that sense, we are *in sport* what we so often hear—a more permissive society.

Or perhaps what has happened in sport suggests primarily that we have less respect for authority. Players don't seem to see the officials as custodians of the game so much as obstacles to work around, to fool.

I find it especially instructive that in the one major sport in which there really aren't any referees—golf—the ethic is still one of honesty. Above expediency. Interesting, isn't it? When the ruling authority is me, myself, and I, we still have respect for the rules. We won't cheat on *ourselves*. Periodically, even with great sums of money on the line, some golfer will volunteer a penalty on himself.

Does that mean that golfers care less about winning? Does that mean golfers are finer people than other athletes? Rather, I hope it means that all of us are capable of being sportsmen instead of gamesmen—if only we can believe that winning is not as important as caring *how* we win.

Gone Fishin'

■   ■   ■

In Colorado last week, I watched two men happily fishing a mountain stream. A day or two later, in Central Park, in the wilds of Manhattan, I paused as a man showed his young son how to cast—over and over, in an empty urban pasture. At a cocktail party not long ago, I was corralled by some people wanting to know if I had seen a wonderful new book, featuring only pictures of . . . trout. And all year, at varying times, friends of mine depart civilization, foregoing even the most modest twentieth-century amenities, to go somewhere primitive, where, for the privilege of being cold and uncomfortable, they can fish.

And the thing that confounds me most—even more than the giving up amenities part—is that while I know many golfers I simply cannot tolerate, many joggers who offend me, and a number of tennis players I cannot abide—I've never met a fisherman I didn't like . . . well, as long as they're not trying to talk to me about fishing.

So I am, all in all, very jealous of fishermen. They must have some secret. Even two thousand years ago, Jesus obviously knew what he was up to when he picked so many of them for his disciples. After all, it isn't just me. Nobody dislikes fishermen. We may not understand them. We may not have a clue why they do to themselves what they choose to do—but we certainly don't harbor any antipathy for them. They're nature's noblemen.

It's ironic, too. A lot of people loathe hunters. Why, in England now, the most pressing national issue concerns the issue of foxhunters. Never mind Princess Di's new beau; the country is torn about outlawing men in pink coats chasing foxes.

But ban their alter egos in high rubber boots seeking after rainbow trout? When you think about it, what's the difference between bringing Bambi down with a rifle slug to hauling in a handsome walleyed pike with a mean hook? It isn't that fish are any less deserving than others of God's creatures. Why, it is certified that salmon know geography better than ninety-two percent of American high-school students, and dolphins are not only cute as buttons, but they are smarter than all talk-show hosts and most football players.

So why don't we get more exercised about killing our marine friends?

Not only that, but when fishermen prey on these dear little creatures of the deep, they use—what? Right! They use *lures*. Lures to kill.

Talk about politically incorrect. Not even rotten hunters gunning down those endangered-species sheep use *lures*.

Moreover, when it comes to fishermen, it is simply assumed that they are liars. They will not tell the simple truth about the size of the ones that got away. Nonetheless, we accept prevarication with our fishing brethren. Nobody, you see, ever wants to say anything bad about fishermen. Why doesn't somebody tell Newt Gingrich to go fish? That way to popularity. In fact, the last president who was a genuine fisherman was Dwight Eisenhower—Ike—the most beloved president. It figures.

But, you see, I don't think you can pretend to be a fisherman. I think the act sorts out the ones who would fish for show, for style, for the wrong reasons. Years ago, I was with a wry old basketball coach named Abe Lemons, down in Oklahoma. Since Abe was the quintessential country boy, I just assumed he fished. So I asked him about it.

"Fish?" he groaned. "Son, I don't like myself that much."

Maybe that's it. Maybe that's why, much as I'd like it, I never can hang that sign on my door that says: GONE FISHIN'.

We Will Rock You

■   ■   ■

Hey, let's go down to the arena and enjoy a ball game. We'll take out a second mortgage so we can afford the ticket prices and some souvenirs for the kids. What a great time we'll have. Of course, games in America now are only single-sense experiences . . . especially basketball games.

You are only allowed to *see* them. You don't hear the wonderful sounds of the ball bouncing, of sneakers squeaking on the floor, of a player crying out "pick him up," or a coach bellowing instructions off the bench.

Instead, all you hear at a basketball game now is a recording—played at a decibel count otherwise familiar only to jackhammers breeding—of a song performed by a bizarre late Englishman, Freddie Mercury, and his unathletic, un-American group named Queen. And, of course, as anyone who has attended a game anywhere in the United States in the noisy '90s knows, it is called: "We Will Rock You."

Oh, what glorious songs used to be associated with sport. "Take Me out to the Ballgame." "Hail to the Victors." "Cheer, Cheer for Old Notre Dame." So many more. Why, best of all, I love the rather obscure fight songs from VMI and the University of Cincinnati. Yes—I'm a real sports song connoisseur. But no more. All we ever hear is: we will, we will rock you.

Puh-leeze.

It isn't much better in the other sports. Baseball, the thinking man's game, also now blazes out so much rock between innings that even outdoors you can't talk. Bugles blare, exhorting *false* cheers. In football stadiums, the scoreboards light up demands to scream out "Dee-fense! Dee-fense!" The opponents can't hear the signals. But then, you and me in the stands can't hear *anything*.

But basketball is the worst. The noise even begins before the game. Basketball introductions now are tacky laser shows, in which even guys averaging five points a game are brought on with more excruciatingly loud fanfare than Cecille B. DeMille ever gave God or Caesar or even Charlton Heston. And then, just when you thought you might actually enjoy a game, it starts: "We will, we will rock you . . ."

Even children's teams play "We Will Rock You" now. And the NHL commissioner, Gary Bettman, says hockey can be made more popular in the United States just by, essentially, playing "We Will Rock You" at hockey games. He calls this perversion the "Americanization" of the game. "We need to add music, video boards, promotions between the periods," the Commissioner says. "Push it into the consciousness of the country."

But we have no consciousness left at American games anymore. We are screamed into submission by Queen. All we hear is: "We will, we will rock you." We can't even hear ourselves cheer anymore. Oh, how I miss that wonderful rising cry that Bob Cousy once called "the last loud roar," when our team poured it on so that the visitors had to, finally, call time-out, in submission.

Oh, to hear a crowd of live people roar again. Oh, to hear ourselves think.

But of course, that wouldn't be modern. That wouldn't be American, that wouldn't be . . . We will, we will rock you.

Sportscasters

■   ■   ■

NBC threw America's premier sportscaster to the wolves the other day, when it publicly apologized for remarks that Bob Costas made during the Olympics' Opening Ceremony—although virtually everybody acknowledges that what Costas said was fair, accurate, and appropriate.

The network's response to his words reminds us once again, though, how sports journalism—print and broadcast—is held to a different standard.

Costas's supposedly offensive remarks were made as the Chinese delegation marched in. What he said was that China had been under fire for human rights violations and that some of its athletes were suspected of drug use. In terms of controversial revelation, this is about the equivalent of Costas declaring that there sure are a lot of cows in Wisconsin. But some Chinese complained, and, before the cock crowed, NBC denied their man Costas before the world.

To be sure, some wise guys say, hey, don't be naive: NBC is owned by GE, and GE can't take any chances that might endanger its exploitation of the huge Chinese market. Oh? Maybe so. But do you really think for a minute that NBC would have hung Tom Brokaw out to dry if he had made the same sort of accurate remarks on *The Nightly News*? Or Bryant Gumbel on *The Today Show*? Or Jane Pauley on *Dateline*? Not likely. Not for sure.

Sports journalism is always viewed differently, though. It is always suspect. Bart Giamatti, the late baseball commissioner and Yale president, once wrote that sportswriting is by far the most superior literature in any newspaper, but that it is also of the blithest spirit, the most glib. The word "allegedly," Giamatti wrote, simply knows not the sports page.

Sports broadcasters are at the other extreme. They often must walk on eggshells, because their station or network has bought the rights to the event they are covering, and so the sportscaster—unlike the sports-writer or the news broadcaster—is the *only* reportorial voice. In Ronald Reagan's famous remark, the sportscaster—his employer, anyhow—has bought this microphone. Sportscasters, like Costas in Atlanta, are expected to be impartial to a fault . . . which is to say: truth must often be the first casualty.

Indeed, sports broadcasters are quite suspect should they dare venture opinions . . . unless they are former jocks. *Allegedly*, in the minds of many fans, if you didn't play the game, then you can't possibly fathom it. John McEnroe even disputes the ability of former female players to cover a male tennis match. Can you imagine listeners protesting to National Public Radio that Mara Liasson be taken off the White House beat because: a) she isn't a former president, and b) she's a woman? But that's the sort of criticism that non-jock sports broadcasters must endure.

Also, since people who watch games on TV love the sports they watch, the slightest criticism of a particular game tends to be taken as a rap against the whole sport. Imagine, if you will, Siskel and Ebert giving thumbs down to one lousy cowboy movie, and then being widely attacked for being cynics who have no spiritual right to review films, because they obviously hate all cowboy movies.

Now, NBC has sent one more message to its sports announcers: be bland, be insipid, and if you do express a harsh truth, even if it is without dispute, understand that sports announcers are not worth our defense.

Playoffs—
The American Dream

■　　■　　■

O nce upon a time, playoffs were looked upon as very inappropriate. Real Americans played only to win it all. In fact, foreigners were appalled at how much victory mattered to us. As Vince Lombardi so famously had it: Winning was not the most important thing—'twas the only thing.

And a tie was like kissing your sister.

Somewhere along the line, though, sometime when we were advised that it really was better for the dollar to *decline*, sometime when we accepted that all theatre had to come from London and that we could blame El Niño for everything, sometime in the middle of all that, Americans lost their harsh competitive way. Oh sure, it was nice to be champion, but it was better to make a buck, and it was perfectly acceptable just to . . . make the playoffs.

And so, America today is the land of the eternal playoff. The sport that doesn't get on the playoff bandwagon is the one that will wither. College football, for example, keeps having silly things called bowl games instead of playoffs, and it is the one sport that keeps declining in popularity.

Baseball, fool that it is, remains ambivalent about playoffs. Baseball sort of invented playoffs, too. A hundred years ago, when there was only the National League, baseball tried something called the Temple Cup, in which the pennant winner played the runner-up. But that was a different U.S. of A. then, and the fans didn't buy it. The winner is the winner, fin de siècle nineteenth-century Americans declared. It was a more quaint place then.

But after playoffs gained some popularity in the National Hockey League—where, commonly, *two-thirds* of the teams qualified—minor league baseball turned to the playoffs in desperation during the Depression. The fundamentalists in baseball may throw fits about how sacrilegious it is that playoffs have come to the majors, but the fact is that playoffs have held an honored place in baseball for decades. Fundamentalists don't want to hear that, though; most baseball purists will even argue that playoffs killed the dinosaurs.

And now—horror of horrors—we also have wild cards. And if you think playoffs were controversial, well, there is just no middle ground when it comes to baseball and wild cards. Wild cards are like liver. I never met anybody who was wishy-washy about liver. Did you? You either love liver or you spit it out. Same way with wild cards.

What drives the fundamentalists in baseball berserk about playoffs and wild cards is this: the best team may not win the championship, because . . . anything can happen in a short series.

Well, yes, that's what's so gripping about short series. Anything can happen. Only in baseball would that potential for surprising excitement be widely viewed as a negative. But baseball is sooo serious. Baseball is mathematics in knickers. There is no room for Cinderella in baseball. (Basically, Cinderella was the first wild card; that's how she got to the ball, didn't she?)

But the fact is that most people adore playoffs—and the more wild cards the better. There are now sixty-four teams that qualify for the basketball NCAA, and some pragmatists argue that with just a couple extra rounds, every Division One team in America could make the playoffs. Hooray! That's even better than the NHL, with its lousy two-thirds worth. Before playoffs, sport was more of an aristocracy. But now, with playoffs, sport is more reflective of the American dream, in which everybody gets a second chance and every child can grow up to be president . . . or a wild card.

Lessons from a Friend

■   ■   ■

Apersonal note to begin with: I remember my grandfather, who grew up in Richmond, telling me about the day when he was a little boy, and they let all the children out of school so they could help pull Robert E. Lee's new statue to its assigned place on Monument Avenue, there to rest amidst the other statues of all the beloved Virginia heroes. And my grandfather would then show me a little piece of frayed rope, which he'd saved all these decades, cut with his penknife from the tow rope after the general's statue was safely set. Virginians have always taken their champions very seriously.

I thought back on that last Wednesday, in Richmond, a century later, when Arthur Ashe, the Virginian, was monumentalized. I tried to imagine how ever I could have explained that to my grandfather—how the hero that came next to Richmond after Robert E. Lee, general in chief, Confederate States of America—that next Virginian—was merely a tennis player, who was also, of all things, black.

As much as that would have confounded my grandfather, it is also still difficult for me to understand quite how deeply Arthur Ashe's death touched so many people. Bill Rhoden, who is black, a sports columnist for the *New York Times*, even observed that the outpouring overshadowed that which had been bestowed upon Thurgood Marshall—not to mention surpassing the affection granted to those other distinguished world citizens who have left us, one after another, in these first sad weeks of 1993: Dizzy Gillespie, Rudolf Nureyev, Audrey Hepburn.

Has any athlete—not to mention *former* athlete—ever been lionized so at his death? It wasn't as if Arthur was the best player ever; why, he wasn't even the best of his time. Rather, he was just a very good tennis player who had come to be recognized as an altogether exceptional human being. I think that, by the time he died, Arthur Ashe had become everybody's favorite athlete. Not just All-American, more just all ours.

Obviously, there was some rare chord that Arthur plucked on people's heartstrings. Probably, too, that twang reveals more about our society right now than it does about the man himself. Andrew Young, eulogizing Arthur at the service in Richmond, may have drawn closest, saying that Ashe had come to represent "the role of innocence in our time." And innocence, like love, sometimes is found in funny places—even in professional athletics.

It was the tennis player who came to triumph in society even as he was grotesquely defeated by fate, the tennis player who was the one who exhibited the dignity and decency that we simply no longer expect from people of consequence. Jesse Jackson characterized it in an intriguing way, saying that Arthur managed to "build a code of conduct for the gifted." Somehow, the public correctly divined that essential goodness of Ashe, so that he really was honored more for his nobility than for his celebrity—which is truly amazing in these Warholian times. That's what a lot of last week was about: us saying, we will pause now for just a moment to honor honor. It felt good, so we were even more profligate in our giving.

Future peril: Nothing, of course, distinguished Ashe so much as the way he handled adversity. It was enough to suffer a heart attack when still in his 30s—while still, for that matter, ranked in the top 10 of tennis players. But then, to contract AIDS from a blood transfusion given after heart-bypass surgery . . . well, that was just impossibly unfair. The intensity of anger that the public feels about how he was subsequently violated by the media, when he was forced to reveal his condition or be "outed" by *USA Today*, remains palpable. Anybody in the press who dismisses the public's disgust at the encroachment upon a private man's privacy does so at their future peril.

But above all, race was forever crucial to understanding the way in which the world dealt with Arthur Ashe. He was, I came to think, in matters of race, *The Universal Soldier*, some kind of keystone figure we need if ever brothership is to triumph. He was black, but he perfectly infiltrated white American society as much as he needed to, and even beyond that he was just terribly interested in everybody everywhere in the world.

Those legions who paid tribute last week kept talking about how Ashe was a "transcendent figure" above tennis, mere sports, but, I'm sorry, the much greater, dearer point was quite the opposite: he was the sort of person who was always down in the ditches, connecting things, tying people together. Arthur would have been mortified to have been reduced to being labeled transcendent.

Anyway, even if we throw around highfalutin words like "transcend," most everybody really sensed otherwise; by the end, all the world wanted to associate itself closely with Arthur. The International Olympic Committee made him the first athlete member of the Olympic Order never to have had anything to do with the Olympics. The bell was sounded 10 times for him at the Bowe-Dokes championship fight, the first time that any but a fallen fighter had ever been so honored. African-Americans exalted him as one of theirs, even though there were occasions in the past when Arthur was painted as effete for failing to scream out and an elitist for failing to go along with politically correct racial dogma. And whites, of course, loved to cozy up to Ashe and cite him as the black ideal—why can't they all be like him?—missing the point that there are precious few whites that live up to that standard, either.

As a matter of fact, nothing blindsided some whites as much as Ashe's recent comment that, as difficult as it was having AIDS, that wasn't nearly as trying as being black. "No question," he snapped.

Arthur Ashe said that? Certainly not Arthur. Not the man who was always so civil and understanding. But the thought wasn't anything new with him. I can remember him years ago instructing me that "equal" though things may seem, he could never achieve that estate because so much of his time—of any black person's time—must be spent simply thinking about race. "You can get up in the morning and just walk outside and start your day. I can't do that. I always have to think: well, here goes a black guy walking outside. So, you see, you'll always have an advantage over me."

Our hope: But the fact that Arthur Ashe could say things about race, however passionately, without bitterness, is what made them so meaningful. Obviously, Arthur Ashe meant more to black people, but, notwithstanding, he was capable of engaging white people; he was capable of causing change in them and their world. In the end, the outpouring of emotion we gave to him spoke selfishly to our hope—that if we could not save his life, what he stood for might help save us.

Although this adulation Arthur received this past week would have embarrassed him terribly, he must have sensed the effluence of affection that would flow with his death. In a way, you see, the revelation of last April that was wrenched from him produced the first draft of his obituaries while he was still alive to read them. His pre-death also, he recognized, made him a more valuable advocate of the causes he cared about, so he could make us cosign for his borrowed time. He wanted to steal a few more months, too, and he thought he would, but he was accepting of what would come of him, whenever it did.

The last time I saw him was only a couple weeks before he died, but it preceded any sense of urgency. Still, he was in the hospital, so he wanted to put me at ease. "You know," he said, "everything in my life is just wonderful now—except for the hospital stuff."

When I looked a little skeptical—as if to say out loud: excuse me, you are reducing AIDS to "hospital stuff"?—he added: "Really, everything is almost perfect."

I left almost believing him. Arthur Ashe had a very good attitude, and it was catching. He was a more infectious person even than what incidentally killed him.

B. D.

Walter Camp, Yale 1880, captain and coach of many great Bulldog elevens, is credited with having invented the All-America. What a wonderful thing. The beau ideal of the breed was Frank Merriwell, who was, of course, a Yale man. Merriwell happened to be fictional, but then that's the point of All-Americas, isn't it? If they were merely real, they would just be class presidents or prelaw students: basic Yalies. The last All-America was Brian Dowling, Yale '69. It has been 20 years since Elis watched him dance between the sideline stripes.

Today, though, Yale—which was to football what Egypt was to civilization—is relegated to something called Onedubbelay, and what were All-Americas are called draft choices and what was America is called a market.

Frank Shorter, the Olympic marathon champion of 1972, and also Class of '69, says that for years he and his classmates have understood that "we were an anachronistic class."

"They entered the old Yale, the last gasp," says Bart Giamatti, the president of baseball's National League, who was a professor of English at Yale then, before being named president of the university in 1978. They entered the same Yale I had"—Giamatti is Yale '60—"but they left campus under completely different assumptions than the ones they'd arrived with. It was the extension of a time that was gone . . . only nobody knew it was gone at that time."

Dowling arrived at a place that was rapidly changing, but even before he got there he was being compared to Frank Merriwell—whom he'd never heard of. At that time, 1965, young Brian had never been defeated in a football game, America had never been defeated in a war, and it was naturally assumed that All-Americas, like Detroit's chromed finest, would roll off the assembly line forever. What Yalie ever really believed the song that went: "We are poor little lambs who have lost our way,/Baa, baa, baa. . . ."?

It's funny, but the America that Dowling lived in then, the one we all inhabited when he began at Yale, is now regularly referred to as Norman Rockwell's America, as if the whole country had been nothing but a quaintly romantic painting. By contrast, the United States is now inevitably drawn, jaded, in thin strokes. The last All-America himself lives on in the comic strip *Doonesbury*, which is rendered by Gary Trudeau, Yale '70. Dowling is the character B. D., who always wears a football helmet. *God have mercy on such as we./Baa, baa, baa.* Harvard 29–Yale 29.

What was so extraordinary about Dowling and his teammates was that somehow they managed to make football important (and even dear) at the very time American colleges were changing forever, when students were marching in the street and sleeping in the dean's office. It was all the more amazing that this devotion to middle-American frivolity should happen in an elitist, Ivy League institution. But it did. "At a time when an understanding gap has frequently separated alumni from students, football has provided a bridge of common interest," the *Yale Alumni Magazine* editorialized, gratefully, in 1968. Hawks and doves could lie down together in the Yale Bowl.

"I should have known someone like you would be calling," Dowling said the other day. "I should have remembered—exactly 20 years. The last time anybody like you called was in '78—10 years." There wasn't any irony in his voice. But then Dowling does not appear to be the sort of fellow who traffics in irony . . . or facetiousness, hyperbole, or aging, either. He looks as if he could glide right into the Yale Bowl now, dodge a couple of Dartmouths and chuck a wobbly one to Calvin Hill in the end zone. At 41 Dowling still has that pigeon-toed gait so common to many fine athletes, and all the boyish aspects: hair not quite in place; blue-green eyes that glint; grins and shrugs. If your mother met him, no matter how old Brian Dowling happened to be, she would say, "My, what a nice boy."

For a living, Dowling runs the Ivy Satellite Network, which specializes in closed-circuit telecasts of traditional games between smaller colleges that organized TV doesn't want to mess with. In this pursuit he dresses in button-down shirt, rep tie, blazer, preppy slacks and loafers. He lives in Fairfield County, Conn., with his daughter, Haley, age 2, and his wife, Betsy, who never knew him when he was at Yale and who gets a little irked at having to tell people that, no, just because she is Brian J. Dowling's wife in exurban Connecticut doesn't mean she is B. D.'s inamorata, Boopsie, in *Doonesbury.*

Dowling shrugs. "My wife still feels that I've never taken enough advantage of it," he says. Then he grins. He's clearly not going to. Ever. At Yale, when he was the last All-America, after he had his wrist broken and his nose broken in quick succession, he told his music teacher—who didn't know the football eleven from the local chapter of SDS—"I walked into a door." Later, when she found out who her accident-prone student really was, she apologized for her ignorance. "Hey, it's O.K.," Brian said. "Your bit's music."

The Yale that Dowling returned to for his senior year 20 autumns ago was still all male. Members of the adult female gender were referred to as "girls" and therefore went to girls' schools, e.g., Vassar, Connecticut College, Briarcliff. "Just hearing one of 'em walk into the reserve room of the library, everybody looked up," Dowling recalls. "Girls even sounded different then. It was still pre-Nike, remember."

By 1968, Yale tuition had soared to $2,150 per year. The university chaplain, William Sloane Coffin, Yale '49, had been convicted along with Dr. Benjamin Spock, Yale '25, of instructing young men in ways to avoid the draft, and William F. Buckley, Yale '50, was having a bloody fit at the depths to which both God and boy had fallen at his alma mater. *Bull dog! Bull dog! Bow, wow, wow,/Eli Yale!*

A front-page banner headline in the *Yale Daily News* in 1967 screamed POT PRICES HIT NEW HIGH. Priorities. A no-credit course in transcendental meditation was offered, but then, as at so many colleges, suddenly all courses at Yale had become pass-fail. Nobody was supposed to be *judgmental.*

Kingman Brewster, president of this new People's Republic of New Haven, announced that in order to prepare for the possibility of girls being admitted into Yale, several hundred of the sex would arrive on campus later in the autumn of 1968 for a trial visit. The *Daily News* (always referred to as the Yalie Daily) put its ear to the ground and whispered that the students were showing "an interest in cohabitation rather than coeducation." The Reverend Malcolm Boyd, the Episcopal priest who had written the best seller *Are You Running with Me, Jesus?*, arrived on campus as a visiting fellow at Calhoun College, one of the university's residential units, and wrote a column for the Yalie Daily entitled "Man and Sex At Yale."

Down in New York City, editors of what would become the Universal Press Syndicate read Boyd's piece. They discussed with Boyd the possibility of his writing a syndicated column. They suggested that Boyd contribute more samples to the student newspaper—opening in New Haven, as Broadway shows had through the years.

Issues of the Yalie Daily spilled into the New York offices, and the editors flipped through them to see if they contained a column by Boyd. More and more, though, they had to read about the Yale football captain: DOWLING BRILLIANT AGAIN. And read about the entire undefeated, untied Bulldog juggernaut. Yale, the nation's original football factory, was cheek by jowl with all the Johnny-come-lately football factories. And there were pep rallies! At Yale!

Somewhat more reflective, Shorter says now: "We were in a bit of an ivory tower. We all knew that outside of Yale there was a lot of bad stuff coming down. We knew that the Rot-cee guys we saw walking around campus might not be around—alive—in another couple years. So to focus on Brian and the football team was an illusion. . . . So we did it."

The fellows down in the syndication offices in New York never did develop much of an interest in either the fortunes of the Yale eleven or in the musings of Rev. Boyd. But as time went on, they did notice something else that was occasionally buried in the inky pages of the Yalie Daily.

Brian John Dowling was born and raised in Cleveland, where his father, Emmett, was president of the Youngstown Steel Door Company. In junior high and then at St. Ignatius High, Brian did not play a complete football game that did not end in victory for his side. One time he was injured and, predictably, St. Ignatius folded without him. As he grew into a 6' 2", 195-pound body, he also became a star in basketball and baseball and played a mean game of tennis. He drew 100 college scholarship offers, coast to coast, but his father opted to pay the full tuition and send Brian to Yale. "Why go cabin class when you can go first class?" Mr. Dowling asked.

As a freshman, Dowling led the Yale Bullpups to a 6–0 record. He was what was known as a Triple Threat: He passed, ran and punted. In the winter, he led the freshman basketball team with 24.5 points per game, and in the spring, after he won a few tennis matches with the Yale tennis team, he switched over to the freshman nine. Before Dowling played a minute in any varsity sport, it was being reported that the living embodiment of Frank Merriwell had at last appeared, in New Haven.

The nonpareil Merriwell, a creation of one Gilbert Patten, who wrote under the name of Burt L. Standish, performed feats of athletic wonder for 17 consecutive years in the Tip Top Library, a series of weekly dime novels that were published from 1896 to 1913. As amazing as Frank was—why aren't kids ever named Frank anymore?—Merriwell had a lot of help because Standish had him play for Yale, the perennial pigskin steamroller in the days of yore.

Dowling, too, was in good company. He is convinced that the team he captained in 1968 could have held its own against any college team in the nation for at least a half, and could only then have been worn down by sheer force of numbers. "We had a lot of really good players, a couple *Parade* high school All-Americas," he says. "And we had one of the two or three best athletes in the whole country."

Dowling is not referring to himself. He is referring to Hill. "Cal was the only player I ever had who could have started at all 22 positions," Carmen Cozza, the Yale coach then and now, says. In fact, one of the reasons Hill chose Yale was that he wanted to play quarterback—and then with Dowling he never got the chance.

"Quite frankly that was a burr, and it stayed with me for a long time," says Hill, now 41, who is a vice president of the Baltimore Orioles.

Long before the Dallas Cowboys surprised the rest of the NFL by drafting Hill in the first round in 1969, there wasn't anybody around New Haven who wouldn't casually acknowledge that Hill was the better *player*. It was just that Dowling only moonlighted as a player, when he got time off from being a legend. When the "dynamic duo" were juniors, the Yalie Daily ran companion profiles. HILL: MORE THAN STATS was the admiring, if rather prosaic, headline for the one. And for the other? GOD PLAYS QUARTERBACK FOR YALE.

The attention focused on Dowling might seem, then, to have been racially motivated—Hill is black—and surely there was something in that; but nobody, Hill included, seems to think that was the primary reason. A study made in 1973 of the Dowling phenomenon by two Yale undergraduates, Christie Bader and J. D. Smeallie, scrutinized Dowling and his exploits as a prize example of American folklore and concluded that while it helped that he was a member of the white race, it meant much more that he simply played the "conspicuous" position of quarterback and was possessor of the perfect personality for an American legend.

Says Hill: "If there was one thing that eased the bitterness of not being the quarterback, it was Brian. When you consider what was going on around him, you couldn't ask for a more super person." The two became good friends, roomed together on the road and still stay in close touch.

Dowling possessed that wonderful Sergeant York admixture of personal self-effacement and professional cockiness. Even now, when a foolish person remarks that the whole experience must have been quite a "fairy tale," Dowling doesn't blink. "No, not really," he says directly. "You've got to understand that I expected to win. After all, I'd won all the games I'd finished since seventh grade."

Oh.

Dowling was knocked out of virtually his entire sophomore season with a knee injury and then missed three games his junior year with a fracture of his right wrist that was supposed to keep him out for six. When Dowling broke his wrist, he told Cozza (and actually meant it): "That's O.K., Coach, I can throw with my left."

In the Harvard game of Dowling's junior year, Yale was behind with barely two minutes left. Said the '67 Bulldog captain, Rod Watson, after the game: "But we never worried. We knew Brian would do something." What he did was uncork a 66-yard TD bomb. Victory.

Without Dowling the Bulldogs were not even .500 (5–6); with him they were undefeated in 21 freshman and varsity games. Going into his final college game, against Harvard, he had led his teams to 65 victories over nine years.

The Yalies liked the fact that their field general was a bold and interpretative player—"a swashbuckling pirate in a sea full of cod fishermen," wrote Bader and Smeallie—who contradicted the stuffy Yale clubman stereotype. He wasn't just Merriwell—or Dink Stover, Nathan Hale, Albie Booth—he was the Great Gatsby coming from the West to show up the eastern swells. Bader and Smeallie, in their study, compared Dowling to Davy Crockett, "a primitive from the West."

As with any legend, the tales grew. Bader and Smeallie counted 23 distinct Dowling fables, each passed along in the ancient oral tradition. The simplest involved a play sequence on the freshman team. Back to punt on fourth-and-11, Dowling ran instead and made the first down. But a penalty forced him to punt again, now on fourth-and-26. So as the Yale coaches pulled out their hair, he faked and ran again, making 35 yards. Pretty good stuff, unvarnished. But soon the tale was embellished and had it that Dowling had run for pay dirt.

More complex was the legend of the big Princeton game in 1967. In this case, Yale people could believe the allegory on only one level, even as they longed to believe it on another. You see, when it started to drizzle at Palmer Stadium, the visiting Yale crowd began to chant: "Make it stop, Brian, make it stop . . ." And he raised his arms . . . and yes, the rain did stop.

Bader and Smeallie concluded: "Brian Dowling is a hero created in the image of a Yale student (much as God has been created in the image of man)—he was atypical, or more accurately, 'supertypical.' " They continued, "The characteristics of a Märchen [folktale] of the English variety" qualify him as a true legend.

Of course, it helped that Dowling had his own modern minstrel to spread the word.

T he chairman of the *Yalie Daily* in 1967, Strobe Talbott, now chief of *TIME* magazine's Washington bureau, remembers a skinny sophomore who "virtually wandered in off the street" with some drawings. That, of course, was Gary Trudeau. His comic strip, which was christened *bull tales*, was soon a campus success, featuring a prototype protester named "Megaphone" Mark Slackmeyer.

Trudeau, as is his custom, will not be interviewed, but we do know that he had no personal connection with Dowling or any of the other Bulldog stalwarts. In any event, on Sept. 30, just after the first victory of the '68 season, the inaugural *bull tales* strip appeared. It featured what was to become the famous huddle motif, with the quarterback, who was not identified, declaring in the first panel: "O.K. team, this play is the same as the last one: 'The Cleveland Clutch.' "

The strips appeared sporadically in the Yalie Daily, evidently depending on how much homework Trudeau chose to do. But during that fall of '68, virtually all of the strips were about the quarterback. By Oct. 14 Trudeau was brassy enough to provide him with Dowling's No. 10 (in that panel the left tackle was giving the quarterback the finger), and two days later one of the other huddle-mates called him B. D.

Hill, No. 30, made a couple of cameo appearances in *bull tales*, but it was B. D. whom the strip revolved around—except for a few brief visits to Mike (the Man) Doonesbury, who was trying to score with girls. The strip was so popular that by Nov. 2 it had earned the sweetest flattery—a parody in a joke issue of the *Daily*. Next to a companion spoof of *Peanuts*, which showed the Great Pumpkin devouring Lucy, the parody of *bull tales*—simply called *bull*—depicted the Yale team assaulting Trudeau.

The strip obviously worked so well precisely because it made Dowling human, a figure of fun—a typical vain and dim-witted jock who wouldn't even take his helmet off. Worldly-wise Yalies, attending this prestigious institution of learning, preparing to spend the rest of their lives as stockbrokers or CIA operatives, had suddenly found themselves going bananas over a silly football team, just as if they were in the Big Ten—and Trudeau gave them back their sophistication. Once they had laughed at the idiotic football players in *bull tales*—and certified their Ivy cynicism—they could go out and be hero-worshippers, just like everybody else.

And so Trudeau sends B. D. off in his helmet ("It's part of my goddamn life style!") to try and make out at Briarcliff—and all he gets is a lousy invitation to a deb party. Meanwhile, back at Yale, Doonesbury, a sort of Everynerd, is all of a sudden scoring with female visitors. The lesson is clear: Football players really are no better than the rest of us. Or, chicks really can like us for our minds.

B. D. was so popular that, although Trudeau's work has since become more and more politicized, the strip kept the electric world of 1968 from intruding into football. Nowadays Trudeau regularly attacks that old Yale baseball captain George Bush; in that campaign year there was only one fleeting reference to politics in the strip, when Hubert Humphrey entered the huddle, seeking to be the new quarterback.

Trudeau's strip fueled the legend of Dowling the student (or anti-student) which grew in concert with the legend of Dowling the athlete. The darkest secret at Ivy League schools is that the hard part is getting admitted. Once in, almost any dummy can get by. Dowling, who had been a solid B+ student in high school and who was, after all, spending hours a day practicing on one or another sports team for the entire school year, was infamous for signing up for the easiest courses—guts, they were called. One of the myths about him was that at the start of one term Dowling entered a lecture hall and the entire room stood up and cheered—not because he was No. 10 for the Blue and White, but because his presence certified that this course was a true gut.

Dowling and Trudeau, though they will go to their graves coupled in their way, met only on one occasion, shortly after the '68 season ended, when Dowling agreed to write a foreword for the first collection of Trudeau's strips. Trudeau came by Dowling's room, the two exchanged bashful, uneasy "hellos," Dowling handed over the foreword, and Trudeau thanked him and left. "I never even got a copy of the book," Dowling says. "That ticked me off a little. But I've never minded any of the B. D. stuff. I've always been able to laugh at myself." He shrugged. "And besides, we won every week."

The last game of his Yale career was against, of course, Harvard. The Game. The Harvards were also unbeaten that year, but they were dismissed as nothing more than a good local act. Although the Eli first string played only fragments of the one-sided games, Dowling broke school career and season records for total offense and passing. He amassed 324 yards total offense against Dartmouth. Against Brown he took five stitches in his face in the first quarter, came back, played barely 20 minutes before he was injured again, but accumulated 303 yards—192 passing, 111 running. Against Princeton, Cozza let him run back a punt, and he took it for 32 yards. The coach then promised Dowling that he could return a kickoff against Harvard; there wasn't much else he hadn't done.

Tickets to the game in Cambridge were being scalped for $100. The Yalie Daily ran *bull tales* on the front page, over the logo, and everywhere Yalies were tacking up posters or screaming out: "Flush the Johns!" For John Harvard. Get it? What is this? Texas A & M? Lincoln, Nebraska?

"Physics majors, art majors, fundamentalists—what we called the Jesus squad—radical atheists, all rallying around us," Hill remembers. "People who had never been to a game got caught up in it. It made people feel better. It was just a nice time . . . all of it. It was a nice time for me. It was a nice time to be at Yale."

Although the Bulldogs lost six fumbles in the game, they led 29–13 late in the fourth quarter. Then Harvard scored and made a two-point conversion with only :42 left—29–21—and Cozza kept his promise and sent Dowling in to receive the kickoff. But Harvard squibbed the kick, recovered onside and started driving.

Dowling dashed over to Cozza and begged the coach to send him in at defensive back. He'd never played that position for so much as a single down at Yale. "I'm sorry, Brian," Cozza said. "I can't. It would ruin that young man for life if I took him out of there now."

So Dowling pawed at the sideline and watched Harvard score on the last play from scrimmage and pass for the conversion. HARVARD WINS 29–29! Roared the headline in *The Harvard Crimson*. "A tie!" says Boyd. "A tie! That was so traumatic it drove everyone crazy."

"You know, I *still* never think of them *coming back*," Dowling says, "because, you see, we never got the ball back."

"The thing is," Cozza says, "that even though he didn't know how to play defensive back, if I had put Brian in, I promise you, he would have figured out some way and we would have won. I promise you." Instead, that game dropped Dowling's career mark to 65-0-1.

Oh, well. Shortly after, Trudeau brought Megaphone Mark back. In June 1969, when the anachronistic class graduated, there were war protests at the ceremony. It was the culmination of a turbulent spring. The whole hockey rink had been turned over to the university community to allow it to vent its revulsion toward the ROTC boys. Draft cards were burned, more pot was smoked, and, says Rev. Boyd, "Everyone was marching toward the Green [the New Haven commons], and everyone was screaming, 'Fascists! You goddamn———— fascists!' And then there was tear gas outside, and it was coming under the door, and you're thinking: But this can't be. This is Yale. This is Yale University."

That summer was Chappaquiddick, Charles Manson and Woodstock, a man from Ohio was walking on the moon, and girls were walking around Yale as students, as women. Then came the trial of the Chicago Eight and in the spring of '70, Kent State. It was, so quickly, as if the autumn of '68 had never been, as if the Yale of that time were nothing more than Brigadoon.

A year later, Dowling, cut by the Minnesota Vikings and wanted by no one else in the NFL, was scuffling for a minor league outfit barely 20 miles from New Haven. He hadn't been drafted until the 11th round. He threw wounded ducks, didn't he? Of course Calvin Hill was chosen in the first round by Dallas and became a star and made everybody think the Cowboys were geniuses. The Universal Press Syndicate passed on Malcolm Boyd, but it signed up Gary Trudeau, changing the name of *bull tales* to *Doonesbury*. (Trudeau published a volume of the original *bull tales* in which many of the panels were redrawn.) "There have been moments when I didn't have the price of a hamburger, when I thought about that," Boyd sighs.

Trudeau obviously kept looking after Dowling, wherever he went— back up to the NFL, to the Patriots in the 1972 and '73 seasons, drifting here and there—always the backup quarterback. A few years ago Dowling wrote the cartoonist, asking for the original of a panel that featured B. D.; it came in the return mail, and he put it up on his wall.

The Ivy League was devalued by the NCAA and is suffered today like some crumbling historical building that stands in the way of a developer's condominiums. It never occurred to anybody in '68 that the Dowling team was the end of the line for the Ivies, the end of where collegiate sport had begun.

But the Ivies award scholarships only for need, and a year at those schools costs around $18,000 now. Calvin Hill has a son, Grant, who is a 6'7" high school basketball guard, and when Hill and Dowling spoke on the phone the other day, they talked about how unfair it would be for Grant to follow his father to Yale. Never mind the $70,000 price tag for four years; how do you ask a great player to perform before a couple of hundred fans, as Grant would at the Yale gymnasium?

"Don't forget," Dowling says proudly, "we drew good crowds. Thirty thousand at least—45 or 50 for Princeton or Dartmouth—and we'd fill the place up for Harvard." Cozza keeps one of the Yale Heisman trophies—either Clint Frank's or Larry Kelley's, he can't remember which— in his office, and he says, "Football is still important to these people around here." But it is never again going to be the way it was.

"We were lucky," Shorter says. "That time we had Brian and Calvin was the end of the time when football wasn't so technical and so chemical. You could still believe then that pure talent could shine through, no matter where it was. Now, if you want to make it, talent isn't enough. You have to go to the factory and take what they give you— and it ain't a milkshake with an egg in it."

Dowling says he always felt that in the pros his big problem was that he didn't know how he was expected to act. "I was never a clubhouse lawyer," he says. "I had always led by example. I tried to explain that in the past I was given the ball and then we won." He shrugs.

You know how it is. That sort of stuff just isn't in the computers that the scouts file their numbers into. It's in . . . well, it's just in the comic strips.

"But that's O.K.," Dowling says. "I'll take what I had. In the pros, I do think I was always in the wrong place at the wrong time, but my high school and college years were so rewarding that I believe I ended up ahead of anybody who has ever played football. I was having a good time, and we were winning, and . . . and"—he looks up and his eyes dance—"and there was this wonderful feeling of the expectation of doing well, and then going out and doing it."

In the old days, there was this curious contradiction, that the more someone was celebrated as an All-America, the less he belonged to the whole U.S.A. He was Yale's All-America or Notre Dame's All-America or Southern Cal's All-America. His college community was so proud of him; he belonged to them; he was All-Ours. Today a college really doesn't possess its good players. They belong to the television networks and the scouting combines. They're generic stars, All-Overs.

And so Brian Dowling, the last All-America, stood on the street corner, getting ready to go back to his office. "Well," he said, "I guess I don't have to do this for another 10 years."

"No, sorry, but probably only five," the other fellow said. "Twenty-five is always a big anniversary, and somebody will call you. But 30 isn't much, so then you'll get 15 years off, and no one's likely to bother you again till the 40th anniversary—2008. Think you can handle it?"

Dowling shrugged and grinned. If only there'd been a huddle around him, he could have peered over it, called a play and, even now, figured out a way.

The Field General

■　　■　　■

The quarterback. Signal caller. Field general. I like that the best: *field general*. There's absolutely nothing else like a quarterback in team sports. Oh, to be sure, there are goalies in hockey or soccer, or pitchers, taking turns every fifth day or closing for a single inning most days—but nobody else is close in influence to the quarterback. There he is: beginning every play, vital to most, utterly in charge. Not even Shakespeare ever wrote a hero so vital to his drama as a quarterback is to his game.

The quarterback, the quarterback—he's our man. If he can't do it, no one can!

In a very real way, in fact, the quarterback is a flaw in football, for while the sport requires entirely too many bodies for one man to achieve victory by himself, the one good man at quarterback is virtually required for victory.

So every Sunday we must hold our breath, praying, in the vernacular, that *our* quarterback will not "go down." Montana goes down, and there goes the 49ers' season. Cunningham goes down and cross off the Eagles. One man down, good-bye to a team.

In fact, now the back-up quarterback has become a vital part of every team—even if he just stands on the sideline with a clipboard. Back-up quarterbacks make much more money than the starters at many other positions. They're sort of the mistresses of sport—kept men. On the other hand, if politicians cared as much about vice presidents as coaches do about back-up quarterbacks, this would have always been a far, far better place. Would you choose a pigskin Dan Quayle to back up your quarterback?

Protecting quarterbacks is a dilemma. He backs up, a stationery target—dead meat if the pocket breaks and he's standing there, naked, arm cocked, or, hardly better, scrambling desperately to escape three-hundred-pounders charging at him.

On the other hand, how do you protect the quarterback with too much favor without making a double standard of what football is—a basic, primeval exercise in which "liking to hit" is the supreme compliment?

It's time somebody came up with an answer. After all, the quarterback as we know him is fifty years old now. Before him was the single-wing tailback, who was more versatile. The tailback ran as well as passed, and sometimes he kicked, too. But for all that, the tailback was not as integral to the team. He did not call the plays. A blocking back did that. Responsibility was more divided. The tailback was a leading man, but he did not necessarily lead. The quarterback is the power and the glory, the brains and the charisma.

Also, of course, it matters that in the NFL, where almost three-quarters of the players are black, most quarterbacks are still white. Maybe this is prejudice. Maybe just because white men can't jump, it doesn't mean they can't throw. Anyway, it is a fact—race—which means that quarterbacks matter more at the box office, just as they do on the field. Of course, quarterbacks do not tend to be as romantic as they used to be. There was a more rakish model once upon a time—as exemplified by Bobby Layne, Dandy Don Meredith, Snake Stabler, Sonny Jurgenson, Broadway Joe Namath. That breed has been replaced by a much more technological version, who is home studying film instead of out chasing beers and chicks.

But if the styles may change, the substance doesn't. The quarterback remains, at once, every team's monster and every team's Achilles' heel. In all sport, there is no other necessary evil like him.

Dressing Up

■　■　■

Through the years several types of sports uniforms have moved into general fashion. Probably the first to make that move was the classic yachting costume—blazer and white ducks. Then, after the war, when more casual clothes became widely acceptable, the colorful golfing outfits moved into everyday style, especially pastels and alpaca sweaters.

Skiing came next. Bright solid parkas were grafted onto Americans who didn't know a slalom from a schluss. In fact, one of the great attractions of skiing was its sexy fashion. The properly attired ski bunny was more likely to be sitting in the ski lodge about the roaring fire than she was to be roaring down the slopes.

Tennis clothes burst upon the general fashion scene next, about a decade ago, when it first became acceptable to wear colored clothes on the courts. Previously, it had not been *au courant* to wear tennis clothes away from the tennis courts, because it looked too much as if you left home in your underwear.

Also, American men had been brought up with the understanding that long pants connoted manhood. The day a boy grew up was the day his momma let him wear long pants. So American men could never get really secure with the British accommodation—baggy Bermuda shorts and long stockings. Somehow, it harkened back to Little Lord Fauntleroy.

Only when tennis became acceptable as a sport could men wear shorts proudly. It seems as if it was almost overnight that short pants went from being sissy to athletic in the United States.

Culturally, tennis boomed at exactly the right time for women, too. Tennis became popular just when it became acceptable for women to sweat. But tennis clothes are cute and properly feminine, so they were the ideal for the new active women. In fact, they were the ideal even if you weren't active. I have heard that up to fifty percent of all the women's tennis clothes bought are never worn on a tennis court.

Now, most recently, I notice that swimming attire is moving into the world at large. It was about a half a century ago that men stopped wearing tops to their bathing suits. Now, tank tops are returning. What's next: spats? Meanwhile, on women, more and more we see the most revealing backless bathing suits being worn in public—with a skirt thrown over the bottom half. And now, the trend speeds up. The ladies are wearing whole coordinated beach outfits—even with high heels, like contestants in a beauty pageant.

I especially enjoy the insanity on display on a windy day. Women come to the pool in floppy hats, which they must fight to keep on with one hand as they struggle with their long gossamer skirts with the other. Like the most modest of Victorians, they grab and slap at their clothes so that not so much as an ankle might be revealed. Then, promptly as the wind goes down, they find a sunbathing spot, whip off their blouses and skirts and lie there in next to nothing.

What does it say about our deep national psyche that, in this hot summer of 1980, for all our libertine displays of flesh, we have exhibited a strange urge to dress up before we undress?

Injury Prone

■　　■　　■

In what is, after all, the very unpredictability of athletics—still, nothing ever makes less sense than these two words: injury prone.

How can that be? Injury prone. After all, athletes are young and strong—the epitome of strong!—and by their very definition they are more advanced physically than the rest of us. How can these heroes be *injury prone?*

So often, too, the ones who do tend to get hurt are accused of lacking courage—of, in the old pejorative: jaking. A broken bone? Hey, spit on it and go back into the game the way the old-timers did.

Yet, the curious fact is that it is often the great players who can be most fragile, who suffer more than the others in sport. How rich in irony is that? To be so good, to be effortlessly in command, yet always, just as mysteriously, to be brought down by some flaw in that same grand body that otherwise rules. Achilles' heel or Samson's hair are, by comparison, easy to comprehend.

Look now at two superb athletes, gorgeously built, square-jawed and handsome, both six-feet-four and two-hundred-plus pounds of grace and muscle. One is named Cal Ripken, and he is indestructible, and the other is Mario Lemieux, and he is, regularly, quite destructible. Look at them together, and it makes no sense whatsoever, the one and the other, so much the same, blessed, but the one, cursed as well.

Somehow, too, what Lemieux has been accomplishing these past few weeks has not been accorded anything near its proper due. Never to put down Michael Jordan, but he was absolutely hoisted to the heavens when he came back from his pleasant sabbatical, during which he played some baseball games. Lemieux has returned to hockey after a year out trying to recover from Hodgkin's disease—cancer.

Before that, he missed whole chunks of other seasons with a broken hand and various excruciating back ailments—ailments so debilitating that he couldn't tie the laces on his own skates—and with anemia from the radiation treatments for his cancer.

Even now, Lemieux must sit out whole games, trying to conserve his energy, to regain his strength, but even then, playing only about three-quarters of the Penguins' schedule, he is the leading scorer in the National Hockey League. Indeed, Lemieux has not faced an opponent yet this season who has been able to deny him; he has made an assist or a goal in every game. He is quite extraordinary.

We hand out comeback awards, but, inevitably, they are given to players who have been laid low for a distinct period of time, and have then come back, whole. Lemieux, though, is forever coming back the best he can, with whatever parts of him he can summon up for the ice. And there is no whining, no pouting, no why must it be me who is . . . injury prone.

It's almost that time for the athlete-of-the-year awards. Hakeem Olajawon, Greg Maddux, Steve Young, Rebecca Lobo, and Michael Johnson lead any list of champions—worthy, all of them. And anything Ripken wins is fine with me. But my vote goes to Mario Lemieux, because greatness of the body is beautiful to see, but greatness that is denied by the body, but achieved by the will, is surpassing of the spirit.

Soccer Moms

■　　■　　■

S o there they were Saturday, all around me, to my left and to my right—short and tall, dark and light, every shape and size, surrounding me, shouting and screaming. They were, of course . . . soccer moms!

This is appropriate. When the most forgettable campaign of '96 concludes in a few days, I suspect that about all we will remember of it will be soccer moms.

Now a lot of inside sporting terms enter the common lexicon—it's a slam-dunk, let's kick off the meeting, he threw me a curveball—but *soccer mom* fits into a somewhat different category. A soccer mom is not of a sport, but something that derives from a sport—like a golf widow, a tennis elbow, or a bowling night.

The closest figure of speech to *soccer mom* has been *Little League father*. But interestingly, that has always been a very negative term. A Little League father is not just an involved dad who supports his boy at the baseball game. Rather, it is a boorish male parent who demands too much of his son, transferring his own old athletic failures to his poor offspring.

Saying *soccer mom*, however, is emotionally neutral. It merely suggests a mother out there being . . . well, maternal.

But the expression also tells us that the adult female is involved in sports now. She is no longer a ballet mom or a piano-lesson mom. Moreover, whereas we understood that the Little League father was browbeating his son, we have a vision of the soccer mom taking *either* a son or a daughter to the child's soccer game.

In fact, the irony of soccer is that while the United States is almost the only country in the world that has never made soccer *numero uno*—or *numero duo, tres,* or *quatro,* for that matter—it is also the only country in the world where soccer is so naturally perceived as an androgynous activity. Indeed, our best soccer-playing women, gold medallists at Atlanta, do better than our men.

But, that aside, what "soccer mom" really means, euphemistically, is "suburban mom." As basketball and football have become sports dominated by African-Americans, soccer has become a more attractive and safe participant sport for white kids. A soccer mom is not racist; it's just that when it comes to her children, she doesn't want them risking their knees and their necks playing that mean and ugly football. Soccer, like football, is an autumn game in America, but soccer is the un-football.

However, that cannot obscure the larger point that soccer has moved a step up in our culture. Like swimming or jogging, though, it remains a participant exercise. The most recent in a long line of failed professional soccer leagues got underway this summer—and it did rather well compared to its predecessors. Its ratings on ESPN rivaled those of ice hockey. But soccer leagues always seem to burst forth, to tease us into thinking that this time America will succumb to the same boring, scoreless game that the rest of the world has always settled for. Then even the soccer players go back to watching the NFL.

What is curious about the American soccer audience, too, is that it is so bifurcated. The second cohort is the one made up of the suburban, upper-middle-class types. The more dominant corps is composed of fairly new immigrants—most of them young Hispanics who have not yet been fully integrated into all of American life and American sport.

Demographically, in fact, the real, most prevalent soccer mom is still, in fact, some poor woman trying to raise a family in a place like Mexico or Jamaica.

Sack

■　　■　　　■

What do you think is the ugliest word in the English language? Well, how about "sack?" At the very least, it must be the ugliest word in the sports lexicon.

Sack. Even worse, it is an AC/DC word—verb and noun alike. He *sacked* the quarterback. That gives him another *sack* for the year. *Sack* is almost synonym-proof.

Why did they have to bring sack into football? *Sack* has always been such an awful word that very few people have done it previously, except possibly for the Visigoths and Attila the Hun. In fact, it is such a dreadful little word that, outside of football, it is rarely even employed anymore. Nobody at the supermarket, for example, ever says: do you want a plastic sack or a paper sack? Receptacles are strictly defined in bag terms.

And understand: *bag* itself isn't any aesthetic delight. But it is certainly superior to *sack.*

Another reason why I am so offended by *sack* is that, historically, other football expressions have always been so unaffected, so downright All-American. *Block* and *tackle* may be tough words, but by God, they are honest words. But *sack*: yucky.

In fact, position titles in football also always got right to the point. The center is in the center and the end is at the end, and if you are a guard, the name may not be fancy, but, indisputably, you know what your job description is. Guards guard. They guard the backs back of them.

Unfortunately, football is succumbing to grandiosity here, too. New positions are getting unnecessarily complicated. I think this started with *nose guard.* "Middle guard" would have been just fine, thank you very much, and in keeping. But because the middle guard lined up on the nose of the ball, somebody had to trick it up. Oh, my, Pop Warner must be jumping offsides in his grave.

But then, everything is going overboard in football lingo now. Nobody anymore simply goes down the field and scores. Rather, they get good field position, and then they put points on the board.

Another major linguistic excess is in the area of passing. It is my understanding that Eskimos have something like a hundred words for "snow." Well, as we throw more passes in football, we are well on our way to tieing this record with names for pass-catchers. Not just ends, but: split ends, tight ends, wide receivers . . . and worst of all: wideouts.

Wideout! You know what that sounds like? It sounds like a position in cricket. Does football know what it is doing to its manly image with these chichi names?

Moreover, passes that are caught are no longer receptions anymore. They are *ree*-cepts, pronounced hard on the first syllable, the way football people like to do it. There is no such thing as defense in football. It is: *dee*-fense.

Now, the latest new word in football refers to emotion. It is "incent." If you want somebody to play harder, you don't give them incentive. Rather, you incent them. As in: "I gotta incent my wideout to get more ree-cepts."

Myself, I would like to sack *incent*.

Yes, Virginia,
There is Sportsmanship

■　　■　　■

On this very day exactly one hundred years ago, at the O'Hanlon residence at 115 West 95th Street in New York City, a little eight-year-old girl sat down to write the most famous letter-to-the-editor in the history of American journalism. A few days later, in the September 21, 1897, edition of *The New York Sun*, an editorial writer named Francis Pharcellus Church replied to the young Miss O'Hanlon thusly:

"Virginia, your little friends are wrong. They have been affected by the skepticism of a skeptical age." And a bit later, that most famous line: "Yes, Virginia, there is a Santa Claus. He exists as certainly as love and generosity and devotion exist . . ."

Perhaps because of this signal anniversary, I received this letter in the mail today:

"Dear Mister Commentator:

"I am eight years old. Some of my friends say there is no sportsmanship left. Papa says: 'If you hear it on National Public Radio, it's so.' Please tell the truth. Is there still really such a thing as sportsmanship?"

And the letter was signed, "Roberta Alomar."

Well, here is how I answered the tyke:

"Roberta, your little friends are wrong. They have been affected by the skepticism of a skeptical age. They do not believe except they see. They only see ballplayers fighting each other and pictures of ballplayers arrested for beating women up, and ballplayers arguing and cheating and, always, they see ballplayers' agents demanding more money, while ballplayers refuse to sign children's autographs for free. But, just because you cannot see sportsmanship does not mean it isn't there.

"Yes, Roberta, there is sportsmanship. It exists as surely as teamwork and the sacrifice bunt and the pick-and-roll exists. How dreary would be the sports world if there were no sportsmanship. Why, it would be as dreary as if there were no Robertas.

"Without sportsmanship, there could be no team spirit and no level playing field and no childlike faith that, even though your hometown heroes are struggling, they might still make the wild card. We must believe in sportsmanship, Roberta, because if we don't believe in fair play, then, at last, we will have no play at all. And then, what would our world be like?

"Not believe in sportsmanship? Why, Roberta, then you might as well not believe in fairies dancing on the lawn or brownies laughing in the cellar. You might as well not believe that Michael Jordan can fly through the air or that Mark McGwire can hit another five-hundred-foot home run or that Martina Hingis is still only sixteen years old.

"You go to a game, and you do not see sportsmanship. You only see beanballs and crackblack blocks and bitten ears and high sticks and cheap elbows, and you assume that sportsmanship cannot possibly survive midst all that. But, Roberta, the most real things in the world are those that neither children nor grown-ups can see.

"No sportsmanship? Thank God it lives on on the field, and for a thousand years from now, Roberta, nay, ten times ten thousand years from now, sportsmanship will still be there to make glad the hearts of those loyal fans everywhere who fill up the luxury boxes and buy one-hundred-dollar souvenir sweatshirts and supply steroids to the players and scream vulgar curses at the opponents and bet the point spread and the over-and-under.

"Yours, Frank Deford.

"P.S. Roberta, I think the more sportswomanship we have, the better, so stay in the game."

Borrowed Time

■   ■   ■

In this modern world, the ancient measures of clock and calendar simply don't work anymore. A large part of this problem is sports. It used to be that even a typically horrid game that the Washington Senators played would be over in two hours, and the various sports seasons corresponded roughly to the seasons of the year. Football was in the fall, basketball in the winter, and so forth. There actually were off-seasons. Remember? But now it takes the Orioles at least an hour longer to do what the Senators did with expeditious defect, and every season tumbles over into every other—just as in life at large everything is on hold, oversold, and out of order.

Since we can't hold back the tide, I suggest we just go along and borrow sports time to measure the new real time of our everyday lives.

For example, since a sports season no longer has any relationship to a season of the year, we definitely need a new term for a sports season, and I suggest *semonster*. Obviously, I've fashioned my new word from the old academic term *semester*. This is especially apt because today's college year, which for some reason now usually concludes around Arbor Day, would itself be more properly known as a semonster.

At the other extreme is the sports minute. When the replay-by-replay announcer advises us that there's a minute left in the game, you know very well that there's anything up to half an hour to go. Similarly, in real life, when somebody says to you, "Got a minute?," you know he really wants a sports minute. Therefore, I'm proposing a new interval of time, which is to be called the *stretch mino*. Now, when the announcer says, "There's a stretch mino left in the half," or a salesman says, "Hey, Cholly, you gotta stretch mino?," you know what to expect.

Some sports, of course, never end. They're like junk mail or traffic. I have in mind, particularly, tennis and horse racing. They constitute a *toursome*. The adjective is *toursomonious*. Presidential campaigns are toursomonious.

On the other hand, golf is tidily arranged in four-day packages. And nothing else in the entire history of the universe has a four-day cycle. There are seven-day weeks, two-day weekends, thirty-day months, and three-day "long" weekends. But, if you think about it, what's the point of adding only one day to the weekend? It would make much more sense to sneak off for four days, and that is what travel agents would recommend if only that portion of time had a name. And now it does: the *golfaway*.

Thanks to incredible research, I have discovered that all sports fights take three minutes and twenty-four seconds. The pattern has been set by hockey. The time to stick somebody, throw gloves down, grab necks, and so forth requires three minutes and twenty-four seconds before the foolish children are finally ensconced in the penalty box. Hockey announcers, chuckling, invariably call this a "fracas."

But, all other such farcical episodes in life—arguing with children about food; discussing Michael Jackson or Elizabeth Taylor's faces; remembering your wife's social security number for the benefit of a medical secretary—have taken the cue from hockey fracases and last exactly three minutes and twenty-four seconds. Thus we have this ghastly but indisputable segment of time that I call the *farcas*.

When you arrive late and say, "I'm sorry, but I had a farcas at the self-service filling station," everyone will understand perfectly.

Half-times at football and basketball games are, for some reason, just the wrong length. If you want to get up, there isn't enough time to get something to eat and drink and go to the bathroom, both. But if you stay in your seat, half-time is an absolute toursome. How many times have your heard someone say: "You mean the other band is going to play, too?"

So, in honor of half-times, we will call any period that is either too long or too short, but just not right, a *half-blind*. You would say, for example, "We got half-blinded when we had to change planes in Memphis." Or: "We wanted a good meal, but he only had a half-blind, so we had to grab a burger and fries."

More and more, I fear, all our days are full of half-blinds. The world—sports and otherwise—is becoming counter-clockdumb. But never mind, I don't want to bother you another stretch mino.

Momentum Has Momentum

■   ■   ■

I know I'm just getting started in this commentary, but please give me a chance to build up a little momentum. This goes for you, too, in your daily lives—especially for those of you who don't usually watch football games, but will be watching the Super Bowl this Sunday.

You've got to have momentum.

Momentum is the most important thing in football, even if I'm not quite sure what exactly it is. It's been around for a long time, too. It even used to be called "Big Mo." But now, momentum is too important to be treated with such familiarity. As football announcers tell us, if a team has momentum, that is good. If it doesn't, a team must get momentum.

As nearly as I can tell, momentum is like oxygen or advertising or bad taste. It's always there. I know that because momentum *shifts*. The announcers tell me this, with great gravity. "Well, it looks like the momentum has shifted." First one team has it, then the other. Nobody ever says: What's completely missing today is momentum. Or: What this game needs is a heavy dose of momentum.

No, the first law of football momentum is that there is always momentum, and if you don't have it, you need to get it. Pronto.

Well, sometimes in a game there are a few seconds when announcers are confused, like when an obscure infraction occurs and the officials have to check the rule book.

This is what the announcers say then: It looks like they've lost their momentum.

It's always spoken that way, too: forlornly, with a great deal of distress, in the same manner as when Peter Pan lost his shadow or Eeyore his tail. But, happily, you do get the idea then that the momentum has not really been lost. It has not disappeared. It has merely been misplaced.

I always try to maintain my composure during these instances, because I know that either: a) momentum will be regained, or b) momentum will shift. It always does. If it's football, there must be momentum. Somewhere.

Rarely, in fact, do we have momentum in other games. Certainly not in baseball. I don't think in hockey. In basketball, occasionally there is momentum, but most times, instead of momentum, a team is "on a run."

What do you think, have I built up any momentum yet in this commentary?

Actually, the one place outside of football where we are told that there is a lot of momentum is during the primary election campaign. A candidate will win a couple primaries, and the pundits will then say that the other candidates have "to stop his momentum."

This is where football and politics are different, momentum-wise. In football, the announcers never suggest that the team that has momentum can have it wrested away. No, momentum belongs to you. It's sort of like your soul. It's up to you whether you will keep it or not. Yes, you may lose your momentum, but you cannot have it taken from you.

The thing about momentum in football is that it is all embracing. I used to think that momentum was, well, in layman's terms, sort of the opposite of inertia. But now, momentum has been expanded to the point where it represents good. If you are playing well, you have momentum. If you are not playing well, you don't have momentum. You have to find some momentum. It's become a very elastic word.

And now, while this commentary has run out of momentum, I hope you can build some of your own momentum to carry you through that interminable Super Bowl Sunday.

There Goes Summer

■   ■   ■

Whenever I think of what summers mean I think first of a time, dead in the middle of winter in Toronto, when I was sitting in a nightclub with Al McGuire. The dance band was playing, but very few people were dancing. Suddenly, the band struck up a familiar old favorite. Memory fails me, but I believe it was either "Unchained Melody" or "Cherry Pink and Apple Blossom White." Anyway, Al turned to me right away and said: "That'll fill up the floor."

"Why?" asked I.

"Summer song," said Al. "More memories with summer songs."

And sure enough, the couples flooded onto the dance floor.

Summers are existentialist. I think that's the word. It's not at all what you *did* on your summer vacation. That was only paying lip service to your teachers when you got back to school. Rather, it's the things you *remember* about summers.

And what makes me mad is that they're taking our summers away from us.

Sports is. Football is primarily to blame. Football is a fall game, and it is also a very serious game (which is why it belongs in the fall, when people get serious). But now they are playing college games in August, and they have a whole new foolish professional league playing games in July, and there goes most of the summer. No wonder students are going back to school too soon. Schools didn't use to start till after Labor Day. Now, schools see people playing serious football in August, so they get confused and they start chaining kids to their desks in August. And there goes summer vacations for the whole family. Shot.

All along, we thought the grinch was out to steal Christmas. But, in fact, it was summer that he was really after.

Pretty soon, we won't even have time to play Wiffle ball anymore. Wiffle ball is the ultimate silly summer game. You can't take it seriously. In fact, the only serious thing I do in the summer is work on my tan. I know, I know. We're not supposed to do that anymore. It's bad for you—tanning. Unfortunately, I never knew anyone who didn't look better with a suntan. It just does wonders. I always tell my black friends that once they understand how important suntans are to white people, they are about halfway there to figuring us out. The easiest way to hurt a person, if they've worked on a serious tan, is not to compliment them.

But now serious football is here in the summer and we don't have time for serious tans, and then the summer is gone all too soon. It worries me. Hockey and basketball are sneaking up on summer at the other end, their seasons lasting deeper and deeper into the calendar. And so if spring and fall sports keep on annexing summer, we're going to pay. To be healthy, we need summer tans and summer memories and summer songs, summer romances, summer games, and summer nights to buffer us from reality. Render unto autumn what is autumn.

Barkley's Last Shot

"It's amazing," Charles Barkley observes, reflecting upon the state of his head. He makes observations all the time, about all manner of things, alternately inducing stupefaction and fatigue from those within earshot. *The Arizona Republic* has even assigned a reporter to shadow Barkley on Phoenix Sun game days, solely for the purpose of recording his sundry and eclectic pronouncements in a column entitled "The Barkley Beat." Surely, in all of human history, this must be a first: having space set aside, regularly, reserved for one man's bons mots, as yet unsaid.

"Yes, it is, very amazing," Barkley goes on. Although *The Arizona Republic* Barkley-observation beat reporter is not on the case at this moment, Barkley is opining about how utterly fascinating it is that while white men with shaved heads invariably look pretty damned awful, black men can grow even more handsome *sans* hair. "If I didn't shave my head I'd have a helicopter look," he reveals, "and I don't like that." I take a helicopter look to mean what was called a monk's pate in less technological times. Barkley grasps his skull tenderly, as Hamlet to Yorick, with the affection born of familiarity.

Not withstanding his noble crown, it is Barkley's body that is truly extraordinary. Charles Barkley's body defies explanation, much as engineers concluded that a bumblebee is aerodynamically impossible. The National Basketball Association persists in listing him at six feet six inches, while he himself acknowledges being no more than six feet four and three-quarters—and with a weight that is a cost overrun somewhere upwards of 250. And yet, playing forward, lost in the timberland of seven-foot behemoths, he's the one who manages to grab the ball, to score. It is mystical, nearly.

Even in Barkley's first year at Auburn University, when the rival team's fans hooted and hurled pizza boxes at the chubby freshman, when he was saddled with such dreadful sobriquets as the Crisco Kid,

Boy Gorge, and Food World, he somehow divined his blessing. "I *knew* then," he says. "I knew I could average 10 rebounds a game for the next 10 years. Wherever I played. I knew." For somehow, in the athletic vernacular, Charles Barkley "explodes." With other great basketball players, you marvel, *Look at him do that!* With Barkley, you wonder, *How does he do that?* At last, struggling, he himself is left to suggest the answer: "God is in my body."

Yet for all Barkley's personal preeminence—he was voted the league's most valuable player in 1992–93, when Michael Jordan was still gracing basketball—he has never led his team to a championship. Not in high school, not in college, not in the NBA. "It's not fair," says Kevin Johnson, a sage young teammate. "No one in the world is more generous than Charles, and he'll always be a great player. But if *we* don't win, *he'll* never be complete."

Of course basketball is a team game. Of course. Of course no single player—especially one so irregularly sized—can will victory for a whole team. But that is rational. That is intellectual. The rare great players whose teams do not once triumph are cruelly cursed, forever to be remembered as what the British call A Nearly Man.

The 1993–94 season was the one meant to be Phoenix's—to be Barkley's—at last. Instead, it was a desultory year for all as Barkley floundered, with injuries to both his back and knees. Despairing, he decided to quit basketball and move on to his next incarnation, which he fancies to be governor of his native Alabama—the first African-American Republican governor in history. But then, this summer, going on 32, he underwent rehabilitation for his back and decided to return for one more season, the one to remember him by.

Barkley needs a victory season all the more because he has no fond memory of a single, perfect game to embrace over time. For all the rebounds and baskets, the only game that remains in his mind, all but obsessing him, is the one a few years ago when Charles Barkley . . . spit.

The usual celebrity façade is the one by which famous people who are absolute sons of bitches in real life artfully maintain a positive image. Barkley is the reverse, the teddy bear who seeks to portray himself as a meanie. "He thinks that gives him an edge," his wife, Maureen, explains. "He thinks it intimidates people." She pauses. "I mean, off the court, too." Barkley hasn't the disposition to stay rude one-on-one, so he must be outrageous publicly. Besides, it's a profitable persona; in modern sport, ogres sell better than do all-American boys.

So, in his Nike commercials, Barkley is paired against Godzilla, monster to monster; he kills a referee in *opéra bouffe*; more shameful yet, he growls thusly at the children of America: "I am not a role model. I am not paid to be a role model. I am paid to wreak havoc on a basketball court. Parents should be role models. Just because I can dunk a basketball doesn't mean I should raise your kids." So, when he was the host on *Saturday Night Live*, his opening monologue consisted of taking on Barney, the hyperlovable purple dinosaur, and mauling him (for which Maureen was all but assaulted by a mother and child at the local Toys 'R' Us a few days later). So, when someone sincere in Phoenix asked Barkley what he would be doing if he didn't play basketball, he declared that he would be in "video porn." So, he calls himself a "90s nigger," infuriating whites, and praises the vision of Dan Quayle, infuriating blacks. So, when he and Maureen were separated, he enjoyed a well-publicized fling with Madonna, infuriating all God-fearing men and women of good taste. And so on and so forth.

Only occasionally does the show boil over for real. In Chicago, there was a saloon fracas. In Milwaukee, he clocked a guy who trailed him. In the first game of the Barcelona Olympics, with the whole world watching the fabled Dream Team, he gratuitously clobbered a poor, gaunt Angolan player, then compounded the assault by protesting, unrepentant: "How was I to know he wasn't carrying a spear?"

I remember chatting with Charles a couple days later, outside his hotel, and timidly venturing that he might lighten up under the glare of humankind. He snarled, "Hey, Frank, they don't like us and we don't like them." *Off the court, too.*

And then, one night in New Jersey, he spit. Purposely. On a fan. No matter what else, that is the moment that counts. "Don't be fooled," Maureen says. "That was a major, major, *major* occurrence in Charles's life. It just eats him alive. Still." That, you see, appears to be the single episode that makes Charles Barkley wonder who he really is. That is his question.

Everything else is his answers.

The private Barkley can be completely unaffected. Like our true-blue heroes are supposed to, he really does visit sick children—and without alerting the Eyewitness News mobile unit or "The Barkley Beat." He suffers fans. Even the press. "People won't believe me," says Howard White, who manages Nike's pro-basketball relations, "when I tell them Charles is one of the best people I've ever known in my life." Barkley is like one of those travel stories—with headlines such as THE NEWARK NOBODY KNOWS or SURPRISING PARAGUAY!—that no one really accepts.

The citizens of Arizona were in awe (and some fear) of Barkley's arrival in 1992, after he was traded from the Philadelphia 76ers to the Suns. But then they were shocked to discover that he just shows up places, like normal people do. The time in Barcelona when he snapped to me so bitterly about foreigners was followed soon enough by one of his famous promenades down Las Ramblas, where he kibitzed and hoisted beers with captivated fans and natives. Meanwhile, his Dream Team colleagues remained holed up in their $900-a-night rooms at their fortress hotel.

Barkley is even a dyed-in-the-wool sports fan. That may not sound surprising, but most hotshot stars really aren't into the games they don't play. Barkley knows statistics and all that stuff. "I just love sports," he gushes. "I love watching greatness." He listens to talk radio, and will call in, just like any Vinny or Bubba. On one occasion, when he heard a lady from Jersey complaining on the air about No. 34, he rang up the station, got in touch with his critic, and sent a limo, with champagne and flowers, to fetch her to his next game.

Barkley makes sense only if you appreciate that none of what has happened to him is logical. Were it not for the freak spontaneous combustion that no one has ever before found hidden in such a body, Charles Barkley would be a very fat and uneducated fellow with a helicopter top down in Leeds, Alabama, punching a time clock and offering unrestrained opinions that none of the other guys on the loading dock would pay any attention to.

Most sports superstars are so naturally brilliant that they are identified by the time they're 13 or 14. Quickly, they become spoiled little princes. But as late as his junior year in high school, Wade Barkley—they still call him by his middle name down home—was an undistinguished, overweight five-foot-ten-inch substitute on an unremarkable team. Incredibly, in barely six years, the pudgy duckling would go from being the sixth- or seventh-best player at a small-town high school to being one of the six or seven best players in the world.

This is why the guffaws that have greeted Barkley's solemn pronouncement that he plans to run for governor of Alabama as early as

'98 should be somewhat restrained; he has pulled off this kiss-a-frog stuff once before. Says the future candidate in his best Horatio-Alger-Meets-the-Comeback-Kid style: "I think if you're good from the beginning it stunts your growth, your drive. Out of everything I've accomplished—everything—I still think the most important thing ever was proving everybody wrong about me. God gave me a special gift, but *I* have taken it a long way." Indeed, Barkley possesses such supreme confidence that by now he has faith that he can mandate victory in any basketball game. "If I'm healthy and if I can get a little he'p"—residual traces of his southern accent pop up occasionally—"I can make the play so we can win. Yes, I believe that."

Really and truly?

"I believe that so much that if we don't win when it gets to that point, I'm in shock."

Of course, as with any politician, we must be wary of Barkley's claims. He is the man, after all, who published an autobiography entitled *Outrageous*, and then, to prove the point, charged he had been misquoted in his own book. But someone most familiar with the high-flown Barkleyan rhetoric—Jerry Colangelo, the Suns' president—offers this formula: "Ninety-nine percent of the time Charles knows exactly what he's saying. Only one percent is he off the wall."

Whether the dream of sleeping in George Wallace's old bed is a quixotic part of that goofy one percent Charles or the adult version of I'll-show-the-world, Governor Barkley is still a work in progress. His platform consists of little more than ending welfare, then passing those savings along to the public schools. Despite having himself been an indifferent, even evasive student, Barkley is passionate on the subject of education. "Maybe you have to come from my background to understand how insecure a kid is if he doesn't have an education," he says, going off on something of an embryonic stump speech. "But, no, all we do is tell 'em on TV, y'all must have a big house and a nice car and fancy clothes, and then we're surprised when they go out and try to get 'em. The first thing we've got to do in this country is find a different message to send to our kids."

Then he snorts at a favorite provision of the Congressional Black Caucus in the crime bill. "Thirty million into midnight basketball—that's a Band-Aid on a bullet wound. The real criminals aren't gonna be playin' any basketball come midnight. Why don't they take that $30 million and put it into scholarships?"

Barkley can be a master of flamboyance, but as a novice candidate, if only because he is still feeling his way, he is more studied and earnest, more . . political. "I guarantee you there won't be a boy or girl who wouldn't take a scholarship if they gave it to him. I give out three scholarships myself, and they're all academic. Not athletic. I'm just so sick of athletics and blacks." His voice rises. He's growing more animated, on more familiar ground. "All you ever hear is we run for 1,000 yards and we dunk. You make 20 points, you get 10 rebounds, they'll find you. Oh, they'll come and find you. But you make straight A's in the same school, they don't even know you're there. And that's sad. That's very sad about this country."

But if his politics are mostly only emotional so far, and his deportment tends to the radical, he certainly is a Republican, culturally and fiscally conservative. For example, his controversial I'm-no-role-model Nike commercial—which he proposed himself—brought down a firestorm of criticism that he was selfish and irresponsible. His prime nemesis in Philadelphia, Stan Hochman of the *Daily News*, labeled it "despicable." Barkley, though, remains proud and faithful to the message, which he sees as pro-family. His point is that athletes are not surrogates, just celebrities; parents themselves must assume responsibility.

The chairman of the Republican National Committee, Haley Barbour, professes to be intrigued by a Barkley candidacy. He cites new congressman Sonny Bono and former congressman Fred Grandy, late of *The Love Boat*, as Republicans who were taken seriously by the voters despite their having matriculated in politics from a weightless professional past. "I mean, Grandy played a stooge, really," Barbour says. And, of course, how can the party forget that a somewhat more serious actor became president, while a former football player may well be the next G.O.P. standard-bearer.

Barkley's color is likewise appealing for Republican cross-casting. Says Armstrong Williams, the black conservative writer and radio host of *The Right Side*, "We have to start somewhere convincing African-Americans to get off the Democratic plantation, and how better to do it than with someone like Charles with a high profile?"

Besides, Barkley is every bit a Republican, well, fat cat. Barkley's mother in 1988: "But, Charles, Bush will only work for the rich people." Barkley: "But, Mom, I *am* rich." He earns $8-million-plus in salary and endorsements, resides in some of the best suburbs in America, possesses all the finest accoutrements, including a Japanese Lexus and an American Ford Bronco, and plays golf with other squires at the nation's most exclusive country clubs.

Apart from alighting from a golf cart to take about 85 to 90 swings a round, Barkley faithfully subscribes to that dictum of another maverick capitalist, the late Henry Ford, who declared, "Exercise is bunk. If you are healthy you don't need it, if you are sick you shouldn't take it." Most players dutifully work out in the off-season, but, in basketball parlance, Barkley is an old 31, his back buckled from the years of fat and lazy summers, then of lugging his avoirdupois at warp speed across the hardwood.

In the late 1980s, as his 76er team began to erode around him, Barkley took a lot of heat from the famously vituperative Philadelphia sports press. "Philadelphia is not a good place to lose," he intones, more didactically than mournfully. By 1991, Barkley was so frustrated in the City of Brotherly Love that he openly petitioned other teams to trade for him. He took to brooding at home. His marriage grew brittle, then shattered. In Leeds, his younger brother Darryl had had drug-related problems with the law, and Barkley felt his fame had belittled and tormented his brother.

Everywhere, too, he began to hear the whispers that he would never quite succeed. He couldn't win in high school, he couldn't win in college, and . . . "Somewhere along the way I got lost," he says now upon reflection. "I let people convince me that I'm nothing if I don't win a championship. If I believe that, I'm stupid. But"—a sigh—"I believed it."

His back began to bother him more. He railed publicly against his teammates. In one silly wrangle, he even got himself in trouble with the league for joking about betting on his own games. It was getting harder and harder to be Charles Barkley. And finally, one night on the road, playing against the woeful New Jersey Nets, it happened. The 76ers struggled; the cries against No. 34 rained down. When the Nets tied the score, Barkley turned to the crowd. He spit. Purposely. He spit on a fan. A little eight-year-old girl.

Although Barkley is sometimes unfairly tagged with an uncomplimentary epithet relating to the area of the central derrière, it is altogether accurate to describe him as anal. This prissy fellow even makes up his bed in *hotels*, and wherever he lives—Phoenix in season, Philadelphia in summer, Alabama on visits—"I just walk around the house looking for dirty stuff." Maureen reports that after a game, at three or four in the morning, she has heard Charles vacuuming downstairs, or awoken to see him zealously Windexing the mirrors that line the long hallway from their bedroom.

This house, which was Charles's bachelor abode, lies just outside Philadelphia, on the Main Line, surrounded by Tudor and fieldstone mansions and tony schools and seminaries. The two commercial establishments closest to the Barkleys are Lord and Taylor and Saks. But just beyond them is the typical franchise effluvia: a 7-Eleven, a Midas, a Holiday Inn, and the Friday's where the famous basketball player first spied the gorgeous blonde. Charles and Maureen were wed in 1989, and their daughter, Christiana, was born later that year.

Within the sports world, checkerboard romances and marriages are casually accepted for what they largely are: the natural result of geography and economic class. Black athletes move to upscale white neighborhoods wherein reside white women. Of course, abroad in the land, the Barkleys attract more notice as an interracial couple, even a call from some ugly Klansman on a recent visit back to Alabama. And not long after Charles spit on the little white girl, a man came up to Maureen, called her "nigger lover," and spit in her face.

Both the Barkleys say, though, that the O. J. Simpson case has failed to produce more unwarranted attention. "The only people who ever seem to be upset," Maureen says, "are black women and white men. I tell the men: Look, if I hadn't married Charles I certainly *never* would have married you anyway, so, really, don't worry about it."

Barkley does cry race occasionally when he's railing about some injustice, and, in a different vein, he enjoys teasing his deficient Caucasian co-stars, rivals and teammates, for suffering from the dreaded "white man's disease." But, he declares, "really, I transcend color. I'm not pro-black. In fact, I think it's even worse for black people to be racist."

In his office hangout across the hall from the kitchen, Charles clicks over from CNN to *Oprah*. He perks up: the theme of today's show is things you want your spouse to learn. One of the guests would like her husband to learn to dance. Exactly what Charles wants of his wife! "Mo, Mo, quick, come in here," he hollers. The couple on *Oprah* starts to dance. But it's not at all what Charles expected. In fact, it is . . . a *fox-trot*. Maureen arrives. "I don't believe this," Charles says, as if he had stumbled on some strange tribal rite on the Discovery Channel.

"But, Charles, *this* is how white people dance," Maureen explains. He shakes his head in wonder. Evidently, his transcendence of race is not quite complete.

Maureen returns to the kitchen, to peel potatoes. This is not unusual. Charles thinks of potatoes as a genuine vegetable, e.g., "The only vegetables I eat are creamed corn and potatoes." Maybe that is why his body is different from everybody else's in the human race, *because he does not eat green vegetables*. Wouldn't that be a kick? All over America mothers would say, "Eat your creamed corn and potatoes so you can grow up as big and strong and fast as Charles Barkley."

Maureen peels some more faux vegetables. Different as she and her husband may be—the poor little black boy from Leeds, Alabama, who was deserted by his father, to be raised by his mother and grandmother, and the prosperous white girl from a big, happy, traditional Catholic family in Bucks County, Pennsylvania—they share one common fundamental. Just as everybody put him down for being fat, everybody kidded her for being a hopelessly skinny twig with big, funny feet. But then he grew up to be Charles Barkley, and she grew up to be a beautiful, willowy woman who dared marry a famous black man named Charles Barkley.

"Whatever problems we've had, color was never an issue," Maureen says. "I promise you that. Never."

He takes all the blame for the separation, I tell her.

"Oh. What does he say?"

I look at my notes and read them to her. "I like to be alone, and the only place I can be alone is at home. They won't *let* me be alone anywhere else. And that alienated Maureen." I look up; she nods. "Because I needed to have peace and quiet at home. She was there, but I needed to be by myself. And then we weren't winning, and I started to rebel at her. I take all the blame."

She smiles softly. "That's very nice of Charles to take the responsibility for our troubles, but I'm sure I nagged him some. He does have mood swings, and I didn't know how to deal with that then. But I understand him wanting to be by himself. I do. *I* value being by myself."

They've been back together for more than a year now and want to have another child, but Maureen thinks they should wait till this last season—the quest—is over. "It's just so different being a celebrity," she says. "You can't even imagine till you live with one." It's probably hardest of all being a famous athlete. Most of the entertainment peo-ple cluster together in L.A. and New York. A Philadelphia or a Phoenix, a Dallas, an Atlanta—big as they are, when it comes to famous people, all they have is their home-team sports stars. *Theirs.* "People expect so much of you," Maureen goes on. "It's amazing to me that Charles copes so beautifully."

Except for that one night, anyway. At the New Jersey Meadowlands in '91. And the heckler was screaming, down by the court, shouting the foulest vulgarities right into Barkley's face. And the Nets' free throw went in, and the man screamed again at him. And Barkley broke. He turned and lunged at the man, spitting at him. Then, satis-fied, he raced downcourt. He didn't know that he'd missed the heck-ler, and, instead, his spittle had flown into the face of a little girl named Lauren Rose.

As soon as he found out what had happened, Barkley called Lauren, apologizing. Without telling anyone, he bought season tickets for the Roses, and he escorted Lauren and her family to a fancy charity dinner. But that was all for Lauren. What about Barkley?

"I look back and I think, Well, the worst case would be if I spit and hit a little girl," he says. "So, I was unlucky. All right? And the best case—the *very* best case—is I spit and hit the asshole screaming at me. But you see—no."

No?

"No, there is no best case, because what does that say about me, that I let a basketball game—a game!—get to me so much that I want to spit on another human being? It was my fault. It was me. It was *all* me." He pauses, then sighs. "After that I started to become a better person."

It's lunchtime at the Barkleys'. Charles has already been to the gym for his daily rehab. He's only 10 pounds over his target weight, and, dutifully, he restricts himself to a dry turkey sandwich with Evian.

He clicks on the TV in his office. His favorite soap, *All My Children*, is over, but the U.S. Open tennis is on. "Hey, Pete Sampras," Barkley calls out with utter delight. Sampras is far and away the best player in the world, at the height of his powers. "Look at him!" Barkley coos. And: "Whatta serve!" And: "Amazing!"

But Sampras is performing with none of the enthusiasm that Barkley displays watching him. His only manifest reaction to even his most spectacular shots is to drop his head over his racket and study the strings. "What is the matter with him?" Barkley finally inquires. Sampras hits a glorious winner, only to return, head bowed, to the baseline. "What is the matter with someone like that?" Barkley asks again, only louder now. "He should be the happiest person in the world. But look at him. Sampras!" He fairly wails at the television screen. "Sampras!"

Sampras remains deeply involved with his stupid strings. "He's No. 1, the best there is," Barkley goes on. "In the world. Isn't that amazing?"

I remind Barkley that he's the best in the world at what he does.

"It's just such a great feeling to be able to entertain people," he says. "You get to bring such joy. But look at him." Sampras mopes about, unwilling to acknowledge his gift to the crowd.

Barkley shakes his head. "Why?" he asks. "No. 1. It's the greatest time of your life. You get to do what you want. The people come to see *you.* Now, when you're through playing, nobody will care then. Nobody will pay to see you. Nobody. Not anymore. You can sleep as late as you want then. Nobody cares." He leans forward in his big leather chair.

"I never forget," he announces. "The best way to keep people away from you is not to be good at anything. There's so many people who could be good, could be great, if they tried. Derrick Coleman [of the New Jersey Nets] should be the best player in the world. Some people are scared to risk it, though. Me, I say, If you're scared, buy a dog."

He flicks the remote control, relentlessly moving onward. He is just plain fed up with Pete Sampras. Soon, Barkley will be departing for Phoenix, for the season of his posterity, his last chance at completeness as a player. He is putting the best face on it, of course, but I believe him when he swears he is secure enough to suffer another year without a championship. "All I ever wanted was ten good years," he says. "I accomplished everything I set out to do in basketball. Be a good player, do the best I possibly could, and make a good living so I could take care of my mother and grandmother."

Downstairs, the garage door opens. Barkley's daughter, Christiana, is back. She has been a bad girl all day, and she knows it, but her mother lets her enjoy a brief amnesty. She runs to her father.

Christiana is precocious and pretty in pigtails, her shade (as you would expect) exactly midway between the pale cream of her mother and the cool beurre noir of her father. He rocks her back and forth in his arms.

For an instant, I can see the same scene taking place next June in a locker room as Phoenix celebrates its championship. Or maybe I can even visualize this tableau a few years from now, on Election Night in Montgomery, Alabama.

Or none of the above.

After all, it is enough that right now Christiana Barkley is in the arms of her role model.

Driven Crazy by Baseball Caps

■ ■ ■

O ften when I ponder the great issues of our time, I cannot help but pause to wonder: When did absolutely everyone in the world start wearing baseball caps? And the companion great question: Why?

Do you think baseball caps are attractive or stylish? I don't. Before they became de rigueur in global fashion, baseball caps had only two first cousins: There were grotesque fishing caps, with exceptionally long visors, made of a dark green acetate material. And there were caps that guys driving tractors wore, which said, simply, JOHN DEERE.

Otherwise, outside of baseball, nobody wore baseball caps. Why would you? Outside of football, who would wear football helmets?

Instead, men wore fedoras, most of which were made in the Hat City, which was Danbury, Conn. If you look at old pictures of people watching baseball games, virtually all of the people were men, all of whom were wearing fedoras from the Hat City. In the late 19th century and first half of the 20th century, if a spectator wore a baseball cap to a baseball game, he would have appeared very affected—like a guy going to the ballet in tights.

Another kind of cap that men wore was of the floppy, flat style. I don't know what it is called. Growing up, we called them "bunny" hats, but I suspect that wasn't their official name. Off the field, Babe Ruth often wore this style of cap. Nobody wears them now except Payne Stewart, the golfer, as part of his hideous throwback outfits.

Other golfers wear, of course, baseball caps. Likewise, if a tennis player wears a cap on court, it's a baseball cap.

Another compelling thing about baseball caps is how many people in other sports put on baseball caps as soon as they stop playing their own games. Quarterbacks, for example. Immediately after they come off the field, they take off their helmets and put on baseball caps. So do race car drivers.

In almost all sports, whenever a team wins a championship, the first thing the players do is don special commemorative championship baseball caps. Often the players put these on before they take the manufacturer's tags off. The Chicago Bulls used to look like a whole squadron of Minnie Pearls. Also, teams in all sports sell baseball caps as souvenirs. This is terribly confusing. Why can't other sports sell souvenir bonnets that aren't baseball caps? Why not hockey berets? Or football derbies? Or basketball cowboy hats? Or soccer bunny hats?

Now women athletes have joined the baseball-cap bandwagon. This has not only made the baseball cap an androgynous item, like sneakers, but also has increased the baseball-cap market by 100%. It has also, in my opinion, brought women down to the level of men—another excellent example of the price we must pay for equality

As near as I can tell, all over the world, "baseball caps" are much better known than baseball itself. In England, which doesn't know baseball from Roller Derby, the head of the Conservative shadow government, William Hague, is derisively referred to by some Laborites as "the nerd in a baseball cap." I suggest to Bud Selig that wherever he goes, he should introduce himself as "commissioner of the sport that gave us baseball caps."

Yes, for whatever reason, baseball caps have become one more American contribution to the world culture—blue jeans for the head, McDonald's for the hair. I don't understand why. Baseball caps are not comfortable; they are certainly not flattering; they are not millinery, not chapeaus. Moreover, the visor shadows the face and makes it difficult to see the person wearing it. It's hard, for example, to French kiss wearing a baseball cap.

Maybe it's just that a baseball cap makes a good billboard. As team insignia have always gone on caps, so can messages and logos be flaunted there: ASK ME ABOUT MY GRANDCHILDREN. Maybe, in this modern time, we wear baseball caps because we don't have enough confidence in our own faces and have to dress them up with brand names or show off resort identification or familiar slogans. Baseball caps have, sadly, turned our heads into bumper stickers.

Next week: Fashion authorities and psychologists discuss why so many people now wear baseball caps backward.

The Grand Old Man

■   ■   ■

In reflection, it is fascinating to recall how Carl Lewis was treated in these Olympics—and what larger conclusions we can draw about how we perceive our heroes over the life of their careers.

With Lewis, then, first we must return to 1984, when he burst upon our consciousness at the Los Angeles Games. He would be the next Jesse Owens. But handsome young Carl was too brash for most tastes, and after one unfortunate press conference when his manager—not Lewis, but his manager—compared him to Michael Jackson, the consensus was instantly established that he was too greedy and egomaniacal. That reputation would hold for years.

Insofar as athletic image is concerned, first impressions are crucial. Moreover, this is especially true in individual sports. In team sports, the athlete can at least count on his hometown fans to come to his defense. Good grief, even Albert Belle has some Cleveland fans to protest that he's really just a misunderstood lad. But in golf or boxing or skiing or tennis or track, the star who gets off on the wrong foot is out there all on his own.

In fact, the brilliant young athlete, like Lewis, who is so instantly marvelous, so natural, so secure in his talent, has little chance to be accepted until he starts to age and show some vulnerability. Jack Nicklaus was the classic case. No one could be better behaved. In fact, he was bland and rosy-cheeked . . . still, he was not at first admired. We punished him for being too good too soon.

Like Nicklaus, Lewis's reputation only began to improve as he suffered challenge and defeat. By 1992, in Barcelona, when he outjumped the record-holder and then electrified the stadium when inserted as the anchor on the relay, his critics decided that he had become a different creature. He appeared then, as they desired, more humble, more forgiving, more human. We adore our athletes when they become The Grand Old Man of their sport. Even Jimmy Connors, still as brash and puerile as ever, was beatified once he moved up into his thirties.

And Lewis? By this Olympics he was thirty-five years old, certified *too* old, and thus an altogether sympathetic figure, symbolic of us all fighting to turn back the tide of years. When he won the long jump in bold and dramatic fashion, Carl Lewis was Our Hero. In fact, over and over again in Atlanta we heard the conventional wisdom about how Lewis was so much more charming and lovable than the unconquerable Michael Johnson.

But unfortunately for Lewis, everywhere he went, after he was congratulated and adored, the interviewer would say: And Carl, would you like to be selected to run in the relay and win a tenth gold medal?

And Carl didn't know the script. He just told the truth and said, yeah, that would be nice. He didn't know that he was supposed to play humble and dissemble, to protest that such a normal thought had never once entered his mind.

So suddenly, Carl Lewis was revealed to be, yes, greedy and egomaniacal. He wanted to *bump* some lesser runner in his selfish quest to rack up another gold.

You see, we had decreed that it was all right for the old man to fight for one more final triumph, but when Lewis wouldn't settle for what we had doled out to his legend, then we turned on him again and put him back in his place.

The moral is: Be respectful as a young athlete, be modest in your prime, be more visibly competitive as you decline, and then be very, very grateful when you are The Grand Old Man. This is the only pattern that the sports ideologues will accept. Cross them at your peril.

Noo Yawk

■　　　■　　　■

Back in the good old days, when men were men and women were broads, when Madison Square Garden was the only arena in the country that mattered, when the Yankees were the only team that mattered, when anybody who was anybody smoked cigars and drank their whiskey neat at Toots Shor's joint, all athletes prayed to play in Noo Yawk.

Mr. and Mrs. America and all the ships at sea, let's go to press: New York athletes had all the advantages—fame, endorsements, contacts, the works.

Oh my, how that has changed. The last athlete who really lusted to play in Gotham was Reggie Jackson, back in the '70s. By now, in many instances, the players who deign to agree to come to the Big Apple must generally be bribed—overpaid—to suffer New York, and it is not uncommon for players to use New York team offers as bluffs to drive up the salaries they can get in other normal American cities.

Bill Madden of the New York *Daily News* pointed out the other day that a prime reason why the Mets have been so disappointing is because the very heart of their order—Coleman, Murray, and Bonilla— is formed of players who would have gone anywhere but New York if only they had had better offers.

The trouble is, New York is too gritty, the press too critical, for spoiled American athletes who have been fawned over all their lives. Most pros today expect the big bucks without having to endure any pressure, and while it is true that yes, as the song has it, "If you can make it there, you can make it anywhere," you don't have to make it there in sport. It ain't Broadway, where everything else is Bridgeport. So the players conclude: Why should I risk criticism and indignity in New York when I can get as much unexamined praise in the sweet, soft hick cities of the south and west?

It is no coincidence that when the Mets were a winner a few years ago, the club was formed of hard-nosed rascals and sophisticates—the vulgar Dykstra, the suave Hernandez, the Yalie charmer, Darling—but then management cleaned house, replacing their street-smart winners with whining losers, who spend all their time complaining about the tabloid press and unsympathetic call-in sports radio bores.

Contrariwise, the Knicks have come to the fore only after management hired a slick, big-city coach, Pat Riley, who brought scufflers to the team—nobodies like John Starks and Anthony Mason, who are the equivalents of the grateful starlet plucked from the chorus line. They win.

Moreover, most New York players today are more transient, seldom as much a part of the community as they are in other, smaller cities. Rarely do any of them venture into Manhattan, except to make their required visits to the arena or stadium. Restaurants? Shows? Concerts? Museums? Hey, how far to the mall? It was, in fact, big news over the winter when Jim Abbott, the pitcher traded to the Yankees from Orange County, got over his depression at that news and actually declared that he and the missus might consider living in Manhattan. Mark Messier of the Rangers might have been the only other current New York player living in the city.

To most players in all sports, New York is alien, its fans and media too exacting. Better to play in less demanding precincts. The fact remains, though, that if a young star can face up to New York, its difficulties and denizens, then it's easier to cope when the game starts and you're only confronting opponents in uniforms that say Charlotte or Cincinnati or Podunk.

Choosing Sides

■   ■   ■

I t would seem to be—as the King of Siam said—a puzzlement that most citizens side with the owners, rather than the players, in the baseball dispute. And nobody much likes the owners, either. Doesn't seem right, does it? Still, when John Q. Public is polled, he sides with the fat old stingy rich men rather than the lean young spoiled rich men.

This is nothing new. Even going back more than thirty years ago, when two of the most attractive, loyal, and ethical guys you would ever want to cheer for—Sandy Koufax and Don Drysdale—banded together to break the one-hundred-thousand-dollar glass ceiling, the public favored the sneaky, snarly Dodgers owner, Walter O'Malley. This was like rooting for Mr. Bumble over Oliver Twist. *Please, sir: more!* But so did the fans choose.

It may be hard to fathom, but I think a large part of this attitude is formed by the fact that a lot of folks simply think that players are lucky to be paid *anything* merely to play a boys' game. So they don't want to hear about anything *more*.

But also I believe that, ironically, there are true democratic instincts at work here. Really. For just as we all fantasize that we will grow up to be ballplayers, so do we also fantasize that we will grow up to be rich—ideally so rich that we can buy a ball club. The United States is a country where limousines are okay because someday *I'll* be riding in one, too.

Athletes may be our heroes, but ultimately, perversely, we side with the owners because they are a more dominant representative of the American dream.

Of course, I also believe that the baseball players' union works against itself now. At least the owners are up-front about it. They're mean, grubby bosses, just like yours and mine . . . well, occasionally like mine. Once in a blue moon like mine.

But the players call themselves a union and try to make themselves out to be the linear descendents of Samuel Gompers. Even the *New York Times* sports page, which features strike coverage that reads like a newsletter from the old Wobblies, came up with the information that the players union has licensing agreements—just like the teams—which average out to $150,000 a player. Walking-around money. The failure of most baseball players to support other real workingmen's unions also furthers the impression that, well, at least the owners aren't hypocrites.

Finally, it is important that fans have never cared how much *certain* athletes make. Nobody gives a hoot how much Mike Tyson will take home from a fight (even if nobody much likes Mike Tyson). Who cares how much Pete Sampras makes playing tennis or Pat Day riding horses? But fans make a real distinction then between these athletes in individual sports getting rich on their own talents and team players coming in on the coattails of stars.

Consider this analogy: Just because Rod Stewart makes, say, five million dollars on tour, no one would argue that some sideman of his, playing drums, should earn two-thirds of what the box-office attraction gets just because he's up on the same stage with the star. Likewise, I really don't think fans are disturbed at what someone like Ken Griffey Jr. makes. But what upsets them is when some sideman utility infielder on Griffey's team argues that he should be rewarded proportionately.

Whether it is fair or not, in this labor dispute and in all the others like it in sport, most fans perceive the owners to be against the players, but they perceive the players to be against *our* team and *our* game.

Time Zones

■　　■　　■

Sometimes I wonder about time zones. Does living in one affect your life differently than another? Bear me out. For example, it is a fact that all network television is divided into two parts. Even though they are three hours apart in the real world, in the television world, the east coast and the west coast get fed programs at the same time. The show that you see in New York at ten p.m. also airs in Los Angeles at ten p.m. The central and mountain zones are also lumped as one. They get shows one hour earlier.

The show that the east and west see at ten, the middle people get at nine. I guess the TV moguls feel that central and mountain folk are still mostly farmers and have to get up earlier than the rest.

But possibly life follows art. Maybe people in the east and west stay up later because television assumes they stay up later and schedules later shows. Sometimes when I have nothing better to do I contemplate whether I would watch Johnny Carson and /or his guest hosts if I lived in Oklahoma where Johnny Carson comes on at a more reasonable time.

Likewise *Monday Night Football*. In the eastern time zone, where I live, *Monday Night Football* does not even start until nine o' clock. And, as you know, these games take an eternity. There is no football game in creation worth my *starting* to watch it at nine o'clock. So I suspect my life would be different, Mondays-wise anyway, if I lived in Tacoma or possibly even Albuquerque or Evansville.

Worst of all is when baseball teams go to play on the west coast. Here we are not even talking about nine-thirty, ten o'clock. We are talking about the game starting at eleven o'clock. If Whittier were writing poetry today, there would be no thoughts of might-have-been. Instead, the saddest words of tongue or pen are these: "Just getting started on the coast."

Coast games are compounded by the problem that afternoon papers have gone out of existence, and so you can't get the scores for another whole day. The decline of America is approximately related to the fact that you have to buy Thursday's paper to get Tuesday's box scores.

However, to be fair, I do not want to present these thoughts merely from my own East Coast bias. I have great sympathy for the people who reside in the Pacific Time Zone, because their days are as screwed up as my nights. Have you ever woken up in California and turned on the television to see a ball game going on? *In the morning, a ball game!* It is completely discombobulating. Hey, there are still some absolutes in life. Saturday morning is cartoons. Sunday morning is politics.

We had better be careful. We are raising a generation of sports fans who are already confused enough about the calendar—what with hockey in May and a new pro football league in July. Soon, they won't even know what time it is, either.

The Subtleties of Sports Lingo

■   ■   ■

T hank you for that introduction, Bob Edwards. As I always say: You are my go-to guy at NPR. A "go-to guy" is what a franchise player used to be.

It's important that we understand sports lingo, because it gets more subtle all the time. For example, Dr. Peter Titlebaum, a professor at the University of Dayton, has started teaching a Golf Networking course to women, explaining to them what "rough," "mulligan," "you're away," "five-dollar Nassau," and other exotic links terms mean, so that female executives can feel comfortable as they try to compete in this man's sports world.

Likewise, Tom Bass, a charming former NFL coach, teaches football terminology to the ladies.

My feeling is that this sort of education should not just be restricted to women. Everybody can use help in being brought up to date on the nuances of the language of athletics. You need a sports vernacular go-to guy, and this morning, I am your big-play man.

For instance, what is the one thing you have to do nowadays to win a game? You have to *step up*. That's the secret.

But then, as my friend John Walsh, the chief honcho at ESPN, points out, nobody loses anymore. They just *don't get the job done*. This circumlocution follows naturally in the lingering football affectation never to use the old-fashioned word "score." Instead, you say, "we have to put some points on the board."

In basketball, though, it's the other way around. Expressions are more shorthand. Players are not even identified by a word position anymore. All the positions are simply numbered. Thus, the erstwhile point guard is now just known as "one," the former shooting guard is "two," and so on, up to the ex-pivotman, who has become "five." A coach will say: "We need a three and a back-up five." And everybody knows exactly what he means.

In baseball, though, there is a new position altogether. Well, new to the brain trust department. He is called "the bench coach." Nobody ever knew what a manager did all game except sit there, arms folded, and chew tobacco. Now, the manager has a bench coach, who is usually an old buddy of his, to sit next to him and chew tobacco with him.

Football formations . . . Oops, excuse me, they *used* to be formations, but then they became "sets," and now they are "schemes." Football is always looking to sound more complicated, and "schemes" certainly achieves that end. A formation sounds like it just sits there, formed. But a scheme sounds like it is in action, doing something.

Jack Betts, an English teacher, reminds me that only in sports do we speak in what I have named "the second-person superlative plural." If, for example, we are talking about great presidents, we simply say: Washington, Lincoln, Roosevelt. But in sports, in the second-person superlative plural, if we are talking about great quarterbacks, we would say: "your Unitases, your Baughs, your Montanas."

There is only one sports injury nowadays. It used to be the rotator cuff. Now it is the ACL—which I previously thought was a railroad. But, in fact, the A stands for anterior, which is enough to stop me cold before I even contemplate the C or the L. Never mind. If ever you see a player in any sport writhing in pain, if you just say, "Looks like an ACL to me," everybody will say, "Wow, you have stepped up with your Einsteins. Now we won't have to go in a different direction."

That's what teams say they do now when they fire the coach. They don't fire the coach. They don't even make a change. Instead, they just say that they have decided to go in a different direction.

Sports Fashions

■   ■   ■

I've always thought that the failure of hockey to expand its sphere of influence probably had a great deal to do with how hockey players look. Really, it is not necessary for Don Rickles to insult you by calling you a hockey puck. It is enough for him to say you look like a hockey player.

In fact, hockey players have always looked to me as if they're wearing diapers. Of course the sport hasn't caught on much outside the Arctic Circle. If you didn't grow up with hockey players, would you be attracted to a sport in which grown men without any teeth are wearing diapers? I don't think so.

On the other hand, jockeys, little as they are, are still the best dressed of all athletes in their work clothes. Perhaps it's just what jockeys call their garb: *silks*. Imagine. Silks. Can we put hockey players in silks?

Soccer players have some style, too. Here is a question to ponder: both soccer players and basketball players wear shorts, but soccer shorts are much cuter. Why? Well, they don't billow and they don't look so glossy. As a matter of fact, the MISL—the Major Indoor Soccer League—is actually basing one of its major sales pitches on shorts. Or, anyway, on what's in the shorts. "Hot Legs," the campaign is called. Attendance is up, too—especially among women. More than one way to skin a cat.

Basketball also has another style problem. How do I say this delicately? Well, I can't. It's just . . . the armpit situation. Basketball is very much an upraised-arm game. Armpits. I was delighted then when, last year, Patrick Ewing of Georgetown took to wearing an old gray practice T-shirt under his regular game tank top. It was drafty in the Georgetown arena, and Ewing, who is originally from Jamaica, obviously didn't have the genes for those kind of temperatures. Good for him. Good for us. Moreover, this year, I'm happy to report that a sneaker company has provided a nicer game undershirt for Ewing.

But, hey, Georgetown, why not go all the way and create a regulation uniform with sleeves? It certainly wouldn't inhibit arm movement, and, for goodness sake, every kid in America has grown up wearing T-shirts. As a matter of fact, this is such a T-shirt world we live in that I suspect that any basketball team, pro or college, that put its players in T-shirts for games would instantly be all the rage.

The last team I knew to officially wear T-shirts were the Evansville Purple Aces. This was about fifteen years ago, and Evansville was not just the only team to spare us armpits, but it also was the perennial small-college champion. The reason the Purple Aces wore T-shirts was because of their coach, a distinguished old country gentleman named Arad McCutcheon. The reason? Well, Coach McCutcheon was Patrick Ewing before his time. He felt that, particularly in the cool midwestern gymnasiums, players were better fighting off the chills with covered shoulders.

But something else. Evansville's uniforms not only had sleeves, but they also were orange—except occasionally when they were pink. Now, if you were listening, you will remember that I said that Evansville was known as the *Purple* Aces. Why, pray, I asked Arad, were the Purple Aces attired in orange, or sometimes pink?

Simple, he replied. The easiest color to see is orange, then pink. And remember, this was before orange tennis balls and Charles Finley agitating for orange baseballs. But Arad had figured it out. On a fast break, you could see an orange blur better than any other color blur—and maybe especially if the blur had sleeves on it.

So it was that, year after year, the Purple Aces won national titles in orange T-shirts.

And it still sounds to me like a good idea for someone to try again.

Why Cowboys Became Kings

■   ■   ■

From his car phone, driving somewhere in the Metroplex, Jerry Jones was explaining why it was that, despite injuries, suspension, free-agent defection and the usual who-shot-J. R. atmosphere that invariably surrounds his Dallas Cowboys, Jerry's Team could very well repeat as NFL champions. "We don't have as much vertical depth this year, but what we do have is horizontal depth," he informed me.

"Jerry," I said, "I'm really not sure there can be such a thing as horizontal depth."

"Well now," came back the reply from the old wildcatter, "if you sink an oil well down deep and then you find a whole rich field all around it, I think what you've got yourself there is horizontal depth."

And, indeed, however oxymoronic, that may be as good a way as any to describe the Cowboys, who are after all not just a football team but a singular cultural marvel. They are not a slice of Americana, as we usually say, but rather, a broad brush of it. While most of our successful sports franchises display some distinct personality, only the Cowboys offer the big tent. In fact, the team has always presented—even boasted—extremes, going back to its very emergence as a power, when devout athletic Christianity was at the helm, cheered on by abject T&A.

The Cowboys' dominion only increases, for Jones has taken what was a benign national phenomenon and turned it into a self-sufficient strike force. No owner in any sport has ever been as influential and creative as Jerry Jones—he, who arrived in Big D unknown, disparaged as "The Crock From Little Rock." Now his credentials are such that the

NFL is suing him for $300 million for trampling league rules, while he is countersuing for more than double that. Incredibly, in a rich consortium of 30 franchises, nearly one quarter of all the NFL shirts and caps and other gimcracks sold bear Cowboy insignias. The team has sold out every game in the '90s, home or away, with the hostile faraway stadiums filled up with Cowboy worshippers. Jones himself has been offered in excess of $500 million for a franchise and stadium that cost him a mere $160 million seven years ago. Naturally, his defending champions will open the NFL season this week on *Monday Night Football*.

There has never been anything quite like this sports dynamo—not even the Yankees of lore. The current Chicago Bulls create a sort of rock-star atmosphere wherever they play, but the reality is that the Bulls as an entity are to Michael Jordan as the Grateful Dead were to Jerry Garcia. The Cowboys are different. This will sound facetious, but the only team they remind me of is the beloved Bay Bombers of the old Roller Derby. Even the most fiendish Derby villains could be transformed into heroes simply by being dressed in Bomber orange and black. In a way, the saddest part of the arrest of Michael Irvin, the Cowboys' star receiver, came when police found him a few months ago in a motel room with drugs and topless dancers. His first words were: "You know who I am." He probably still doesn't understand that it doesn't really matter that he is Michael Irvin, star. He is just another player currently wearing Cowboy number 88.

Jones, of course, is able to see a silver lining even in this scandal. "We all love seeing people get up off their knees," he says—and his history is good. With the Cowboys, redemption has always been as marketable as idolatry.

Now, with the team's hegemony safe from sea to shining sea, Jones is turning his flank south. The Cowboys are already Mexico's Team, and a major appeal is directed to Hispanic-Americans. At a *scrimmage* in El Paso this summer, a record 51,000 showed up. The opponent was Houston, which after years in Dallas's long shadow is departing for Tennessee next year. There is a certain symbolism in this. Once Houston and Dallas were the municipal twins of the Lone Star State, but one can legitimately argue that strictly because of the Cowboys—a football team! —Dallas now stands alone, while Houston has fallen into the next lower tier, on a level with the likes of San Antonio and Austin.

Certainly no city has ever been so attached to a sports franchise as Dallas. Even the slightest feather that falls amongst its heroes is whirled into high drama by the local gum-flappers of the airwaves. Last year, there were 37 different Cowboy radio shows in the metropolitan area, where listeners could follow every twist in the strained relations between All-Pro quarterback Troy Aikman and his rapscallion coach Barry Switzer and every hint of sedition, racism or homosexuality on the team. Cowboy books are churned out at a rate that would do Martha Stewart proud; another happy season begins with the release of "Hell-Bent," a raw account of last year's ugly success by Skip Bayless, the team's most perceptive observer.

Notwithstanding, Dallas seems to find its municipal identity in its team. It is widely believed that the city's redemption from its darkest day—Nov. 22, 1963—came with the rise of the Cowboys, their glamour and their glory sprinkling stardust upon the discredited city. Once it was blithely assumed that Dallas had somehow killed President Kennedy. Now, no matter who else may be accused of that crime—the CIA, the Mafia, Cuba, aliens—Dallas is no longer impeached. And J. R. is gone, too. Dallas is just the home of the Cowboys, the NFL champions, a franchise that has never seen its equal. *You know who I am.* I am Dallas: I am the Cowboys.

Pregame Shows— Coming at You!

■ ■ ■

I am very upset that I don't have a pregame show for this, my weekly commentary. You see, every event of any consequence now in sports has a pregame show. And if NPR got me a precommentary show, then Bob Edwards could say, "Frank Deford's commentary will follow the precommentary show," and some experts could come on then and argue how my commentaries have been lately, and how exactly they expect me to do this morning. Some authority might even say, "This is a must-win commentary for Deford!" A pregame show that doesn't talk about a must-win situation is simply a pregame show that has lost its bearings.

Pregame shows as we know them started a couple of decades ago, Sundays on CBS. The original featured a very diverse cast, including Jimmy The Greek, who picked games, and Phyllis George, who provided the women's angle.

Now, unfortunately, no matter how many pregame shows there are, they all duplicate each other. There is a professional sports announcer host and a bunch of loud ex-players or a few ex-coaches who are between jobs. It's all very inside stuff. The host starts off a question, usually by saying: "What about . . . ?" Like: "What about the Bears?," or "What about that John Elway . . . ?" And then all the ex-players jump in with their opinions. Everybody talks very fast, because if you take a breath, somebody else will swamp you. The Fox baseball pregame show actually has an ex-player on it they call "Psycho," with his expertise portion called "Psycho Analysis." The pace on all those shows is accelerated by a lot of laser noises, which are employed instead of periods and commas.

Pregame shows are so popular that ESPN has a football pregame show Sunday even though it doesn't have any games that follow the pregame show. ESPN's big brother, ABC, has also added a pregame prime-time show this year to "Monday Night Football." What about . . . that?

Football fans certainly do have a choice, though. The ESPN pregame show makes up for the fact that it has no games, postshow, by being very frantic. The host is Chris Berman, an announcer known—familiarly and accurately—as Boomer. Boomer dispenses a lot of cross-cultural pop references about music and movies. But everybody else on ESPN is terribly intense, trying to get a word in edgewise.

The closest alternative is "Fox NFL Sunday," which comes from Hollywood. In fact, the correspondents say: "And now, back to Hollywood"—which doesn't sound properly footballish to me. Anyway, the Fox pregame show is hosted by James Brown, a Harvard man, who is known as J. B. He acts sort of like the social chairman at a frat party, and sometimes J. B. and the old jocks even go out on a little artificial-turf football field in the studio and run plays. At any moment you expect the guys to goose each other and tap a keg. The roundup portion is called "Check It Out!" and J. B. screams: "Coming up! Coming at you!" My head spins.

In contrast, there is CBS, the granddaddy, which is now hosted by Jim Nantz, who is known as . . . Jim. It's by far the most sobersided show, and sometimes the ex-players even sit with Nantz around a little table that has flowers on it. Nantz regularly says "some kind of." CBS is some kind of an escape from the other two bedlams.

So, hey, what about I get my precommentary show, which would be some kind of way to Check Me Out! Coming Up! Coming At You!

Kenny, Dying Young

September 27 last was a beautiful clear day in Connecticut, kissed by the first crispness of the early autumn. The leaves were only starting to turn, but in a couple of weeks the hills around Ledyard would be in full blaze. September 27 was a football Saturday. If the day had been warmer, in another season, the shooting would have taken place at the beach instead of out in the quiet woods, among the cedars and the pines.

Around one in the afternoon, Brian Taylor came by and picked Kenny Wright up at the trailer where Kenny lived with his divorced mother. Wright was 24 then but still known for the fine and fearless high school football player he had been; he had set school records, and in his senior year, as a tight end, had made all-conference.

As the two young men departed, Kenny told his mother, Phyllis, that they were just going for a ride. Kenny knew this was a lie. He knew he wanted to stop first at his father's house to get a sawed-off 12-gauge shotgun, to use as a weapon, not for recreation. He and Brian picked up another friend of theirs, Billy King. And, even though Brian and Billy were far away from Kenny when he fired the awful shot a few hours later, they have been charged as accomplices in manslaughter two.

We overemphasize sport in so many ways. Colleges sell their souls to stock winning teams. Grown men take games they watch on TV more seriously than their wives and children. Every year so many little boys from the streets trade in their chances for an education to chase after the rainbow of play-for-pay. Say this for Kenny Wright: he never let himself be deluded by athletics. They were never a means to an end. He only dealt in them for love.

His father, the older Ken Wright, pleaded with him to go on to college, to buy a diploma and more childhood with four more autumns on the gridiron, but as much as the boy adored football, he knew that he couldn't take four more years of studying, that it was time to get a job.

But to be in sports, to be active—that was always what motivated him, diverted him from the less active pleasures of life

"My youngstah just lived for his sports," Phyllis Wright says. She always calls him that—"my youngstah"—in her native New England accent.

There are so many kids like Kenny. Even when he wanted to be by himself, to be contemplative, in his way, it had to involve sports. He could not sit and read or even remain long before the TV. He didn't watch a whole lot of television except for sports. Instead, he would take a gun and tramp through the woods, hunting small game, rabbits or squirrels or birds. His father had schooled him in that when he was still a young boy.

But it was never important to Kenny that he find something to kill. He wouldn't even consider going off with his uncle in the autumn to shoot deer up in Maine. In a way, the only shot, that ever mattered, in the woods, was the one he fired on September 27. "He just liked being active so," Phyllis says. "Lots of times he'd never even shoot at all. He just liked it out there: life all around him, but still alone."

The other thing Kenny did by himself was build up his body. Brian remembers that Kenny started that at a very young age, before other boys got into weights. He bought his own equipment. He read body-building magazines and followed their guidance. Bill Mignault, the football coach at Ledyard High, says, "Kenny was very proud of his athletic ability. He was very proud of his strength. And he was very proud of his appearance."

When Kenny graduated in 1974, his classmates voted him Class Bod (male division), and he posed with Kathy Nason (female division winner) for the yearbook. In that old photo, there is a smile playing across Kenny's face, but in those jet eyes of his there seems to be an underlying sense of pride, too. Class Bod was not just a gag honor. Kenny Wright wore his body well, and it mattered to him in ways that were right. He was always a physical person.

Oh sure, he liked a lot of other things. He liked parties. He liked girls. He liked to go to the Brookside Inn in Preston and drink a few beers with his buddies and shoot some pool and play some electronic TV games or punch up the James Taylor and Neil Young numbers on the jukebox.

But he couldn't be happy long if he wasn't active. "He was such an aggressive-type guy," says Brian, the best friend Kenny ever had. "We were very tight," Brian says. Some people said Kenny could be too tough, could be a brawler. "No, he was never malicious," Brian says. "The fun, sports—that's what he lived for." That is almost exactly what Phyllis says.

Sports put a lot of structure into Kenny's existence. At Ledyard High his grades were inevitably better during the football season, even though that was when he had to devote so much of his free time to practicing. His temper was contained during football. "Football kept Kenny involved and more active in everything," says Mignault.

And it is true that the only time Kenny really floundered in his life was after he finished school and there was no more football to point to in the fall. He had never been afraid of a fight, but now he grew afraid he might miss one. Fighting was fun for him, and nobody frightened him. Once, in a diner, he took on half a dozen sailors. And he started it. Another time, Kenny flailed out and hurt a cop who was trying to break up a fight. "He wasn't the goodest boy then," Phyllis says. Kenny cooled off in the slammer a couple of times for breach of the peace. It was a very exasperating time for everybody. In dismay, Kenny's father once said to Phyllis, "How can you still love him?" But it was mostly a matter of understanding. As Brian said, Kenny wasn't malicious. He just hadn't grown up yet, and liked to scrap. Everybody knew that, and that would be his bad luck.

And, anyway, he found another, healthier outlet soon enough. He began to scuba dive, to spearfish. Ledyard, where Kenny lived, is in from the water, colonial rural. There are stylish riding horses here and there, but also, as one sees out in the wide-open spaces, the road signs have been dimpled by sharp-shooters and there is a Grange Hall. Yet the sense of the sea is great, even in the hollows. Ledyard lies near the Thames River, and 10 miles downstream, toward where it flows into Long Island Sound, are New London and Groton, the U.S. Coast Guard Academy and the nuclear submarine base. The college boys from Harvard and Yale race their shells on the Thames, just south of Ledyard, every June.

A few miles up the coast to the east of the Thames is Mystic, a restored whaling town, and it was there, where the Mystic River pours out toward Mason Island, that Kenny did most of his diving and fishing. There was no stopping him once he had mastered it. He would put on his wet suit and go in no matter how cold it was. Even if there was a thin layer of ice, he'd sometimes go under. He had confidence that he would break out through the surface if it came to that.

He loved to pop up out of the water like some briny monster from a Japanese movie, over near a bridge in Mystic, where a lot of old black fellows fished. They'd be sitting there, all cold and gray, all empty lines, and Kenny would appear out of the deep, brandishing a whole line of fish. "Hey, you've got to go *after* 'em," he'd call to the old gentlemen, and then he'd climb into his pickup and go home.

"There were a lot of happy times," Brian says. Kenny had usually worn a beard, going back to when he was in high school, but now he wore only a trim mustache. It was almost debonair, and with his ebony eyes he was handsome; with his powerful physique, he was a striking figure of a man. He had a pretty girl friend, named Karen, whom he loved, and had a good job where he'd always wanted one, working for Pfizer, the drug company, down in Groton. Around southeastern Connecticut, Pfizer is known as an especially fine employer—good people—and for three years Kenny had driven there, week after week, applying for work. He had a relative who worked there, but Kenny was determined to be hired by his own hook. And finally he was, as a chemical worker, in the spring of 1979. He and Karen celebrated. "He was happier'n a pig in slop," Phyllis says. Everybody was pretty sure that in time Kenny would marry Karen and start a family. "It sure was starting to jell for him," Brian says. "Everything was going in the right direction."

K enny even took up boxing—with gloves—and had a couple of amateur bouts. And a semipro football club named the Sea Hawks had come to the area, so he made up his mind that even though he hadn't played in five years he'd go back to the gridiron.

At Ledyard High, Kenny had carried about 180 on his 6'1" frame, but now he had filled out more, to 200 at least, maybe 225. And the extra weight was muscle. It was common for people around Ledyard to characterize him as "strong as an ox." But tough as he was, Kenny had gentle hands. He was a tight end, he could block, but he could also catch the ball so well that Mignault put in a special pass play for him.

The other receivers would stay in, as if it were going to be a running play—except for the back on Kenny's side, who would come over the line and cut in a little, taking the defender with him. Kenny would delay a count, as though he were going to block, too, and then he would go down and out, and the quarterback would look for him over by the right sideline. The play was so successful that Mignault kept it in the Colonels' playbook even after Kenny graduated and lesser lights took his spot. In fact, the last time Kenny went to his old school for a game, he asked, "Coach, you still got my special play in?"

Ledyard High was opened in 1963. The school colors are navy blue and white, but when Mignault fielded his first varsity, in 1966, the Green Bay Packers were big, so he designed the football uniforms after Green Bay's with blue where the Packers' green would have been, only touches of white, and heavy on the gold. The gold catches your eye much more than the blue or the white. Mignault's teams have been strong year after year. They have had only one losing season in their 15 years of football, but Kenny is still second in career passes caught and third in touchdown receptions and total yards receiving. As a senior, he was voted to the All-Eastern Connecticut Conference team. He wore big No. 86.

So he was pretty sure he could make the Sea Hawks, even after the long time away from the game. The only problem was that he had a shoulder that dislocated easily, so he decided he would have a pin inserted. He was going in for the surgery around Memorial Day of 1979, so he'd be fully recovered for the football season, but during his final checkup the doctor found some kind of boil on Kenny's left shoulder, where he was going to operate, and thought it would be unwise to cut into this infected area. There was no great rush. But that was too bad. If Kenny had had the operation, he'd have been in the hospital on June 3.

On that Sunday night, going on two years ago now, Kenny left the party early. He had to work at Pfizer the next morning, so he wanted to go home and get a good night's sleep. Friends called him names and what-not, urging him good-naturedly to stick around and have a couple more drinks, but Kenny was firm and laughed back at them, and climbed into his Ford pickup. He had a good job now.

But there was a big guy there, an acquaintance of Kenny's, and he knew Kenny liked to tussle, and so the big guy opened up the truck door and yanked Kenny out. Playfully, they scuffled, full of whiskey and youth. Then Kenny was down, trying to catch his breath, sort of half sitting up, his head bent forward some, between his legs, and the big guy took a flying leap onto him, right onto his neck.

A lot of people were laughing, and it took them a while to realize something might be wrong with Kenny. Even at the hospital, it didn't seem to be much: the skin wasn't broken; no bone was broken. All it was was a bruise. Isn't that something? All it was was a goddamned bruise. Or, officially, a cervical cord contusion, C-7. All the football, all the wrestling, the boxing, the fights, all that he'd done for his body. And then a bruise: henceforth and forever, Kenneth W. Wright would be a quadriplegic.

When he was released from the hospital he tried living with Karen at first, but, in many ways, living with her made things more difficult for him. So he moved into his mother's trailer. Mr. and Mrs. Wright had been divorced some time before. Phyllis does private duty work in a nursing home. She was more than qualified to tend to her son, but she had to quit her job to manage him properly. "I told my youngstah: I will always take care of you, but I can't help you," Phyllis says.

And, at least, Kenny was not completely wasted. There was some movement in his upper body, and he worked with his hands so that, in a sort of gnarled manner, he could hold things and write his name. Once, he took an hour and a half to fix up a fishing rod. "I did it, I did it, Ma!" he cried. But, as we know, he was never much for that sort of sedentary stuff. He began to work out, though, building himself back up again as best he could. At his worst, his weight had gone down to 143. But soon he was as powerful across his chest and shoulders as he'd ever been. People could see it. But that was small consolation. "My youngstah always needed his legs to live his life," Phyllis says.

He told her, "Ma, I know my body. If there's one thing I know about me, it's my body. And I know I'll never walk again." Soon he began to talk about suicide.

The 1979 football season came and went. He got taken to see a couple of the Colonels' games, and once or twice he was also carted over to St. Bernard's High where the Sea Hawks played their home schedule. Some of his old friends carried him in to see the closed-circuit telecast of the first Duran-Leonard fight, too. So Kenny at least tried, the best he could, to divert himself with sports from the pain and the depression.

By now, though, a lot of his old pals had stopped coming by; they couldn't deal with this Kenny. Only a few never stopped sacrificing for him. Billy, who is employed by the maintenance department in the nearby town of Stonington, was one; Brian, who works for a plumbing-supply company, was another.

Brian is 25 now; an uncommonly good-looking young man. He has difficulty talking about his old friend; after all, they were so close. They had known each other since they were nine, in Little League baseball. Brian would try to carry Kenny around. He even took it upon himself to transport Kenny down to New London for his haircuts. Or he'd come around in his truck and drive Kenny and his wheelchair out to the woods, where Brian would park and then push Kenny along the paths. In better times, they had hunted a lot of these places together. Brian was never a scuba diver but, like Kenny, he loved hunting. The best is being out there by yourself, nobody bothering you," he says.

But possibly Kenny was happiest when someone took him fishing, because that was a thing he could *do*, even if he couldn't do it at all the way he used to. Buckled into his wheelchair, he could hold the rod in his twisted hands and even reel in some of the snapper blues he hooked. One time he got hold of a big fish and it yanked, and just then he had one of his muscle spasms; somehow he held on, kept on fighting, and pulled in the fish. But it embarrassed him to almost lose control. Phyllis says, "He just couldn't cope. He was an athlete."

It was hard for Phyllis and Kenny to get by, too. Pfizer's medical insurance had paid a lot of the bills, but Phyllis couldn't leave Kenny to go to work, and they had hardly enough to live on. Soon, Phyllis began to sell off his scuba equipment, item by item—his fins, his wetsuit, his spear gun and so on. She used this money mostly to buy one thing: Old Grand-Dad for Kenny.

In their wisdom, the doctors wouldn't prescribe any pain-killing drugs for Kenny, because they didn't want him to become addicted. "Fine, he'll become an alcoholic instead," Phyllis would yell into the phone at them. Three stiff shots of bourbon, cut with a little cola, and Kenny could at least get some respite from the pain.

By now, Kenny was talking about suicide a lot, and each piece of his equipment his mother sold seemed to symbolize the draining of hope. "This isn't living, this is existing," he said. The 1980 football season approached. "Don't worry, Ma," he told Phyllis, "I'll never do it here, where you'd have to find me. It'll be at the beach or in the woods. My two favorite places."

By fall the last piece of his scuba gear had been sold for Old Grand-Dad. "Summer was over, so it wouldn't be at the beach now," Phyllis says.

Brian came to pick Kenny up on the afternoon of September 27. As he took Kenny out the door of the trailer, onto the ramp that his mother had had built for him, Kenny called back to her, back to where she was pinning up some draperies. "Hey, Ma," he said. "See you later. Take care of yourself."

She started, holding the curtain tight, for just an instant. Kenny was never very expressive. He wasn't "a kisser" at all. If he had kissed his mother, she would have known right away that he was going out to kill himself. What he did say—"Take care of yourself"—was the most he could manage under the circumstances. He was just as relaxed with his father, when he dropped in to pick up the sawed-off 12-gauge. "Kenny was in real good spirits," the elder Wright remembers.

They stopped for Billy King, and then Brian drove his truck along Route 214, the old Pequot Trail, Indian territory. Out of Ledyard, on the road toward Preston, they drove by the high school. It's located at the top of Spicer Hill Road, and the Pequot Trail winds half a mile below. When Kenny passed by, at the bottom of the hill, the Ledyard Colonels, in their navy blue and white and gold, were playing a game. It was a fine football Saturday, a crystal-clear afternoon, the sun reflecting off the gold helmets. And the view to the northwest from that field, down Spicer Hill, was so glorious that not even a football game on a football Saturday had any business intruding. The whole sweep, as far as one could see, was thick and green, touched with fire colors, hiding everything below the foliage. The Pequot Trail was obscured from sight, as was the old Western Reservation—and the place about 3 1/2 half miles away where Brian pulled his truck off the road, just before the turnoff to Preston and the Brookside Inn. Brian and Billy wheeled Kenny into the woods for what he knew would be the last time.

While they were there, under cover of the trees, the Ledyard Colonels won their football game, 20–0.

By late afternoon, Phyllis was through with the curtains, and she sat down and started to crochet. A large clock ticked loudly in the trailer, and, suddenly, she looked up and it dawned on her. Out loud she said, "Oh my God, Kenny's gone. He's never coming back."

She knew, even though he hadn't told her. That was the point: not to tell anybody. The reason for his shooting himself was that his body didn't belong to him anymore, and he was tired of troubling other people with it. But for what Brian and Billy did that day, for no more than driving Kenny out to the woods and standing their friend to a few beers—for that, under Connecticut law, they face the possibility of 10 years for assisting in the commission of a suicide.

At about the moment when Phyllis realized what Kenny intended to do, he asked his two friends to go get some more beer. They were gone only a few minutes, half an hour at the most. When Kenny heard them drive off, he took his gnarled fingers and unbuckled his seat belt so that he could bend his torso forward and make a better target for himself Then he aimed the 12-gauge up at his heart and pulled the trigger. It was a difficult thing to manage, physically. But then, Kenny had always been capable, physically. The last things he saw were the bright trees of autumn and an azure sky the shade of the sea.

The athlete now rests in the Elm Grove Cemetery, on the banks of the Mystic, very near to where he used to go spearfishing. At first Phyllis went to the grave every day, but she doubted that was good for her, so now she mostly just visits on Sundays. Sometimes she says a prayer over Kenny's grave, but other times she stands there and looks down and snaps at him. "Oh why, you bugger?" Phyllis says. "Why didn't you fight longer?"

She glances up now, in the trailer, as she talks. The clock is ticking louder. "Oh why? I think if he'd been a bookworm, he . . ."

He what?

"He'd have adjusted better." Phyllis shakes her head. "You know, I don't really get mad at Kenny when I shout at him. You see, even if there had been a miracle, if he'd somehow been able to walk with braces and crutches, I don't think Kenny would've been happy. Not my youngstah. Not the way he was."

At the head of the grave there is a small marker, set flush in the ground. Phyllis has ordered a larger, upright one. There's no hurry on its delivery, though, because the earth by the Mystic is frozen now, and the stone couldn't be set in place till the spring thaw. It will be specially engraved. In one corner of the stone there will be an outline of a football and a jersey, No. 86. In the other, there will be fins, a mask and a snorkel. Phyllis explains, "These are the things my youngstah loved the most," which is why she is having them cut in the stone, to go with Kenny's name and the dates he lived and played, 1956–1980.

Jocks

■　　■　　■

When the news of the horrific school massacre in Colorado began to emerge last week, I found myself wondering what in the world some foreigner would make of one of the young murderers shouting that they were out to shoot minorities and . . . jocks.

Even allowing for the fact that hatred is irrational, how do you explain that boys who admire Hitler would despise athletes as much as they do racial groups? As despicable as ethnic hatred is, at least it appears to be a traditional part of the worst of the human condition—and one that is also, too often, passed along; in the chillingly lyrical words from *South Pacific*: "you've got to be taught to hate." But be taught to hate athletes? The schoolboy killers and their friends obviously had learned to despise athletes from their own everyday experience.

Of course, those grotesque boys were deranged, but altogether, as Americans, how torn are our feelings about athletes. What ambivalence we feel about . . . jocks. How we like them too much and dislike them too much.

It's important to remember that American schools are about the only ones in the world that so intertwine competitive athletics with academics. In most countries, youthful sport is the province of clubs, like our Little League baseball. But we have developed a school system whereby sports not only matter a great deal, but often even provide the main identity for a school. The high school athletes themselves— even junior high!—are lionized.

From an early age, jocks in America enter some sort of a samurai class. They are treated specially, cosseted, even lied for by adults. Only athletes can win college scholarships based on their extracurricular activity. As there *are* student-athletes, there are *no* student-actors or student-singers being fought over for scholarships. Are there?

So, it is easy to understand how so many children in America who are not blessed by athletic genes come to envy jocks—even, perhaps, to despise them. The jocks are so prized in our society. They get the girls. They get the laughs. And because they are on teams, they belong, *ipso facto*. And everybody wants to belong in adolescence, don't we?

It's natural that those children who are not so coordinated, not so comfortable, would turn their wrath toward those smug S.O.B.s who get all the attention, who get along so easily. It was that way when I was in high school. I'm sure it's worse now.

Because now there's even more of a division, when so many kids are totally a-athletic. Today's younger generation is the most sedentary in our history. And, of course, the grown-ups celebrate athletes more in our society than ever before. Our samurai, our musketeers, our heroes.

I do not know whether movies or TV shows or rap music or video games have an adverse and compelling effect upon children. But I can understand how sports does upset lots of kids. The jocks are real and they are right there in school with you, and if you are a boy adrift and insecure, I think it would be easy to hate them.

It may well be that in honoring young athletes so much, and in concentrating so on the games they play in school, we have made even more of a competition between those children who are and those who are not . . . jocks.

Peterose

■   ■   ■

I n Greek mythology, there is the familiar tale of Peterose—the son of Mercury and Diana, the huntress—who, given those great genes, was a terrific athlete. From an early age, Peterose would play and play, play games so well that Zeus told him: Peterose, you may play all you want, but you must go and listen to Athena, the goddess of wisdom, so that you will also learn to play fair.

Alas, on the very day he was to meet with Athena, Peterose ran off to shoot his bow and arrow (and also to chase some wood nymphs).

Peterose grew up, though, to win the gods' archery championship year after year, until one time when Zeus believed that Peterose broke the rules. Did you listen to Athena? Zeus asked him. And when Peterose admitted that he had not, Zeus banned him from Mount Olympus, allowing Peterose to come back for only one day a year, to attend the grand banquet after the gods' archery competition. Even then, though, Peterose would not be permitted to sit at the banquet table and wear a laurel wreath like all the other champions (many of whom were lesser champions than Peterose). No, he could only watch the feast at a distance.

But, an ironic development. So great had Peterose been that all the others present paid more attention to him, afar, than to the champions who sat right there with Zeus. And this infuriated Zeus, who swore again that he would never allow Peterose entrance to the banquet of the gods.

So goes the mythology—which, as a matter of fact, I made up completely. I made it up, because there *should* be mythology that relates to the tale of Pete Rose—or, anyway, an Aesop's fable or an old Bible story or Indian folklore. Something. The Pete Rose allegory is that of a lesser god, destroyed by his own excess and obsession but revived by the unyielding vengefulness and sanctimony of those who would punish him in perpetuity.

Rose made far more hits than anybody in baseball history, but, as a manager, he seems to have bet on baseball games. Probably. We know for sure that he bet on everything else. In effect, then, Rose pleaded *nolo contendere* to the gambling charges, accepting a lifetime suspension from the diamond Valhalla.

But . . . no sooner had Rose struck the deal than did the commissioner, Bart Giamatti, allow that, well, yes, he personally did think that Rose was guilty. To Rose, that inside acknowledgment violated the spirit of the arrangement. And, sadly, Giamatti dropped dead but days later—the victim, many of his friends still believe, of a heart weakened by the stress of the Pete Rose morality play.

Now, after all these years, Rose has appealed to Bud Selig, the head of baseball's executive council, for reinstatement, so that he, the greatest hit maker of all time, can be inducted into the Baseball Hall of Fame at Cooperstown.

Selig adored Giamatti. To overturn his judgment, to support the scoundrel who may have helped cause Giamatti's death? It's unlikely.

But remember that banquet on Mount Olympus? Like that, the people who go to the Hall of Fame now barely notice the plaques on the walls that celebrate all the other gods of baseball. Rather, Pete Rose is more evident by his singular absence from Cooperstown than he would be by his blurred presence. The fans, baseball pilgrims, leave the Hall of Fame, and as they go forth back into the world, what they remember most is the one plaque they did not see in the shrine.

Perhaps that is mythology enough.

Lovers and Fighters

■   ■   ■

Many people who watched "Monday Night Football" last week were apparently quite taken aback at Lawrence Taylor's distress after he participated in the tackling of Joe Theismann, which broke Theismann's leg and probably ended his career.

As the replays clearly showed, the play was entirely bad luck. No one was at fault, so Taylor's concern seemed all the more misplaced. What's the big deal, Lawrence? It's a contact sport and injuries are all part of the game.

But the fact is that as rough—as quite simply violent—as many athletes are on the field, few of them are dirty players, malevolent beings. And there's a big difference between intensity and intent.

Part of this is human nature. Anybody who gets the reputation as a headhunter may get his own head handed to him. Part of it is the nature of the beast. Unlike you and me, athletes get a chance to release. As a rule, they don't play angry. It's my experience that the most dangerous time in any game is not in a close game when nerves are allegedly taut, but in a one-sided contest when the loser's frustrations begin to show. Remember how some of the St. Louis Cardinals came apart at the seams in the lopsided seventh game of the World Series? The Cards could endure a pressure-packed pennant race with grace. A shellacking got to their pride, their heart, their shame.

Also, I submit a stereotyped reason. Big guys don't like to fight. People want to fight big guys to prove themselves, but most big guys back off. And most athletes are big guys. It's the Napoleonic little terriers like Billy Martin who start the scraps. Lawrence Taylor doesn't need to hurt anybody.

Boxing, of course, is the most contradictory sport, because it is the only one in which the combatants are supposed to try to hurt one another. Mencken once observed that when he saw two women kissing it reminded him of boxers shaking hands before a bout, but the fact is that few boxers bring antipathy into the ring. The classic exception took place a quarter of a century ago when Emile Griffith ended up battering Bennie Paret to death. At the weigh-in Paret had taunted Griffith with homosexual slurs. Then, in the ring, the referee, the veteran Ruby Goldstein, was so shocked at Griffith's unusual fury that he froze as Paret was pounded. But most boxers seem to retain the most affection for the fellows they shared the most blood with.

Retaliation is part of the human condition, of course, and most athletes think it should have a place in every game. Never mind the rule book—let us have our own page or two on the law of the jungle. Many players still argue, for example, that the problem with the designated hitter in baseball is that the pitcher can now throw at batters without having to worry about getting thrown at himself.

Of course, as lethal as a hardball can be, it's always important to distinguish between shaking someone up and hitting them. If you want to keep a batter loose, you throw at him. *At* him. That brushes him back, away from the plate. If you want to hurt or maim a man, you throw just below and behind his head. By reflex, then, the batter will duck *into* the pitch himself.

One of the reasons I think hockey has never caught on with most of America is that its intentional, codified violence disturbs most of us. Who likes goons on any team? We want to believe that our big, rough and tough athletes are really soft and caring inside. Like Lawrence Taylor. And it's true; in the old cornball phrase, most of the best athletes are lovers, not fighters.

Spring Training

■   ■   ■

There are only three places I have ever been in sports that are always beautiful and evocative and special.

One is the backside of a racetrack at dawn when the first sun catches the breath of horses snorting, when everybody there has a sure thing in their pocket and knows they'll be rich by the time the sun goes down. The second place is a golf course, uncrowded and dewy, when the morning sun is higher now, just starting to burn. Nothing did God and man fashion so well together as a golf course.

And then there's Spring Training—the Grapefruit League or the Cactus League or whatever you prefer. I'm down there now, training for spring myself.

It's all quite overdone, of course. No well-toned athlete needs weeks and months to get ready. In the old days, around the turn of the century, spring training's real purpose was to dry the ballplayers out after a winter of drinking.

Nowadays, the businessmen-ballplayers stay pretty much in shape all winter and come to the subtropics needing only to touch up their muscles and their skills. Mostly, Spring Training is for the spectators and for the players' wives and children more than it is for the players.

A few years ago the *Los Angeles Times* sports department decided that it had seen through this ruse. Why send a reporter all the way from Los Angeles to Vero Beach, Florida, in order that he might faithfully report back that so-and-so had a pulled muscle and somebody else went one for two in an intrasquad game? No, decided the *Times,* we will use the telephone to report these crucial moments, until perhaps the last week or so of Spring Training when it really gets serious. Well, logically, of course, the *Times* was correct. Of course

Spring Training is repetitive and even superfluous. But that misses the point.

The decision did, however, send shivers up and down the spines of all baseball reporters and other hangers-on who have been going to Spring Training for years in order to get spring and news—and in that order.

And, I must say, it burned me up. Los Angeles has no business trying to steal the spring and the harbingers thereof from us poor souls in the temperate north. Wouldn't that be just like Los Angeles.

Well, luckily, the solid north held together. The newspapers and the TV and radio stations refused to be so studiously practical and they kept flooding Florida and Arizona with reporters and cameramen and editors and commentators and columnists, all faithfully reporting bumps and bruises, practice bunts and bingles. And, boys and girls, they are there to this day.

One of a Kind

■   ■   ■

E ven allowing that we might overstate the point, it is not uncommon for the most memorable of our athletes to reflect their times. Certainly, the Babe was at one with the Roaring Twenties, just as Jackie Robinson perfectly represented the grand societal advances of the postwar years, and as Ali and Billie Jean so symbolized the turmoil of their period. Likewise, Michael Jordan is not merely so extraordinary for what he does. He also has been the right, best athlete for us now, for this relatively serene and altogether prosperous *fin de siècle,* when the United States rules alone, as much superculture as superpower.

By now, is not Jordan a figure as cultural as he is athletic? Even several years ago, for example, in a vote of *Chinese* students, he tied Chou En-lai as "the world's greatest man." And, most would ask, whatever happened to this Chou En-lai? Nowadays, it is blithely accepted that the tall, dark and bald young man has become the most familiar face on the planet Earth, that with the death of Diana, Princess of Wales, Michael Jeffrey Jordan, late of Wilmington, N.C., has become the First Celebrity of the World, positively ubiquitous, the human Hard Rock Cafe T-shirt.

Yet it is instructive that all his global renown—and his domestic fortune—could not have been achieved if Jordan's American sport (one barely a century old) had not, at the very moment of Jordan's appearance, risen to challenge football and baseball in the U.S., and soccer everywhere else. Still, eminence through basketball? Through hoops? If Jordan is most like anyone else today, it is probably Bill Gates, who clambered to the top of the world in business and wealth in an enterprise that didn't even exist a brief time ago.

With such stature has come criticism. Still, it is a measure of these boom times—of Michael Jordan's times—that the bulk of the reproof leveled against him by the likes of Jim Brown and unrelenting anti-Nike fanatics relate to the businessman, not to the athlete or the person. This Jordan is a conglomerate, they say, too greedy, lacking social responsibility. Why isn't this Jordan spending more time in the inner cities, handing out Christmas turkeys there? Funny: No one ever lambasted Larry Bird for not spending his idle hours demonstrating his largesse in Appalachia.

Oh, how quickly do times change! Or, how greatly did Michael Jordan change them. It was but a short while ago that every profile about a black athlete would emphasize how he—unlike his white alter egos—couldn't attract endorsements. As that other famous athletic Mike, Mr. Tyson, laments his commerciallessness even now: "I don't run around with no shoes on." But here is Henry Louis Gates Jr., in *The New Yorker* no less, proclaiming that "Michael Jordan has become the greatest corporate pitchman of all time." The irony of the charge that Jordan has allowed crass white men to pass him off as some kind of cartoon character away from the court is that if Jordan is at all resonant of Disney, it is not because he is a cartoon, but rather a family-entertainment empire.

All this is quite amazing, and all quite '90s. Also, much of it is above—beyond? beneath?—race, Jordan has become like a handful of other public black people, notably Colin Powell, Bill Cosby and Vernon Jordan, who don't seem to be creatures of color. Well, at least not to whites, they aren't. Nobody admits it, but the subtext to "Oh, gracious, what ever is the poor NBA going to do without Michael Jordan?" really is, *What ever is the NBA going to do without such a terribly appealing black player?*

Certainly, as unbelievably great as Jordan is on the court, his popularity is related in no small measure to his engaging persona. Let us merely consider, first, his attire. In mufti he always presents himself in a magnificent suit, complete with a tie, tied. (God, if just once we could see an I'm-cool movie star in a coat and tie. And shaved.) Yet with this downright old-fashioned presentation, Jordan also wears an earring. Talk about something for everyone. He pulls it off, too! Anybody else wears a coat and tie with an earring, it's like DockSiders with a tuxedo. But on Jordan it's real. Real nice. The jiggy gentleman.

Too bad the classy Jordan mode hasn't caught on. Other athletes dress up only when they're indicted. But, then, you see, the greatest paradox about Jordan is that, for all his majesty, he's neither seminal nor progenitive. Jordan is simply spectacular, by himself, of himself, of his time. Babe Ruth, for best comparison, not only saved baseball, but also changed the sport. It's not Jordan's fault, but he did neither for basketball.

In fact, long before he ascended to new heights, black basketball had become accepted as the theater of levitation. Why, before number 23 was even born, it was said of the playground legend Jumpin' Jackie Jackson that "he could take a quarter off the top of the backboard and give you change." Later, the silken Elgin Baylor—who was the first entertainer, in showbiz or sports, to be deemed "superstar"—brought that same ability (and more) to the NBA; it was Baylor who was the Manet of the Impressionist school of basketball, which Jordan, in time, would attend.

None of this is to diminish Jordan. If he didn't come first, he has improved on everything. Consider jumping, which, by itself, isn't the least bit sexy. Quick, name the Olympic high jump gold medalist. Hell, name any high jumper. But Jumping by Jordan is equal parts art and optical illusion. It must be the tongue.

Yet as he is not a true original, neither will there be any legacy. Indeed, apart from Andre Agassi's "Image is everything," Jordan's "Be like Mike" must be the greatest commercial curse.

It isn't just that no one can possibly be like Mike, but rather that in the impossible attempts to imitate him, the sport has been diminished. Bird and Magic Johnson not only saved the NBA, but also gave us a better game, one that was focused upon the ideal of team. Give Jordan fair credit: He was too good for that—"God disguised as Michael Jordan," as Bird famously called him—but the faux Jordans who have come after him have only proved that imitation is the sincerest form of vulgarity.

If lesser lights find it hard to knock off his game, trying to copy Mr. Jordan's demeanor is an even more imposing task. In a world where celebrity wannabes feel they have a right to be whiny and boorish, Jordan has been remarkably dignified. His vaunted competitive spirit—all that tedious he'd-try-and-beat-his-own-grandmother crap—is absent off his fields of play. His extreme penchant for gambling only makes him more human to most people. This is, after all, a man who has somehow made a handsome asset of baldness, the first athlete since Dorothy Hamill to affect hairstyle fashion.

Likewise, we appreciated his relative failure at baseball. Really, to have pulled that off would have been a bit much. After all, a great part of Jordan's popularity is that he seems, away from basketball, remarkably well adjusted. Consider: the stable, middle-class family upbringing, the early disappointment—not making the high school team, an episode that has, by now, been raised to Jordanian scripture—then the overcoming of this rejection, learning to play at the foot of the wise and sainted Dean Smith, finding success leading his team, winning a number of "rings" (what we used to call championships), becoming a doting father, being blessed with convenient tee times, etc., etc., etc.

We admire, too, that the good son's evident devotion to his father and his anguish at that terrible death are matched by the privacy that Jordan, the husband, carves out for his young family. Do you have any idea what his wife's name is? What she looks like? How many children they have? How many times must Barbara Walters have tried to get into his living room? To be sure, Jordan is no paragon—enough already with the golf!—but we can imagine the enormous demands that are put upon him and we marvel at the way he lives such a life, most graciously. In a time when we're crying out for heroes, it is sufficient that we understand that Jordan is man enough.

It is, though, time for him to leave the stage. Yes. Bill Bradley wrote that the athlete had an obligation to live out the full arc of a career, and probably this should be true for most athletes, even the best ones. But Jordan is a special case, the athlete for our time, and to see him tarnished at all, even occasionally to see age overtake him, is only to be so cruelly reminded how temporal and fragile we all are, how elusive and brief is perfection. For all his majesty, for that perfectly celestial final minute against the Jazz on Sunday, still, we also saw the first leaf of autumn in these playoffs. No more, thank you.

It's like that old question, What do we look like in heaven? Do we look all wizened, the way we do when we died at 80, or do we get to choose to be at our youthful best? Because, if there is a heaven on earth, it certainly includes a vision of Jordan at the height of his powers, effortlessly kicking everyone's ass. It serves no purpose for society to have to remember his struggling to force up another tagged fallaway that . . . falls away.

Besides, what actor had a better exit than the one Michael Jordan wrote for himself in Salt Lake City?

What has been so amazing is that Jordan has achieved a certain mythology without benefit of our fevered imaginations. Everything he's done is on tape, and has been viewed and reviewed from every angle.

None of it has been dreamed or exaggerated. Let the movies depend on special effects, let the politicians rely on spin. Michael Jordan is neomillennial, our first literal legend. And so much of it has been so beautiful. That above all. He made sport into art in a way that we really haven't seen, haven't admired, quite so, since the Greeks chose athletes, foremost, to decorate their amphoras.

In the end, whenever the end, it wasn't so much the basketball. It was the beauty. It truly was a thing of beauty.

Football and Basketball Coaches

■　　■　　■

I t is presently one of those periods of the year when two major sports overlap—in this case basketball and football—and so now it is especially obvious how different are the typical coaches in these major sports.

Now, coaches in general were best summed up once by Eugene McCarthy, the former senator and presidential candidate, who is also a sports fan of great devotion. McCarthy said, "Coaching is like politics. You have to be smart enough to know how to do it, but dumb enough to think it's important." And certainly, in that singular respect, coaches in all sports share a commonality of delusion.

But why is it that the gentlemen who coach football tend to be so different from the fellows who coach basketball? Close your eyes now and visualize the typical football coach. He has his arms folded. He wears some kind of silly little hat. His clothes are somber and solid. His arms are still folded. An eighty-seven-yard punt return has just unfolded before his eyes—never mind whether it was for or against him—and his arms are still folded. Wait, he listens to an earphone held to his ear. With great emotion, he taps his clipboard and then folds his arm again.

Clipboards. I always think of football coaches when I see clipboards. Football coaches are military men, and clipboards are very military. Some of my fondest memories of the army were of clipboards. If you held a clipboard when you were in the army, nobody would ever tell you to do anything. If you held a cup of coffee, the sergeant would say, "Listen, when you're finished with the coffee, do this." You were temporarily inviolable with coffee. But as long as you held a clipboard you were permanently inviolable in the army. This is why I have such a warm spot in my heart for clipboards. Once I figured this out, all I did in the army was drink coffee and carry a clipboard.

Now, have we got that straight? So, let's move on and close our eyes again and visualize a basketball coach. He's squeezing the life out of a rolled-up program. He wears a loud jacket, open at the neck so we can see his beads and chains. He screams and makes many hand signals—numbers and the letter T, etc. He wears his hair down in front and tries to look like one of his players.

Football coaches are addressed as Coach. Basketball coaches are known as Teddy and Nicky and Bucky.

Basketball coaches never amount to anything, either. They are, as their clothes suggest, perennial adolescents. If they can't coach well enough to keep a job, they vanish. The height of their life is coaching basketball. This is not true for football coaches. They are little generals, putative administrators. They have a staff of a dozen assistants and a team made up of hordes of players.

Even bad football coaches get bumped up. They becomes assistant athletic directors if they are losing coaches or head athletic directors if they are winners. Football coaching is a career. Basketball coaching is an ego trip. Basketball coaching is acting. Football coaching is directing.

But no matter what, half of 'em still win and half of 'em still lose.

How We Lost Our Pastime

■   ■   ■

Nineteen ninety-six marked by two impossibilities in baseball. First, the New York Yankees, historically America's most insufferable conglomerate, became absolutely lovable, lending to the Big Apple a downright small-town, Capraesque air. Moreover, baseball management and labor actually found it possible to sign a peace pact. But forgive me: do you get the feeling that perhaps baseball will not be crossing that crowded bridge to the 21st century? I do. I fear that the national pastime has forever lost that mystic ability to provide us with any sense of who we are.

Nothing brought this home to me more than last month, when the National Basketball Association was jubilantly celebrating its 50th anniversary. It was not only much clever mingling of marketing and reminiscence. No, what you heard clearest was wise men proclaiming that basketball is now *the* American game, the one in rhythm with our hectic, cybermanic boomer-X lives.

But wait. There is also what is everywhere else called "American" football. A run-of-the-mill "Monday Night Football" tilt attracts more viewers than a World Series showdown—even one with the Yankees playing. Football is glamorous and violent and one big casino, and what could be more all-American? Why, the Super Bowl has superseded the World Series, both as an athletic and a cultural event, even if, mostly, people only end up talking about which commercials fared the best.

And hockey—ice hockey!—heavens to Betsy, even the sun belt is now peppered with NHL franchises. The movies that Hollywood used to make about the Bad News Bears being cutesy-poo playing baseball are now made about the Mighty Ducks. Moreover, most incredible of all, alien soccer is also struggling to squeeze into this Athletic-American smorgasbord.

In the face of all this, I really don't worry anymore how baseball is doing, now that it is just another prime-time fill-in to help Fox win a week. No, but what I do worry—anyhow: wonder—about is whether *we* as a country have lost something of ourselves now that we no longer have a game that, maybe, helps explain the *us* in our "heterogeneous." Jacques Barzun's famous observation from 1954 that "whoever wants to know the heart and mind of America had better learn baseball" simply has no currency anymore.

I'm probably being a bit sappy. Have any other people ever needed a National Pastime that seeks to illuminate them? I mean, the Canadians claim hockey as their totem, but I have never yet met a single Canadian off the ice who at all resembles the Canadians on it. And soccer is everybody else's identifying sport—from Brazil to Norway—so it is really nobody's.

And yet, dammit, maybe it is good to have yourself a National Pastime. Even the coming of spring to America seemed more defined back when Spring Training heralded that; and for the whole country to listen with one ear every afternoon to the "October Classic" bound us in a special way that neither "Seinfeld" nor "E.R." nor Michael Jordan could ever hope to in this niche America. And I know this: of all the games I ever saw, ever, anywhere, the one that touched me the most was one nation's team playing its national sport.

I was in the city of Douala, which you have never heard of, because it is not in any league and has no nickname. Where Douala is, is in Cameroon; and the Cameroonian national team had somehow gotten to the quarterfinals of the World Cup, playing England, and so the whole city, the whole nation, was involved in this one game. The people thronged together in the streets to watch on public TV sets, or massed in bars, with dirt floors, if they had the wherewithal to buy one beer and the emotional forbearance to nurse it.

Nowhere, ever, have I seen people care so about their one thing, this game of their country. This was not overemphasizing sport. It was overemphasizing belonging. That is what baseball did for us in America, when the game was singular and we were young and struggling to find ourselves. When Cameroon scored the go-ahead goal, a stout lady grabbed me and danced with me, her eyes so joyously beaming, and someone snapped a photograph of that ecstasy, and I still keep it on my wall, because it is the best "sports picture" I have.

Unfortunately, Cameroon lost the game. And now we have lost our National Pastime. Someday, I think, we will regret that baseball failed to accompany us across that span to the 21st century.

Our American City

■   ■   ■

I could not help but notice that Cardinal Bernadine of Chicago died last Thursday just hours before the musical *Chicago* opened in revival on Broadway.

Of course, there is no equating the two links in this coincidence. The Cardinal was not only this unbelievably good person, but this force for good, somehow able in this adversarial world to bring us together with grace and civility. And *Chicago*, the musical, however good, is just a play.

What constructs the paradox, though, is that the musical succeeds, wonderfully, darkly, by celebrating exactly all those things that the Chicago cardinal was not—hypocritical, cynical, venal.

Naturally, any metropolis, any large institution, is a creature of extremes, but never, it seemed to me, has anything been writ so contradictorily, so clear, so stark, so perfectly about one place—Chicago!

Chicago—the city of Michael Jordan and Oprah Winfrey!

I think Chicago is the one place that best stands for America. It calls itself the second city, but really, New York is more of the world than the United States, and Los Angeles is only marginally a city, without a core—just people and cars and images all living uneasily together, in motion. Chicago is us.

Hey, after all, Chicago is the city of the greatest *losers* in the nation—the Cubbies!

And Chicago offers the most obvious representation of the sport football—Da Bears—they from Sandburg's "city of big shoulders . . . stormy, husky, brawling . . ." Da Bears!

Maybe Chicago is so much more American because all the swells and dandies really *do* fly over it, going coast to coast, or only deign to meet out there at the O'Hare Hilton. Can't soil the place that way.

Could Siskel and Ebert have worked in New York or L.A.? No way. Neither could have Northwestern . . . or Mike Royko . . . or Ernie Banks . . . or Harry Caray.

But Chicago was *due* Michael Jordan . . . from us to you. It was serendipity.

As one extraordinary American athletic figure of the first half of the century, Babe Ruth was somehow meant to end up in our apex— New York. So, it seems, was the one extraordinary American athletic figure of the second half of this century properly destined for our model—Chicago.

Always before, things in sport started in Chicago, then moved on. So much of modern baseball was formed in that cauldron. Even sports-writing as we know it developed with Chicago baseball. The Cubs and the White Sox ruled the National Pastime when the Yankees were still something called the Highlanders, but after the Black Sox scandal of 1919, the diamond power flowed out of the Windy City.

Likewise, the glamour of pro football in the beginning centered around Chicago—George Halas and The Monsters of The Midway. When the NFL became fashionable, though, it left the Bears behind, bruisers from another time.

But maybe Chicago learned a lot from these lessons. It allowed other cities to carry the early load in pro basketball, even masquerading its own great team with a New York name: the Harlem Globetrotters. But the Chicago Gears, Chicago Stags, Chicago Zephyrs—all failed. Then, though, when pro basketball became stylish—aha, then came the Bulls and Mister Jordan.

Now, of course, for better or worse, the Bulls' owner, Jerry Reinsdorf, who also owns the downscale, stockyard White Sox, rules baseball, controlling his puppet *pro tem* commissioner. Yeah, well that's Chicago, too, isn't it? The back room. And Chicago is on Broadway and in heaven and in all the standings and just about everywhere else, too. Chicago, more than ever, is our American city.

The Van Horns of a Dilemma

■　　■　　■

Keith Van Horn is quickly being recognized as the premier rookie in the NBA. His loquacious teammate on the New Jersey Nets, Jayson Williams, even gushes that Van Horn is the best player to come into the league this whole decade. Why, led by Van Horn, the woebegone Nets—inevitably unknown, altogether unloved—suddenly appear to be genuine contenders, and, incredibly for now, are the glamour team for all sports in the whole metropolitan New York region.

Even more amazing, Keith Van Horn is . . . well, the basketball player is white.

Already, in fact, the obvious surface comparisons to Larry Bird have started—which is pretty ridiculous because Bird was altogether an original, some kind of mutant, irrespective of race. But yes, like Bird, Van Horn is a six-feet-ten country boy with skin the color of Ivory Soap. Van Horn compares himself to Derrick McKey, a solid African-American forward with Indiana. But nobody, besides Van Horn, is looking at style. Only color.

Poor Keith Van Horn. It isn't anything he asked for, but he is going to be the cause for a great deal of cynicism and perhaps almost as much guilt.

Now, the cynicism is easy to perceive. A lot of people will try to use Van Horn's race to sell whatever it is that they're selling—products, ratings, tickets . . . even basketball itself. Conversely, a lot of other people will dismiss him as a fraud, simply because he is white. A certain amount of reverse racism does exist.

The guilt is more complicated, though, because even a lot of sensitive, sincere, dyed-in-the-wool white liberals are going to be cheering for Van Horn at night and not respecting themselves in the morning.

Well, all right, who do we fans cheer for?

Basically, those conditions which most create a rooting interest in sports are allegiance, anomaly, and underdogness.

The last is the easiest. If for no other reason than that we want a good game, we will invariably cheer for the team that's behind.

Allegiance is a bit more complicated. Sure, we support the teams where we live—or where we grew up—or where we went to school. But allegiance can also take on more personal forms. For example, an American of Nigerian descent probably cheers for the Houston Rockets no matter where he lives in this country, because the great Rocket star, Hakeem Olajawon, is from Nigeria. Many Italian-Americans still unabashedly root for The Azzurri, the Italian national soccer team, instead of their own U.S. team.

Moreover, everybody pretty much appreciates these special tugs on the heart and accepts that there are different types of loyalties, and that sometimes heritage can trump residence.

Anomaly also wins our affection. We root for the little guy in the big man's game. Or: Hooray for the Jamaican bobsledders! For the American sumo wrestler! Tiger Woods, the lone prominent black golfer in a white sport, is another obvious example.

But that leads us back onto the Van Horns of a dilemma. Should whites, the majority, the power in this society, be granted the same sort of emotional dispensation when the roles are reversed, when whites are the rare bird? And they certainly are in the NBA, where whites are not so much a minority as they are an endangered species.

The issue is complicated further in that whites behaved atrociously for years, desperately seeking a great white hope to be a heavyweight champion to somehow prove Caucasian superiority. That was nasty. That was unremittingly racist.

But Keith Van Horn is no symbol. As a matter of fact, it is someone like Tiger Woods who bears a far heavier burden. To hear some people talk, Woods is supposed to lead a whole generation of young African-Americans onto the links. Van Horn? White kids already have had every chance to succeed at basketball, and the proof is in the pudding. Only a few of them can cut it, and no matter how good a player Van Horn is, it isn't going to help any little white boy anywhere pull down a rebound.

But what's the rooting etiquette? What's the morality? Isn't Keith Van Horn just a Tiger Woods in sneakers? And if white people do cheer for him—and they will, because that's human nature—does that make white people racist? Or does it just stamp them as another benign example of being proud of your own . . . like everybody else everywhere?

The Team Player: Bill Russell

It was 30 years ago, and the car containing the old retired basketball player and the young sportswriter stopped at a traffic light on the way to the airport in Los Angeles. (Of course, in the nature of things, old players aren't that much older than young writers.) The old player said, "I'm sorry, I'd like to be your friend."

The young writer said, "But I thought we *were* friends."

"No, I'd like to be your friend, and we can be friendly, but friendship takes a lot of effort if it's going to work, and we're really going off in different directions in our lives, so, no, we really can't be friends."

And that was as close as I ever got to being on Bill Russell's team.

In the years after that exchange I often reflected on what Russell had said to me, and I marveled that he would have thought so deeply about what constituted friendship. It was, obviously, the same sort of philosophical contemplation about the concept of Team that had made him the most divine teammate there ever was.

Look, you can stand at a bar and scream all you want about who was the greatest athlete and which was the greatest sports dynasty, and you can shout out your precious statistics, and maybe you're right, and maybe the red-faced guy down the bar—the one with the foam on his beer and the fancy computer rankings—is right, but nobody really knows. The only thing we know for sure about superiority in sports in the United States of America in the 20th century is that Bill Russell and the Boston Celtics teams he led stand alone as the ultimate winners. Fourteen times in Russell's career it came down to one game, win you must, or lose and go home. Fourteen times the team with Bill Russell on it won.

But the fires always smoldered in William Felton Russell, and he simply wouldn't suffer fools—most famously the ones who intruded upon his sovereign privacy to petition him for an autograph. He was that rare star athlete who was also a social presence, a voice to go with the body. Unafraid, he spoke out against all things, great and small, that bothered him. He wouldn't even show up at the Hall of Fame when he was inducted, because he had concluded it was a racist institution. Now, despite the importunings of his friends, he is the only living selection among ESPN's 50 top athletes of the century who hasn't agreed to talk to the network. That is partly because one night he heard an ESPN announcer praise the '64 Celtics as "Bob Cousy's last team." Cousy was retired by then.

Russell says, "They go on television, they're supposed to know."

Cousy says, "What the Celtics did with Russ will never be duplicated in a team sport. Never."

Of course, genuine achievement is everywhere devalued these days. On the 200th anniversary of his death, George Washington has been so forgotten that they're toting his false teeth around the republic, trying to restore interest in the Father of Our Country with a celebrity-style gimmick. So should we be surprised that one spectacular show-off dunk on yesterday's highlight reel counts for more than some ancient decade's worth of championships back-before-Larry&Magic-really-invented-the-sport-of-basketball?

Tony Heinsohn, who played with Russell for nine years and won 10 NBA titles himself, as player and coach, sums it up best: "Look, all I know is, the guy won two NCAA championships, 50-some college games in a row, the ['56] Olympics, then he came to Boston and won 11 championships in 13 years, and they named an f----- tunnel after Ted Williams." By that standard, only a cathedral on a hill deserves to have Bill Russell's name attached to it.

But then, too often when I try to explain the passion of Russell himself and his devotion to his team and to victory, I'm inarticulate. It's like trying to describe a color to a blind person. All I can say, in tongue-tied exasperation, is, You had to be there. And I'm sorry for you if you weren't.

Russell was right, too. The two of us did go our separate ways after he dropped me at the airport. He left the playing life exactly 30 years ago this week, on May 5, 1969, with his last championship, and my first child was born on May 7. So there were new things we both had to do, and in the years that followed we were together only a couple of times, briefly.

Then a few weeks ago we met at his house in Seattle, and for the first time in 30 years I climbed into his car. The license plate on the Lexus reads KELTIC 6, and on the driver's hands were two NBA championship rings: his first, from '57, and his last, from 12 years later. We took off together for the San Francisco Bay Area, there to visit Bill's father, Charlie, who is 86 and lives in a nursing home. It was 13 hours on the road. We stopped along the way at McDonald's and for gas and for coffee and for a box of Good 'n' Plenty and to pee and to buy lottery tickets once we got over the California line, because there was a big jackpot that week in the Golden State. In Oakland we found a Holiday Inn and ate a fish dinner at Jack London Square, where a bunch of elderly black ladies sat at the next table. "I was thinking they were old," Bill said, nodding his gray head toward them. "Then I remembered, I'm probably their age." I laughed. "Hey, what are you laughing at?" he roared. So, like that, wherever we happened to be going in the car, our destination was really back in time.

Back to the Russell Era. Back to the Celtics and the University of San Francisco Dons, to the Jones Boys and Cooz. Yes, and back to Wilt. To Satch and Heinie and the sixth men. Red, of course. Elgin and Jerry. But more than just the baskets, more than just the '60s. Russell's family experience describes the arc of a century. Why, when Charlie Russell was growing up in Louisiana, he actually knew men and women who had been slaves. He told me about "making marks in the ground" to help his illiterate father calculate. I was baffled by that expression. "It's from the old country," Bill explained. That is, from Africa, centuries before, passed along orally. And as we were talking, and the old man— wearing a jaunty red sweat suit and a green hat—reminisced about more recent times, he suddenly smiled and said something I couldn't quite make out. I leaned closer, "What's that, Mr. Russell? How *what?*"

"No, *Hal,*" he said. "All on account of Hal DeJulio." Charlie remembered so well, after all this time. You see, if young William hadn't, by chance, been there on the one day that DeJulio showed up at Oakland High in the winter of '51, none of this would have happened. None of it at all. But life often hangs by such serendipitous threads, and sometimes, like this time, we are able to take them and weave them into a scarf for history's neck.

The long trip to Oakland was not unusual for Russell. He enjoys driving great distances. After all, he is most comfortable with himself and next most comfortable with close friends, cackling that thunderous laugh of his that Cousy fears he'll hear resonating in the afterlife. *Playful* is the surprising word that former Georgetown coach John Thompson thinks of first for Russell, and old number 6 himself always refers to his Celtics as "the guys" in a way that sounds curiously adolescent. Hey, guys, we can put the game on right here!

Cynosure on the court though he was, Russell never enjoyed being the celebrity alone. "I still think he's a shy, mother's son," says Karen Kenyatra Russell, his daughter, "and even now he's uncomfortable being in the spotlight by himself." Maybe that's one reason the team mattered so to him; it hugged him back. "I got along with all the guys," Russell says, "and nobody had to kiss anybody's ass. We were just a bunch of men—and, oh, what marvelous gifts my teammates gave to me."

"He was just so nice to be with on the team," says Frank Ramsey, who played with Russell from 1956 to '64, Russell's first eight years in the NBA. "It was only when others came around that he set up that wall."

Russell loves nothing better than to talk. "Oh, the philosophizing," recalls Satch Sanders, who played with Russell from '60 to '69. "If he started off and said, 'You see,' we just rolled our eyes, because we knew he was going off on something." Yet in more recent times Russell went for years without permitting himself to be interviewed. "If I'm going to answer the questions, I want them to be my questions, the right questions," he says—a most unlikely prerogative, given the way journalism works. O.K., so no interviews. Privacy edged into reclusiveness.

On the other hand, as upside-down as this may sound, Russell believes he can share more by not giving autographs, because instead of an impersonal scribbled signature, a civil two-way conversation may ensue. Gently: "I'm sorry, I don't give autographs."

"You won't?"

"No, *won't* is personal. I don't. But thank you for asking." And then, if he senses a polite reaction, he might say, "Would you like to shake hands with me?" And maybe chat.

Utterly dogmatic, Russell wouldn't bend even to give his Celtics teammates autographs. One time this precipitated an ugly quarrel with Sanders, who wanted a simple keepsake: the signature of every Celtic he'd played with. "You, Satch, of all people, know how I feel," Russell snapped.

"Dammit, I'm your teammate, Russ."

Nevertheless, when the shouting was over, Russell still wouldn't sign. Thompson, who was Russell's backup on the Celtics for two years, is sure that Russell never took pleasure from these sorts of incidents. "No, it bothered him," Thompson says. "But doing it his way, on his own terms, was more important to him. And that's Bill. Even if it hurt him, he was going to remain consistent"

Russell speaks, often, in aphorisms that reflect his attitudes. "It is better to understand than to be understood," he told his daughter. "A groove can become a rut," he advised his teammates. And perhaps the one that goes most to his own heart: "You should live a life with as few negatives as possible—without acquiescing."

So, alone, unbothered, one of the happiest times Russell ever had was driving around the West on a motorcycle in the '70s. When he takes a long automobile trip by himself these days, he listens to National Public Radio, CDs and tapes he has recorded to suit his own eclectic taste. On one tape, for example, are Stevie Wonder and Burl Ives. On another: Willie Nelson and Aretha Franklin. But also, always, Russell sets aside two hours to drive in complete silence, meditating. He has never forgotten what Huey Newton, the Black Panther, once told him: that the five years he spent in solitary confinement were, in fact, liberating.

Russell returned twice to the NBA after he retired as the Celtics' player-coach following the 1968–69 season. As coach and general manager of the Seattle SuperSonics from 1973 to '77, he built the team that would win the championship two years after he left. A brief tenure with the Sacramento Kings during the '87–88 season was, however, disastrous and unhappy. On the night he was fired, Russell cleaned out his office; returned to his Sacramento house, which was contiguous to a golf course; and stayed there, peacefully by himself, for weeks, venturing out only for provisions and golf. He didn't read the newspapers or watch television news. "To this day, I don't know what they said about me," he says. He put his house on the market immediately, and only when it sold, three weeks later, did he return to Seattle, where for 26 years he has lived in the same house on Mercer Island, one tucked away into a sylvan hillside, peeking down at Lake Washington.

Divorced in 1973, Russell lived as a single parent with Karen for several years, until she left for Georgetown in 1980 and then Harvard Law. Alone after that, Russell says, there were times when he would hole up and practice his household "migratory habits." That is, he would stock the kitchen, turn on the burglar alarm, turn off the phone and, for the next week, migrate about the house, going from one couch to another, reading voraciously and watching TV, ideally *Jeopardy!* or *Star Trek*—just bivouacked there, the tallest of all the Trekkies, sleeping on various sofas. He was quite content. The finest team player ever is by nature a loner who, by his own lights, achieved such group success because of his abject selfishness. You will never begin to understand Bill Russell until you appreciate that he is, at once, consistent and contradictory.

Russell began to emerge from his most pronounced period of solitude about three years ago. Shortly after arriving in Seattle in 1973, he had gone into a jewelry store, where he hit it off with the saleswoman. Her name is Marilyn Nault. "Let me tell you," she sighs, "working in a jewelry store is the worst place to meet a man, because if one comes in, it's to buy something for another woman." But over the years—skipping through Russell's next, brief marriage, to a former Miss USA—Marilyn and Bill remained friends. Also, she impressed him as a very competitive dominoes player. When Bill's secretary died in 1995, Marilyn volunteered to give him a hand, and all of a sudden, after more than two decades, they realized they were in love. So it was that one day, when Marilyn came over to help Bill with his accounts, she just stayed on with him in the house on the hill under the tall firs.

There is a big grandfather clock in the house that chimes every hour. Like Bill, Marilyn doesn't hear it anymore. She has also learned how to sleep with the TV on, because Bill, a terrible night owl, usually falls asleep with the clicker clasped tightly in his hand. Usually the Golf Channel is on. Imagine waking up to the Golf Channel. Marilyn has also learned to appreciate long car trips. Twice she and Bill have driven across the continent and back. Their lives are quite blissful; he has never seemed to be so at peace. "They're the ultimate '50s couple," Karen reports. "They have nothing but kind things to say about each other, and it's part of their arrangement that at least once a day, he has to make her laugh."

Yet for all the insular contentment Russell has always sought in his life, his play was marked by the most extraordinary intensity. If he threw up before a big game, the Celtics were sure everything would be all right. If he didn't, then Boston's coach, Red Auerbach, would tell Russell to go back to the toilet—order him to throw up. Rookies who saw Russell for the first time in training camp invariably thought he had lost it over the summer, because he would pace himself, even play possum in some exhibitions, to deceive pretenders to his throne. Then, in the first game of the real season, the rookies would be bug-eyed as the genuine article suddenly appeared, aflame with competition. It was as if the full moon had brought out a werewolf.

Cousy says, "The level of intensity among the big guys is different. You put a bunch of huge guys, seminaked, out there before thousands of people, and you expect them to become killers. But it just isn't in their nature. Kareem [Abdul-Jabbar] probably had the best skills of all big men, and he played till he was 42. If he'd had Russ's instincts, it's hard to imagine how much better he'd have been. But he'd have burned out long before 42."

Sanders: "There's no reason why some centers today couldn't block shots like Russ did. Only no one has the intestinal fortitude. A center blocks one shot now, the other team grabs the ball and scores, and the center stands there pouting, with that I-can't-do-everything look. Russell would block three, four shots in a row—I mean from different players— and then just glower at us."

Russell: "Once I blocked seven shots in a row. When we finally got the ball, I called timeout and said, 'This s--- has got to stop.' " Some years Russell would be so exhausted after the playoffs that, as he describes it, "I'd literally be tired to my bones. I mean, for four, five weeks, my bones would hurt."

Russell believes that Wilt Chamberlain suffered the worst case of big-man syndrome; he was too nice, scared that he might hurt somebody. The year after Russell retired, in the famous seventh game of the NBA Finals at Madison Square Garden, Willis Reed, the New York Knicks center, limped onto the court against the Los Angeles Lakers, inspiring his team and freezing Chamberlain into a benign perplexity. Russell scowls just thinking about it. "If I'm the one playing Willis when he comes out limping," he snarls, "it only would have emphasized my goal to beat them that much worse." Russell would have called Six—his play—again and again, going mercilessly at the cripple, exploiting Reed without remorse. The Celtics would have won. Which was the point. Always.

"To be the best in the world," Russell says, all but licking his lips. "Not last week. Not next year. But right now. You are the best. And it's even more satisfying as a team, because that's more difficult. If I play well, that's one thing. But to make others play better . . ." He grins, savoring the memory. "You understand what I mean?" Bill often says that, invariably when there is no doubt. It has to do with emphasis more than clarity. In fact, I can sort of visualize him saying that after he blocked a shot. *You understand what I mean?*

Yes.

It is difficult to comprehend whence came Russell's extraordinary will on the court. Karen recalls only once in her life that her father so much as raised his voice to anyone. "I just never saw the warrior in him," she says. "As a matter of fact, as I got to understand men better, I appreciated all the more how much of a feminine side my father has." Ironically it was Russell's mother, Katie, who appears to have given him his fire, while his father, Charlie, instilled the more reflective component.

What do you remember your father telling you, Bill?

"Accept responsibility for your actions. . . Honor thy father and mother . . . If they give you $10 for a day's work, you give them $12 worth in return."

Even more clearly, Russell recalls the gritty creed his mother gave him when he was a little boy growing up in segregation and the Depression in West Monroe, La. Katie said, "William, you are going to meet people who just don't like you. On sight. And there's nothing you can do about it, so don't worry. Just be yourself. You're no better than anyone else, but no one's better than you."

One time, when he was nine, William—for that is what he was called till basketball made him just plain Bill—came home to the family's little shotgun shack after being slapped by a boy in a gang. Katie dragged him out to find the gang. She made her son fight every boy, one by one. "The fact is, I had to fight back," Bill says. "It wasn't important whether I won or lost."

When he and I visited his father, Charlie said this about Katie: "She was handsome and sweet, and she loved me, and she showed it by giving me children." Bill was very touched by that, subdued. Then Charlie smiled and added, "She played some basketball too—the bloomer girls."

Bill shot to his feet, screaming, "Daddy, I never knew that!" Then there was such vintage Russellian cackling that the old fellow in the next bed woke up, a little discombobulated by all the fuss.

If Katie Russell had any athletic instincts, though, they paled before her passion for education. It was an article of faith with her, a high school dropout, that her two sons—Charlie Jr., the elder by two years, and William—would go to college. Bill has a vivid memory of his mother taking him to get a library card. That was not mundane; that was a signal event. And this is what he remembers of West Monroe, altogether: "I remember that my mother and father loved me, and we had a good time, but the white people were mean. But I was safe. I was always safe. In all my life, every day, not for one second have I ever thought I could have had better parents."

Then, in 1946, when William was 12, his mother died of kidney failure, with very little warning. Katie Russell was only 32. The last thing she told her husband was, "Make sure to send the boys to college." The last thing she told William was, "Don't be difficult for your father, because he's doing the best he can."

The Russells had moved to Oakland not long before, after Charlie was denied a raise at the mill in West Monroe because he was black. Now the father and his two sons boarded the train with Katie's casket to return to Louisiana to bury her. It was after the funeral that young William heard Katie's sisters arguing about which one of them would take the two motherless boys to raise. That was the custom in these matters. Charlie interrupted. "No," he said, "I won't let you. I'm taking the two boys back with me." Though there was still much protesting from the aunts, that was that.

"I told my two boys they'd lost their best friend," Charlie says, "but we could make it if we tried." The goal remained to get them through college. Charlie Jr. was developing into a pretty good athlete, but his father couldn't spend much time thinking about games. After all, he'd had to quit school to work; unlike Katie, he'd never even been able to play basketball. It certainly never occurred to him that now, for the first time, there were people like Hal DeJulio around, scouting black teenagers eager to give the best ones a free college education just for playing some ball.

The radar detector on the Lexus beeped. Russell slowed down. A bit. We had driven through Washington and most of Oregon, too. A billboard advertised the Seven Feathers Casino. Ah, fin de siècle America: casinos, cable, cosmetic surgery and scores from around the leagues. Russell, who just turned 65, is fairly pragmatic about the new ways of the world. He never put on any airs—witness that amazing laugh of his, which is the loud leitmotif of his life. "I try not to stifle anything," he says. "It isn't just my laugh. If I have to sneeze, I just let it go. You understand what I mean?"

He is also helped by the fact that even as a young man, he looked venerable. Other players would dart onto the court, all snappy and coltish. Number 6 would stalk out hunched over, stroking that dagger of a goatee, and stand there dark and grim. We always talk about teams "executing." All right, then: Russell appeared very much an executioner.

Jerry West, who was denied about a half-dozen championships strictly because of Russell, remembers. "When the national anthem was played, I always found my eyes going to Bill. He did that just right, stand there for the anthem. He was a statue, but there was a grace to him. Even just standing still: grace."

Whereas Russell is disappointed by much that he sees on the court today, he does not lambaste the players. He is just as prone to blame the coaches for taking so much of the spontaneity out of basketball. "The coaches dumb players down now," he says, clearly irritated. "They're stifling innovation. They're not letting them play outside the system." Pretty soon, it seems, the Celtics' fast break, which was the most gloriously coordinated rapid action in sport, will be nothing more than athletic nostalgia, like the dropkick.

And the players? Well, it's not just them. "All the kids in this generation—they really don't have a clue," Russell says. "They don't know, but they really don't care. A lot of my peers are annoyed that the players accepted a salary cap. I'm not. I know there's not supposed to be a limit on what you can make in America, but then, the NBA may also be the only place where there's a high roof for a minimum. When I speak to the players, I just say they have a responsibility to be caretakers. When you leave, there should be no less for those who follow you than there was when you arrived."

We started up Mount Ashland, whose other side goes down into California. Russell said, "Of course, a lot of my peers are also annoyed with all this money these kids are making. Me? I love it when I see a guy get a hundred million, because that says something good about what I did. You understand what I mean?"

This is, however, not to say that some of the guys making a hundred million—or getting by on only 50 or 60—have a clue about what Bill Russell did. It took years of hectoring by some of his friends to persuade Russell to step out of the safe shadows, to display himself again. His legacy was fading. John Thompson fairly bellows, "Nobody cares when some turkey like me won't give interviews. But Bill Russell! I say, Bill: You owe it to the people you love not to take this to your grave. I want my grandchildren to hear you talk about all you were."

So, while sometimes it mortifies Russell that he is, like everybody else, marketing himself—"I can't believe I'm doing all the things I swore I'd never do," he moans—there is the reasonable argument that truth nowadays must be packaged; otherwise, only the hype will survive as history. So Russell is planning a speaking tour and an HBO documentary about his life, and Karen is working on a book about motivation with her father, and a huge charitable evening to honor Russell is scheduled at the FleetCenter in Boston on May 26, where his number 6 jersey will be ceremonially re-retired. Russell is even selling about 500 autographs a year, and when we went to ship some signed basketballs to a sports collectibles store, I felt rather as if I had gone over to Handgun Control and mailed out some Saturday Night Specials.

So, O.K., it's the millennium, it's a different world. But we're not that far removed from the old one. Look at Bill Russell in 1999. His grandfather Jake was of the family's first generation born free on this continent. When this fading century began, Jake Russell was tying to scratch out a living with a mule. The Klan went after him because even though he couldn't read or write a lick, he led a campaign to raise money among the poor blacks around West Monroe to build a schoolhouse and pay a teacher to educate their children at a time when the state wouldn't have any truck with that.

At the other end of Jake's life, in 1969, he went over to Shreveport, La., to see the Celtics play an exhibition. By then his grandson had become the first African-American coach in a major professional sport. Jake sat with his son, Charlie, watching Bill closely during timeouts. He wasn't quite sure what he was seeing; Celtics huddles could be terribly democratic back then. It was before teams had a lot of assistants with clipboards. Skeptically Jake asked his son, "He's the boss?" Charlie nodded.

Jake took that in. "Of the white men too?"

"The white men too."

Jake just shook his head. After the game he went into the decrepit locker room, which had only one shower for the whole team. The Celtics were washing up in pairs, and when Jake arrived, Sam Jones and John Havlicek were in the shower, passing the one bar of soap back and forth—first the naked black man, then the naked white man stepping under the water spray. Jake watched, agape. Finally he said, "I never thought I'd see anything like that."

Of course, it was hardly a straight line upward to brotherhood. Nor was Bill Russell afraid to point that out to America; he could be unforgiving and sometimes angry, which meant he was called arrogant by those who didn't care for his kind. Russell invested in a rubber plantation in Liberia, and at a time when African-Americans were known as Negroes, and the word black was an insult, Russell started calling himself black. In the civil rights movement he became a bold, significant figure far beyond the parquet.

Thompson says, "It took a long time for me to be able to accept him as a person, as another guy, because I admired and respected him so. Russell made me feel safe. It was not that he was going to save me if anybody threatened me. Somehow I knew it was going to be all right so long as I was with him. I was going to be safe."

Often, edgy whites misunderstood him, though. Once a magazine quoted him as saying, "I hate all white people." Russell walked into the cramped old Celtics locker room, where equality reigned: Every player had one stool and two nails. Frank Ramsey glanced up from the magazine. "Hey, Russell, I'm white," he said, "You hate me?"

The two teammates looked into each other's eyes. "I was misquoted, Frank," was all Russell said. That was the end of it; he and Ramsey remained as close as ever. A few years earlier, too, there had been a big brouhaha in Kentucky, Ramsey's home state. Russell and other black Celtics had pulled out of an exhibition game there because the hotels were segregated. There was a lot of talk that Russell should not have embarrassed Ramsey that way. None of the talk came from Ramsey, though. Then, in 1966, when Russell succeeded Auerbach and became the first black coach (while continuing to play), he accepted the job only after trying to persuade Ramsey to return to basketball, from which he had retired in 1964, and coach the Celtics. Russell thought that would be better for the team than for him to make history.

The Celtics really did get along the way teams are supposed to in sports mythology. Russell threw Christmas parties for his teammates and their families. In 1962 he took the astonished rookie Havlicek around town to get a good price on a stereo. "All of us were strangers in a place far from home," Russell says, "But we made it into a unique situation. Cousy started it. He was absolutely sincere about being a good teammate."

Still, it was different away from the warm cocoon of the Celtics. One night in 1971 the team assembled in the Boston suburb of Reading, where Russell lived, to be with him as the town proudly honored their captain. It was the first time Heinsohn ever saw Russell cry, he was so happy. A few months later some people broke into Russell's house, rampaged, smashed his trophies, defecated in his bed and spread the excrement over his walls. They didn't want any black man in their town. But in the locker room Russell never talked about the terrible things that happened to him so close to the Celtics' city. "He was too proud to let people know," Heinsohn says.

Cousy still feels guilty. "I wish I'd done more to support Russ," he says. "We were so close, as teammates, but we all should have been more aware of his anger." Cousy draws a deep sigh. "But you know jocks—all into the macho thing. Always afraid to let the conversation be anything more than superficial. We mature so much later than anybody else."

So they just had to settle for winning.

Russell drove the Lexus into Oakland. When he was a little boy, after rural Dixie, his big new California hometown seemed such a wondrously exciting place. But Oakland wasn't Valhalla. "I couldn't even go downtown," he says. "The cops would chase the black kids away. And you still have those soldiers in blue in the streets. In terms of economics, things are certainly better in America today. But the criminal justice system hasn't improved."

Still, even if the police ran young William out of stylish Oakland, he grew up in contentment. Even after Katie's death, the Russells enjoyed the sort of family embrace that is denied so many black boys today. Charlie Jr. would graduate from college and become a social worker and a playwright. William, for his part, was a bookworm. For someone who ended up 6' 10", he grew very late and wasn't much noticed on the basketball court. But then, he also wasn't much good. Frank Robinson, the great baseball player, was on the McClymonds High basketball team with Russell, and he says, "He couldn't even put the ball in the basket when he dunked." Russell was scheduled to graduate in January 1951, whereupon it was his intention to get a job in the shipyards and save up to go to college part time.

This is surely what would have happened, too, except that Hal DeJulio, who had played at the University of San Francisco and occasionally steered young players toward the school, went to an Oakland

High–McClymonds game one day to help the Oakland coach. USF was a struggling urban Catholic college that didn't even have a gymnasium; the team had to settle for leftovers and overlooks. As a consequence, DeJulio noticed McClymonds' center, the unknown string bean with the incredibly long arms, who had a rare good game that day. A week later DeJulio showed up unannounced at the Russells' house and offered William a scholarship to San Francisco. Only then did he tell Dons coach Phil Woolpert about his find. Woolpert was skeptical but agreed to take William on.

It was that close to there never being a Bill Russell. "It gives me chills," Karen says.

Even as Russell won his first NCAA title, in 1955, his coach—like most everybody else—couldn't yet fathom that Russell was this genius who had, in effect, created a whole new game of basketball. For instance, Woolpert concurred with the conventional wisdom that to play defense you must not leave your feet, "and here I was airborne most of the time," Russell recalls. Although the Dons' victories piled up, Woolpert kept telling Russell he was "fundamentally unsound." He would say, "You can't do that!" Russell would respond, "But I just did."

Nevertheless Russell liked Woolpert—"a fine and decent man," he calls the coach—who was being excoriated for starting three black players: Russell, K. C. Jones and Hal Perry. Woolpert was flooded with hate mail, and rival coaches snidely called him Saperstein, after Abe, the coach of the Harlem Globetrotters. Although the NCAA championship won by the 1965–66 Texas Western team, with five black starters, has over time been painted as a watershed event, the fact is that Russell was as much pioneer as avatar. The African-American domination of basketball traces to two teams, his teams: USF in college, Boston in the pros. Texas Western was but the end product of what Russell inspired— and what he had suffered through—a decade earlier.

K. C. Jones remembers an occasion in Oklahoma City, where USF was practicing, when local citizens threw coins at the players as if they were clowns in the circus. Inside, Jones raged. But Russell, smiling sardonically, picked up the change and handed it to Woolpert. "Here, Coach, hold this for me," was all he said.

"Then," Jones says, "he took it out on the opposition."

"I decided in college to win," Russell says matter-of-factly. "Then it's a historical fact, and nobody can take it away from me. You understand what I mean?"

Indisputably, his race diminished Russell in the eyes of many biased observers, but, withal, it was the rare fair-minded expert who could comprehend the brilliance of this original force. Indeed, even as Russell won every year in the NBA, the fact that Chamberlain averaged sky-rocket numbers was more beguiling to the unsophisticated. Meanwhile, in Boston, the stylish—and Caucasian—Cousy continued to hold the greater affection. Auerbach recalls one time when Cousy was injured but the Celtics swept a five-game road trip, with "Russ blocking a million shots." When the team returned home, it was greeted by a headline that made no reference to the victory streak, asking only, WILL COUSY PLAY TONIGHT? "This coulda killed my team," Auerbach says. He felt obliged to order the exhausted players to go directly from the airport to the Garden, there to air the matter as a team.

Russell was a great admirer of Cousy, though, and the two led together. If they called a team meeting, they'd start off by soliciting opinions on how they—Cousy and Russell—were lacking. After that, who could bitch about anybody else? Jones cannot recall a single instance, either in college or in the NBA, when Russell "jumped on anyone's butt. But Bill definitely had his Machiavellian side. Anybody who didn't fit in, he'd just dismiss him."

Russell's simple key to a successful team was to encourage each player to do what he did best. "Remember," he says, "each of us has a finite amount of energy, and things you do well don't require as much. Things you don't do well take more concentration. And if you're fatigued by that, then the things you do best are going to be affected." The selfishness of successful team play—"I was very selfish," he declares—sounds paradoxical, but a team profits if each player revels in his strength. Still, Russell points out, there is a fine line between idealistic shared greed and typical self-gratification. "You must let your energy flow to the team," he says.

And sometimes, of course, you simply must sacrifice. For instance, one of the hardest things Russell had to learn to accept was that if he filled one lane on a fast break and Heinsohn was on the other flank, Cousy would give Heinsohn the ball—and the basket. Every time. "He simply had so much confidence in Heinie," Russell says. "So I had to discipline myself to run that break all-out, even if I knew I wasn't going to get the ball."

Above all, though, the key to Russell's success was that his greatest individual talent was the one that most benefited the team. It was not only that he blocked shots; Auerbach estimates that 80% of the time Russell could also direct the blocked ball into Celtics hands, usually fast-break bound. Moreover—and here is why statistical analyses of Russell's play are meaningless—the mere threat of a Russell block made opponents think twice about shooting, while the other Celtics could gamble aggressively on defense, knowing that number 6 would save them. "Other teams, all you hear is 'Switch!' 'Pick!' 'Help!' " Thompson says. "On the Celtics you'd only hear one word: 'Russ!' "

Although Russell made his team nearly invincible, the singular image that survives is of that one extraordinary athlete. That's the trouble with old sportswriters: They remember the beauty they saw far better than people today can visualize it from reading statistics. "It wasn't just that Bill was the whole package—and he was," West says, "but there was such presence he brought to the game."

By himself, in fact, Russell was hugely responsible for changing the way the public thought about big men in basketball. Before Russell, the giants were often dismissed as gawky goons or, like Chamberlain, bully-boy Goliaths. But Russell was as comfortable in his shape as he was in his skin, and it showed. "I am tall," he says. "O.K.? And if that's the only reason I can play, that's all right too. Don't deny your biggest asset. I'm a tall black guy. O.K.? No apologies, no bragging." In a game that was much more choreographed than the one today, no one could fail to see the elegance of Russell—this great winged bird swooping about, long angles that magically curved, rising high before your eyes. In fact, Russell saw himself as an artist, his play as a work of art. "If you can take something to levels that very few other people can reach," he says without vanity, "then what you're doing becomes art."

Unashamed, he sought to play the perfect game. "Certain standards I set for that," he says. "First, of course, we had to win. I had to get at least 25 rebounds, eight assists and eight blocks. I had to make 60% of my shots, and I had to run all my plays perfectly, setting picks and filling the lanes. Also, I had to say all the right things to my teammates—and to my opponents." Ironically, the closest he ever came to achieving that ideal was one night when he lived up to all his standards except the most obvious one: He did not make a single basket in 11 attempts.

Never mind. There were many discrete exquisite moments that made up for never quite attaining that comprehensive dream. "Sometimes," Russell told me in the car, breaking into a smile at the recollection, "sometimes if I could do something exactly the way I wanted, it was such an exhilarating feeling that I wanted to scream."

That memory was so joyous, in fact, that he missed the turn to the airport. Yes, 30 years later, he was driving me to an airport again. We had seen his father that morning, so our mission was accomplished. And now Karen was coming up to visit Charlie, so three generations of Russells would be together, Bill in the middle.

Karen returned, not long ago, from her first visit to West Monroe. "We're like so many other Americans, all scattered to the winds," she says, "and it was, for me, like finding my lost tribe. It also put my father's incredible journey into a context I'd never been able to put it before." She visited Katie's grave, and it made Karen think: "She had the vision for my father, as he had the vision for me."

Charlie was touched when Karen hugged him and told him this. Bill looked at them—the father who had a sixth-grade education and the daughter who'd graduated from Harvard Law. There they were, a whole century's worth of one American family. When Bill was young, in his game, players like him were known as pivotmen. Now, in his family, he is something of that again, the axis on which the Russells, ahead and behind him, turn. But then, it was the same way with basketball. Bill Russell was the pivot on which the whole sport turned. You understand what I mean?

A Gentle Goliath: A Tribute to Wilt Chamberlain

Seven feet, one and one-sixteenth inches tall was Wilton Norman Chamberlain. No one, however, believed him. He once said to me, "I could tell a little person, 'Oh, I'm 10' 3",' and he would answer, 'No, you're taller than that.' " To almost everyone he encountered, Wilt appeared simply larger than life, a human optical illusion. He loomed. It was as if he blocked out the sun.

Were it only that. Were it only everyone else's perception. But the irony was that Wilt Chamberlain, who died of a heart attack last week at 63, was never quite big enough even for himself. Especially in his prime, he constantly felt compelled to do more, to be better, to go higher. For someone so curious and sensitive, he was too influenced —seduced, even—by his own physical preeminence. In a world where he knew he was the Most Man, he never would allow himself the legal dictum *res ipsa loquitur*: the thing speaks for itself. No, Wilt needed numbers to validate himself. If the most points were not enough, then he would get the most rebounds, then the most assists. Never take a rest. Never foul out. Alas, near the end, when he crowed of having had assignations with 20,000 women, that numbing statistical braggadocio made him a figure of fun. Always before he had been controversial, often even villainous, but never foolish.

As bad as his judgment was in that case, he didn't deserve ridicule. Wilt's other flaw, you see, was that he was a very nice and gentle man. His best friends called him Dippy, which is hardly a name we associate with ogres and giants. David and Dippy? I don't think so. Bill Russell even pointed out that if Wilt had possessed a mean streak, there would have been no stopping him. On the one occasion when Wilt was very angry at me, he delegated Jerry West to suggest that I depart from the Los Angeles Lakers' locker room; he couldn't bear such confrontation himself.

In fact, I rarely recall that great deep voice rising in anger, although, coincidentally, the last time I saw Wilt, we fussed as friends. "Sometimes, my man, you take a right turn, and I just don't know where you are going!" he groaned, alluding to something I had written. By chance, someone snapped a shot of me then, pointing what appears to be a menacing finger at Wilt. I look at that photo now—Wilt in some outrageous *Arabian Nights* outfit and I'm amazed at how surprised and cowed (well, he was sitting down) he is, reacting to my impolite gesture. It shames me because I know Wilt never would have acted so intemperately toward me or any other mere mortal. He was careful not to scare the little people. A little late, but: I apologize, my man.

This night in question was last May, in Boston, where Russell was being celebrated. Wilt had flown across the country on his own hook, even though he knew that he was traveling 3,000 miles just to be the evening's appointed bad guy. No matter. He had learned to endure the cape of villainy slung round his shoulders.

Wilt always recognized that the loss that hurt the most—and that set the precedent for his being perceived as a loser—was his Kansas team's triple-overtime defeat by North Carolina in the 1957 NCAA final (in which, in fact, he played valiantly). Afterward, he morosely walked the rainy streets of Kansas City, and when he left college after the next season, it would be another 40 years before he returned to the campus. The shame he inflicted on himself for this defeat simmered for that long. "That goddamn one against Carolina," he would mutter. Worse, at the beginning of the game Tar Heels coach Frank McGuire had sent out his shortest starter, 5' 10" Tommy Kearns, to jump center against Wilt—or, really, to call mocking attention to Wilt's height. Cruelly, it worked; it hurt him. Yet McGuire would become Chamberlain's coach with the Philadelphia Warriors in his greatest quantitative season—50.4 points a game, in 1961–62—and Kearns would become his friend and stockbroker. So there Wilt was in Boston for Russell, too, ready to take his public lumps to help honor his old friend and foe.

Oh yes, the January before last Wilt finally went back to Kansas, where he put on his old letter jacket (which still fit perfectly) and watched as his jersey was raised above the court at Allen Fieldhouse. "I felt like I let the university down," he told the crowd.

"No, no!" the Kansans cried back.

"Rock, chalk, Jayhawk," Wilt said softly, and he cried.

There was that sweet side the hugeness screened. For example, for all his masculine swagger and the sexual stats, Chamberlain counted many women among his friends and personally financed women's track and volleyball teams. He was a devotee of women's tennis. In a phrase almost Victorian, Wilt always decorously referred to his women as *young ladies*, even as he felt he had to total them up. He never married, and he told one of our mutual friends that only once, when he was playing in San Francisco in the mid-1960s, did he ever contemplate such a possibility. He simply didn't want to forgo his independence, and anyway, in an overpopulated world, he said, "I feel no need to raise any little Wilties."

Although he always lived alone, Wilt never seemed to be a lonely man. He had learned to love Goliath. He was accessible. He relished a debate, adored travel and delighted in an eclectic range of the globe's roster of human beings. Indeed, it may be most revealing that, of all his basketball years, the one he enjoyed most was the one between leaving Kansas and joining the NBA, when he was a Harlem Globetrotter, globetrotting with no pressure on him to perform heroically, to quantify anything. I always thought that Chamberlain would have been much more content in an individual sport—such as track and field, in which he excelled, disparately, in the high jump and the shot put. The conflict between team and personal supremacy forever confounded him.

There's no doubt that he could do, by himself, almost anything he ordained. I learned that myself, just as the centers he toyed with under the hoop did. In 1969 I wrote a cover story on Chamberlain for *Sports Illustrated*. He was 32 then, his great scoring days were behind him, and I ventured this memorable line: "There is a growing school of thought that he no longer possesses sufficient moves to make him a bona fide high-scoring threat." It had, in fact, been more than a year since he had made 50 in any game. So: The very next game he played after the magazine came out, Wilt went for 60. Yet in the seventh game of the NBA Finals that year, Russell's swan song, the man who never missed a moment of any importance on the court took himself out of the game, sore-kneed, when the Lakers fell behind the Boston Celtics. Only when Los Angeles rallied without him did Chamberlain petition to go back in, but coach Butch van Breda Kolff refused. It cost van Breda Kolff his job. It cost Wilt more, his image.

His defenders—and it almost defined what sort of a person you were, whether you fell into the Chamberlain or the Russell camp—always maintained that Chamberlain would have won as many championships as Russell did if he had been lucky enough to be surrounded by the deep Celtic green. "No," Bob Cousy said not long ago. "To play with Wilt you had to go down, set up and wait for him. We couldn't have played that way."

It was not, really, that Chamberlain wasn't a team player. That's simplistic. In his great cathedral house in Los Angeles he kept not a single trophy attesting to his individual achievements, except for his Hall of Fame certificate. He gave all the others away. "They make other people happier," he told me matter-of-factly. Rather, I think, he was just so dominating a presence that he overwhelmed his own team. He was, ultimately, primarily an opposing force. Whereas players like Russell made their teammates better, it was Chamberlain's fate to bring out the best in the opposition. Finally he awoke one summer's morning on vacation on an island somewhere in the Adriatic and understood that. "There was always so much more pain to my losing than there ever was to gain by my winning," he explained. It was time to quit basketball.

The rest of his life was much happier. He went barefoot and could play at being Wilt more than having to *be* him all the time. And if there is a heaven, my man, it's a place where nobody has to shoot free throws.

Athletes Dying Young

■   ■   ■

A. E. Housman, the poet and pessimist, wrote of the particular and ironic sorrow of "the lads that will die in their glory and never be old." We are somehow saddened all the more by death too early when it is a sportsman who is taken from us.

Recently, two athletes died young in the line of competition: Greg Moore, an automobile racer, and Colby Goodwin, a rodeo steer-roper. Another, Payne Stewart, perished in that bizarre airplane crash on his *way* to compete. So now three times again we have heard the echo of what Houseman wrote in "To an Athlete Dying Young": "And silence sounds no worse than cheers/ After the earth has stopped our ears."

And yet we are not only particularly touched when an athlete dies when he is still in his prime—we also find ourselves uncommonly affected in special, difficult ways when we learn that the flame of the former athlete has been extinguished. The deaths this fall of Wilt Chamberlain and Walter Payton remind us of this again. We react quite differently, I think, to the passing of such sports stars from how we do when we learn that some other comparable famous person has gone.

Part of it is probably because athletes are such amazing physical specimens. Their death too soon makes us seem even more—and hopelessly—vulnerable.

No doubt this fragility touches us especially now in our twenty-first century rational overconfidence, in which we're convinced that if we just live prudently, and don't eat junk food and don't smoke and watch our alcohol intake and exercise regularly, why we're going to stay around so much longer than all those promiscuous saps who still live so foolishly.

And then Payton, this incredible dynamo, this dear person— "Sweetness"—contracts a dreadful disease, and Chamberlain, who may simply be the most imposing human presence you could ever see—fades away in his sleep, far short even of three score and ten.

We are taught that inequity rules, and we accept that premise—but in the cold way of an insurance salesman reading an actuarial table. Ah, but when it is a great athlete, a Payton or a Chamberlain, so strong and beautiful, who dies too soon, we are obliged to accept a much greater truth: that it is really not unfairness we are dealing with. It is powerlessness.

Beyond that, though, athletes connect us to youth—ours and theirs alike. We encounter politicians and other serious figures only after they're already middle-aged. And even if we grow up with young movie stars, most of them stay in the business; they are not put out to pasture at an early age.

So even if entertainment figures might, like athletes, enter our consciousness so young, we watch them grow old. They're not trapped in their youth. Someone like James Dean, who *is* forever young and who is much more passionately held because of that, proves the point.

Athletes, though, remain singularly in our memory, always doing the glorious physical things that only the young can. Suddenly then, when we hear that some sports hero is *dead*, it forces us, so very dramatically, to confront the uncomfortable inevitable.

For baby boomers, the Wilt of their childhoods and the Sweetness of their early manhoods have once again with their deaths become powerful symbols. The athlete dying young is a tragedy . . . for him. The athlete dying too soon is an anxiety . . . for us.

Ruthian

■　　■　　■

Roger Maris certainly looked like an athlete. And he was indeed a very good athlete. It was just that he didn't look like a home-run hitter. And there was, likewise, the sense that he didn't *deserve* to hit sixty-one home runs in one season. In a very real way, for a lot of people, Maris has just been keeping Babe Ruth's record—temporarily, on hold—until the next rightful owner comes along.

And never mind that temporarily, on hold has stretched into thirty-seven years.

The home-run record was identified with The Babe. The Babe was the very vision of a home-run hitter. What seemed like a little twig of a bat would leave his hands in a flip as he stared after the deep damage he had done. We want—we expect—every slugger ever after to live up to that.

Why, I think if there was just one thing I'd like to be able to do just once in my life, it would be simply to stand there at home plate, admiring a huge home run I'd just blasted. It may be the most godlike thing a human being can do, staring out after a home run he has wrought.

And then picking up what is always called the home run "trot." I have no reason to doubt that the expression—"the trot"—originated with Ruth. Certainly it should have. The swing. The long look. The bat flip. The trot. The tip o' the cap. The handshakes . . .

This brings us to Mark McGwire.

It has been decided, in some form of national referendum, that Mark McGwire is the person that Roger Maris has been holding Babe Ruth's record for all these years.

McGwire looks like The Babe's heir, an absolute monster of a man—and yet, like Ruth, so obviously warm and gentle. McGwire's home runs do not merely clear the fence. They are not parabolas. Rather, they just go out and out until they run into something. In fact, McGwire is, really, the first athlete since Michael Jordan who does something that so evidently, to the naked eye, seems to defy physical laws.

Remember: superiority is not all that easy to discern in athletes. How many baseball fans could pick out Kerry Wood, the Cubs' new hundred-mile-an-hour pitcher, from a bunch of guys throwing ninety or ninety-five? Could you go to a gym and watch boxers and tell which one possesses a knockout punch? But McGwire, like Jordan, is simply and obviously different from every other of us Homo sapiens.

Ever since he shook off a series of major injuries and settled in a year ago, McGwire has been drawing crowds to batting practice. At his home St. Louis park and every National League stop, thousands of people are showing up a couple hours before game time simply to watch him take practice swings against seventy-mile-an-hour puff balls. As far as I know, there has been nothing like this in the entire history of spectator baseball—which is approaching 150 years. Did huge numbers of fans show up to watch Ruth practice? I never heard of it.

McGwire, a California boy who has fallen in love with St. Louis—as it with him—is still a bit confounded by all the attention. He keeps talking about how somebody or other is also hitting lots of home runs. McGwire doesn't quite understand about myths yet. Roger Maris was a mere athlete who did one legendary thing, and that didn't astound us so much as it irritated us—because it was so out of context. But, as for McGwire, it's the other way around. We've already made him a legend, and now we will be disappointed if he *doesn't* do the Ruthian thing.

Good Sports Towns

■　　■　　■

The hockey franchise known as the Atlanta Flames is on its way to Calgary. This news may be less than earthshaking, but there is some obscure significance in it. Now that Atlanta is watching one of its teams leave, Denver and Detroit remain the only large American cities never to have lost a franchise in a major sports league.

This means, I suppose, that Denver and Detroit can now lay claim to being the finest sports towns in America. This is, after all, something all American cities love to boast. It is a universal speck upon the American psyche. If Sinclair Lewis were writing now, he wouldn't call his classic booster novel *Main Street*. Instead, he would title it: *Great Sports Town*.

In fact, wherever I go in this country, local residents always assure me of two things: number one, they have the most beautiful women; number two, they have the best sports fans. Not the best athletes, you understand. That can be proved on the field. But enthusiasm, like beauty, is subjective. So we have the best sports fans.

Probably this reveals some insight into our national character. Nobody wants to go into the army anymore, but everybody still loves a parade.

It is important to people that they are known as good fans, as a good sports town. Wherever you go in America, you will discover that when the attendance is announced, the people on hand will cheer—effectively, for themselves. If it is a rainy night, people in the stands will say to one another, "This is a pretty good crowd for a rainy night." If you don't think that, then you're a pretty stupid minority to be sitting out in the rain.

I don't know whether this sort of concern applies itself in other areas of entertainment. Is there such a thing, for example, as a good movie town? Do people in the carnival business talk about good Ferris wheel towns? There used to be a widely held opinion in show business that Milwaukee was a bad vaudeville town. The expression was that there were three bad show weeks every year: Christmas, Easter, and Milwaukee. I've often wondered if this hurt Milwaukee, because I do know that people get upset if you suggest that their city is a bad sports town.

My own view is that no section of the country, much less any one city, is more sports-minded than any other. In fact, I'm not altogether sure what criteria we should employ to decide what makes a good sports town. Does just high attendance, for example, make you a good sports town? Columbus, Ohio, is supposed to be a wonderful sports town because one hundred thousand people show up every week to watch the Ohio State Buckeyes play football and very seldom lose. But I think it is just as fair to say that Manhattan, Kansas, might also be a very good sports town because the university team there, Kansas State, loses all the time and vast numbers there *don't* go to the games.

Generally speaking, I *am* very suspicious of cities that boast that they are a good sports town to "support" a losing team. This encourages bad performers and enriches stupid management, and it is nothing to be proud of. City boosters might just as well boast that they support corrupt government by voting crooks back into office.

As a rule of thumb, you should also be suspicious of sports towns where a large percentage of the fans take radios to the games to find out what is going on right before their eyes.

In fact, you should be suspicious of lots of things. Probably the only reason that Detroit and Denver have never lost a franchise is that no one in their right mind would want the Detroit Pistons or the Colorado Rockies.

Game Faces

■ ■ ■

nasmuch as it's all a game, and it's the day after the midterm elections, I thought it would only be proper to now imagine what our most familiar political heroes would be if they were in sports. For example:

AL GORE would be wearing earphones and hoping, finally, for his chance as the back-up quarterback for the Tennessee Oilers.

KEN STARR would be an umpire with a very large strike zone.

JESSE HELMS would be Juan Antonio Samaranch.

BOB DOLE would be Sammy Sosa. Politics been bery, bery good to me.

COLIN POWELL would be Michael Jordan. Except, if Michael Jordan comes back and plays again, then:

JOHN GLENN would be Michael Jordan.

NEW YORK MAYOR RUDOLPH GIULIANI would be George Steinbrenner. But you already knew that.

GOVERNOR GEORGE W. BUSH would be president of the Texas Rangers.

MONICA LEWINSKY would be Anna Kournikova.

TRENT LOTT would be a nondescript offensive lineman whom nobody notices until he's caught holding.

TOM DASCHLE would be a soccer player nobody ever notices in a soccer league nobody knows exists.

ROSS PEROT would be Dennis Rodman.

MADELEINE ALBRIGHT would be Bud Selig. No, excuse me, WARREN CHRISTOPHER *was* Bud Selig.

ORREN HATCH would be the perfectly exquisite drum major, leading the band at halftime.

JAMES CARVILLE would be Hulk Hogan.

MARY MATALIN would be Stone Cold Steve Austin.

BILL BRADLEY would be Mike Tyson's next opponent. Well, maybe, perhaps, if, possibly . . .

GEORGE MITCHELL would be the referee in Mike Tyson's next fight, whomever he fights.

BILL CLINTON, comeback kid, would *be* Mike Tyson, comeback kid.

HILARY CLINTON would be Don King, promoting Mike Tyson's next fight.

PAT BUCHANAN would be the Daytona 500.

DAN QUAYLE would be Spring Training.

TEDDY KENNEDY would be the left-field wall at Fenway Park.

STROM THURMOND thinks he would be Cal Ripkin, but really he would be George Foreman.

RICHARD GEPHARDT would be Pete Sampras.

NEWT GINGRICH would be Andre Agassi.

VERNON JORDAN would be Nike.

And everybody else in politics would be a free agent, dreaming that they would be Mark McGwire.

Coming of Age
in America

■   ■   ■

I t was not, the officials explained, a "sophisticated" bomb. Somehow, it would seem that any bomb that kills you is sophisticated, but the fact is that, very quickly, it is we who have all grown very sophisticated in the matter of bombs.

"Hey, it's not Oklahoma City," a fellow named Steve said, walking into the Olympic Stadium with his wife the morning after. Steve was, however, troubled by the drizzle. Might it turn into a rain hard enough to affect the competition? They had good tickets.

But he was not insensitive. No, in fact, Steve was pretty much representative of the general attitude of Atlanta, of the citizens of the Olympic Village, the fandom of the Games. The Olympic Bomb did not, above all, evince shock or horror. Oh yes, of course those of us in Atlanta were sorry for the victims. But then, we are saddened, in a passing way, when we hear about some stranger dying in a car crash or in a robbery down at the mall or in the other quotidian tragedies of our time. No, after the explosion came to Centennial Olympic Park, the primary response was simply one of . . . well, *Why not* . . . Why not here . . . Why not here now? Terrorists have, you see, taught us well to understand how they think. So, by now a cowardly attack on the Olympics seemed almost inevitable to us who have learned that planes can fall in little pieces from the sky. As awful as it is to acknowledge the fact, the day of the Olympic Bomb—July 27, 1996—will be primarily remembered as America's coming of age in accepting these incidents of random public carnage.

"It sounds sort of unfeeling, but you can't let it bother you," said Lance Deal, an American hammer thrower. Steve, the fan, and Lance, the athlete, are both practical men. So are we all, practical men and women now.

What is most instructive about our sophisticated reaction was that there was no outcry—not even a whimper—to call off the Games. Now, think back 24 years ago, in the midst of another Olympics, when it was all foreigners murdered. At that time, the public sentiment in the United States was almost hysterical in demanding that the Munich Games must be canceled. Americans eviscerated their own Avery Brundage, the IOC president, as a heartless ghoul.

But the fact was that in Israel, which had lost its sons, the attitude was altogether different. Israel was already a province of terrorism. Israel believed that to call off the Olympics was to award victory to the monsters. Years later, I went to Israel and spoke with the families of the murdered weightlifters. To a person, every one of them—parents, brothers and sisters, widows and fatherless children—remained gratified that, though the men they loved had been killed, the Games of Munich had only been wounded.

The Israelis knew. And now, you could sense that cold attitude palpably here in Atlanta. You could feel it. We of the United States are in Israel now. Starting last Saturday morning, we are, too, in Belfast and Mindanao and Beirut and Saudi Arabia and in all the other places where terror has become potluck.

The athletes took it, perhaps, even more in stride, for they had their competition, and so, in that favorite overused sports word, they had to stay *focused*. Soon enough, though, would some Olympians begin to learn about the everyday personal service charge that terrorism deducts from our emotional ATM. For example: the morning after the Olympic Bomb, Barbara Byrne, a former member of the U.S. rowing team, managed to get out from Atlanta to the rowing venue to see some of her old teammates compete. However, a few of her friends' parents were delayed so much by the suddenly more vigilant security that they were unable to arrive in time, robbed forever of the chance to watch the prime moment of children's youths. "Every Olympics you ever go to, you can look right up and see your mom," Byrne said. "And then they even took that away from us."

But that, of course, is why the Olympics must be such an attractive target to people who can only view dreams and joy and excellence with savage envy. Blood you spill, and take the memory of mothers, too. Moreover, the Olympics, of all sporting events, sets itself up with its pretensions of spirituality, of being a quasi-religious "movement." Others of the world's great international competitions are content with being mere fun and games—which is, truly, what all the Olympics are. But, typically, the IOC spokesman immediately embraced the Turkish photographer who died of a heart attack after the explosion as a "member of the Olympic family," when, in fact, the poor man was not; he was a working journalist covering their Olympics.

The Games may have grown huge, but largest of all in their own bloated image. Surely, that Olympian posturing invites trouble from the fanatics and the friendless who would prefer to prick our happiest balloons with bombs.

So, now that our fears have been answered, the question becomes: what city in its right mind would want the Olympics? If Atlanta can hardly be taken to account for terrorist murder, it will always be linked somehow; besides, even before the Olympic Bomb went off, Atlanta was held up in some derision before the world. What city needs to risk that just for a fortnight in the summer sun?

People will surely say now: this tragedy only reminds us how unimportant sports really are. On the contrary. Sports are the *lingua franca* of the world, so very important in bringing us together. And that only means all the more to those who are bent on blowing us apart.

The Rabbit Ball Conspiracy

■   ■   ■

Even as baseball moves into the second half of its season, there continue to be sinister reports that the ball is hopped up this year. These dark suggestions pop up regularly, about every third year, but what no one has ever even remotely tried to explain is this: if there is more rabbit in the ball in a particular year, who reorders the same every year?

I mean, the baseballs are made down in Haiti, to some kind of secret formula, like Coca-Cola, and all I want to know is, how does the word get to Haiti to change the formula? Are we to believe that the owners in baseball, not one of whom can keep a secret till lunch time, all get together and decide to juice up the ball, oh, say 4.3 percent, and then they send an emissary off to Port au Spain with the word—and then the owners take this secret to their graves?

Or possibly it works like this. Whenever there is a new commissioner, the old commissioner takes him aside, and they cut their wrists slightly, and when their blood intermingles, the old commissioner tells the new commissioner that he has one secret function—to determine each year how much rabbit to put in the ball. And so, last November 14, Peter Ueberroth woke up, decided that the ball must be juiced up 4.3 percent, put on a disguise, and took a secret plane to Haiti to convey this message.

Aha. Or possibly there is a mysterious figure somewhere in baseball, like the tooth fairy or the gnomes of Zurich or the Nielsen TV ratings families, whom nobody knows but whose sole function on this earth is to decide how much to juice up—or juice down—the baseball.

Otherwise, you see, I just don't understand how it's done, unless of course the Haitians in the baseball factory just sort of do their own thing, depending on what side of the bed they got up on this morning.

And yet every year that the hitters start off a bit better than the year before, the cry goes out that they—they!—have hopped up the ball.

What I don't understand is, if they keep making the ball go further, why don't the best players hit more home runs? In the last quarter of a century, since Roger Maris hit sixty-one, only two players have hit as many as fifty dingers in a single season. The American league is supposed to be the power league, with more accommodating parks to boot, but Maris—and Mickey Mantle that same year—were the last American leaguers to reach fifty. And, of course, in every other sport we're told that people are getting bigger and stronger. Are we to believe that only mediocre baseball players are improving?

If you know who's getting these balls changed and keeping it completely secret, please let me or the *National Enquirer* or Jack Anderson know.

The Cult of Celebrity

■   ■   ■

Sports stars have rarely had to deal with the paparazzi in the way that movie stars have. Yet it is also undeniable that, of all the celebrities' cases that bear the most resemblance to what happened to Princess Diana, driven at breakneck speed to her death in that Paris tunnel, the attack on Monica Seles is the closest.

To be sure, the Princess died an accidental death, whereas the tennis player survived a premeditated assassination. Nonetheless, both tragedies were caused, at base, by the cult of celebrity, by that obsessive attachment that fans develop for those famous distant people whose experiences and countenances press close upon their imaginations.

The larger difference between sports stars and the other "names" is that jock heroes are so much more accessible. Spectators watch them live, in action. The media has regular close access to them. Why, in the United States, the press literally talks to athletes when they are naked. Or: do you want to take Michael Jordan's picture? Easy. He comes out of an arena a hundred times a year. He walks through a hotel lobby just as often, pretty much on schedule. Why should the paparazzi bother him when every kid can take his own personal snapshot?

Maybe this is something of a safety valve for athletes. Movie stars—and Diana fit into that broad category—are more insulated and cosseted. This protects them, yes, but it also makes them forbidden fruit, makes their stories and their photographs so much more valuable.

Also, their love lives matter so much more. Nobody cares a great deal about who athletes are going out with, except in those cases in which they cross over and pair off with entertainment figures—Andre Agassi with Brooke Shields, David Justice when he was married to Halle Berry . . . and on back to Bob Waterfield and Jane Russell and Joe DiMaggio and Marilyn Monroe. It was who Diana was seeing that, ultimately, killed her. Monica Seles? It was who she was competing against that caused her stabbing.

Nevertheless, precisely because sports stars *are* so physically approachable, they must endure everyday fans in ways that show biz stars are rarely forced to. Think about it. All the hundreds of photos we have seen these past few days of Diana, and not one portrays her signing an autograph. Movie stars only slow down to smile and show off their gowns, or their new lovers on their arms.

Athletes are asked—expected—to stop and sign autographs. Everywhere. Yes, even standing at urinals.

I think it is revealing that the European athletes, who are not quite so accessible as their American counterparts—either to fans or media— must suffer the paparazzi menace more. Both Steffi Graf and, before her, the French star Yannick Noah, moved to New York—of all places— to find privacy. In fact, Graf, who has always been a photographic specimen in the German laboratory, herself greatly admired the Princess for how she endured in the face of relentless attention. And it was, of course, a deranged fan of Graf's who stabbed poor Monica Seles.

Certainly, a great many American athletes may despise the press, but still, they do not suffer the perennial intrusions into their privacy so much as foreign athletes or show business grandees do. I suppose it is, finally, something of a trade-off. The price of personal freedom for the famous is . . . autographs. Pause and sign your name over and over, so that whenever you dare step out into public, you ransom an escape that eminent celebrities like Princess Diana have never been allowed.

Give unto us that little piece of you that is your name or we will steal your face again and again . . . and maybe, steal even more.

Waiting for (the Next) Jordan

■   ■   ■

We have been diverted too long by the question: Who will be the next Michael Jordan? We should know the answer by now: nobody. Sometimes there just ain't a next. But as we have all sat about fretting, waiting for Godot, the NBA has been eroded by all those players who have been given the license of our dreams to dare audition to be that *next*.

The result is that, right now, the National Basketball Association doesn't need to look ahead for the successor to Mr. Jordan. It needs to look back to the way it was *before* he arrived on the scene.

Maybe basketball just hasn't been prepared to accept its new respect and eminence. It was, for so long, a seedy sport that couldn't compete with baseball, which fostered family and community, or football, which was a party game, a spectacle. But basketball? It was downscale, played in tacky gymnasiums—sometimes even enclosed in wire mesh. It's been all but forgotten now, but at one time (and not that long ago), basketball players were not "hoopsters," but "*cagers*" because they existed in this athletic zoo.

Then, overnight, thanks to some magnificent talents and clever marketing, basketball was turned right side up. Suddenly, the grubbiest game was the most glamorous. The word "artistic" began to appear, although, in truth, basketball didn't become art so much as show biz. Instead of prizing plays, we began to celebrate *moves*. And, as with some other forms of theater, the performance became subsidiary to the performers.

Certainly it is instructive that in hockey, where Wayne Gretzky is likewise planning to depart the stage, there is not nearly the demand for "the next Wayne Gretzky"—and Number 99 was every bit as important to his smaller sport as Number 23 was to his. In a way, in fact, Gretzky might even be more significant to hockey. After all, it is a faceless sport in which Gretzky is the only player with any Q-rating at all.

Certainly, both Jordan and Gretzky rose above their games. Indeed, it isn't Jordan's fault, but maybe the worst thing that ever happened to basketball was that he was too good for the sport. Whereas Bill Russell, and then Larry Bird and Magic Johnson, were renowned for *leading* their teams to championships, Jordan is known for carrying his.

And so, the players today tend to play in his image, each for themselves. Selfishness rules and culture excuses. Why, even if there was to be a next Michael Jordan, it is unlikely that the next would be like the original off the court. Those players who would be the future king only seek to emulate the present one on the court. Jordan has been almost as impressive as a gentleman off as he was a star on.

But this appears to have been lost on the younger generation. "It's all right on the street, so . . . " Pat Riley sighed the other day, justifying another fight on the court. In that way, venerated and forgiven, the stars constantly proclaim their manliness. They pout, whine, demand, taunt, fight, and, by all accounts—as *Sports Illustrated* detailed so graphically last week—live sybaritic lives, siring more offspring than do Kentucky Derby winners. It's all me, all now, and it's just all become so terribly tawdry.

At the annual awards dinner last week of the National Association of Sportscasters and Sportswriters, Dave Kindred of *The Sporting News*, who was voted Sportswriter of The Year, used that occasion to announce that he was sorry for all these years supporting the players over the owners. He couldn't do that anymore. And it wasn't that he liked the owners any better.

Kindred's proclamation—for he is a most respected voice in the profession—had the ring of that time a generation ago, when American officials began to declare that, sorry, but they had changed their minds completely, and now they stood against the war in Vietnam.

For now, at least for a few more weeks, we remain in the glowing presence of Jordan—one so brilliant we don't usually stop to consider the shabby world he gives shine to. But when he does depart, the NBA will finally have to understand that there can't be any next to guide the future if nobody can stomach the here and now.

The Highlighting of America

■   ■   ■

Boring. The one word that everyone in sports fears—and hears. Boring. That's boring. That's really boring. Soccer is boring. Running the football is boring. Pete Sampras is so boring. Nothing else matters, if the fans—especially the young fans—find it . . . boring.

Tony Gwynn was trying to explain the other day why so few African-Americans play baseball anymore. Well, he said, "Baseball is perceived as boring." That's all. Tony Gwynn himself is the greatest hitter of our time. Plus, he's a gentleman of the first order. He took a breath. "I'm boring," he sighed. Nobody wants to see such a boring genius.

But on the other hand . . .

Because Mike Tyson is a total loose cannon, he is not boring. He can't box, but promoters were lined up to vie for his next fight as soon as Iron Mike got out of jail the other day.

Wrestling is scripted, so it is never boring—and setting ratings records by the day, as TV networks fight for more wrestling. Neither is Shaquille O'Neal boring. He plays the Jolly Green Giant on the court, with slam-dunks that are always called "awesome." All season long, NBC showed Shaq's Lakers team to the exclusion of all others. But free throws are boring. Practicing free throws is even more boring. So, Shaq's team got whipped by the San Antonio Spurs, whose stars, Tim Duncan and David Robinson, are complete, solid, team-oriented players. Yeah: boring. Nobody wants to see them just *win* games.

I'm convinced that a large reason for this burgeoning attitude is the *highlights* on TV—which fill up the local sports reports and the network roundups. Highlights consist of holes-in-one, hockey fights, automobile race crashes, and desperation basketball shots taken from half-court that go in. In slow motion. Naturally, if you grow up watching game highlights, actual games are boring.

And unfortunately, I'm afraid that this is also starting to become true in other aspects of our existence. Life follows sport. The highlighting of America. If you'll notice, the main thing we hear about the presidential candidates is simply that they are boring. Except, of course, President *Clinton* isn't. Like The Shaq and wrestling, he's always had good highlights. That's the key. And I'm sorry, but an air war does not have good highlights.

And whereas everybody said that the Academy Award-winning movie, *Shakespeare in Love*, proved that everybody adored The Bard, *Shakespeare in Love* was basically just a Shakespeare highlight film. Of course nobody's going to see *A Midsummer Night's Dream* now. It's not as good as the Shakespeare highlights. In *Shakespeare in Love* you didn't have to sit through all the boring stuff. You just got the good quotes, like "Romeo, Romeo, wherefore art thou?" and a sword fight, plus you get to see Shakespeare's girlfriend rolling around in bed naked. Stupid Shakespeare never once had Portia or Ophelia or Lady MacBeth naked.

I'm telling you, as a Shakespeare highlight film, *Shakespeare in Love* is the worst thing that could have happened to the real Shakespeare. Now, his plays will forever be boring.

And so that you won't have to hear this whole boring thing again, here is the highlight reel from this commentary: Mike Tyson is out of jail. Wrestling ratings. Shaq dunks. Awesome. Hole in one. Hockey fight. Crash. At the buzzer, from mid-court. Romeo, Romeo, wherefore art thou? Sword fight. Awesome. Rolling around in bed naked. Innn . . . sloooowwww . . . motionnnnn.

When There Were Still Elusive Barriers

I. A Pivot in Time

Now, at the end of this 20th century, we famously celebrate America as "the world's only superpower," but the fact is that in the middle of the century, when much of the rest of the earth lay in ruin, we were far more the monarch of this planet. There was no such thing as a global economy then. There was only an American economy, and what embers still glowed elsewhere after World War II did so only by the sufferance of American generosity. Oh, to be sure, something menacing lurked behind the Iron Curtain, but we, the blithe nieces and nephews of Uncle Sam, lived off the fat of the land. The U.S. in 1954 made up only 6% of the world's population of 2.7 billion, but it owned 60% of its automobiles, 58% of its telephones and similarly vast amounts of breeziness and arrogance. For the first time, we were getting fat and happy.

A young Oxford student, Roger Bannister, visiting the States in 1949, was astonished not only by Americans' enthusiasm but also by their sloth. "It seems quite impossible to walk in America," he wrote in his 1955 autobiography, adding that he "acquired a reputation for madness" by occasionally requesting to go on foot rather than ride. Somewhat later, from New Zealand, came a young beekeeper named Edmund Hillary, who was even more appalled by this blessed land. Its enchantments, he admitted, offered a "constant appeal to my baser instincts," and since Hillary perceived, correctly, that he was looking at a preview of the new global model, he concluded, "I feel a deep sadness for the future of America and the world."

Perhaps because of the war, those who had lived through it had come to expect more of humankind; mere peaceful prosperity must have seemed selfish and tawdry. Hillary, especially, wrestled with moral dilemmas. Before he had joined the Royal New Zealand Air Force during World War II, he had been a conscientious objector. The American desire to run roughshod toward success wasn't part of his makeup; in all his life, the only competition that Hillary has ever won was when, as a child, he was honored for building the best snowman. Instead, he said, he was "a reader and a dreamer" who was most comfortable alone, with nature. So, one day in January 1940, "weighted down by my mental turmoil"—to fight or not to fight?—he had journeyed from his home in Auckland down to the majestic South Island of New Zealand, to the Hermitage, a lodge at the base of Mount Cook, the highest mountain in the antipodes. There, looking up at the snow and the heights, young Hillary had an epiphany: He wanted to climb. And he did. It was, simply, "the happiest day I had ever spent."

Bannister had been too young to fight in the war, but he remembered the air-raid sirens and the deprivation. Besides, even while he grew to manhood, as the '50s wore on, England remained grim and impoverished. No wonder that, in his visit to the States, Bannister was taken aback by the self-satisfied American athletes against whom he faced off. They were so driven, so mad for victory that, it seemed to him the American middle distance runners had lost "freshness and sparkle," and sport itself was being transformed "into a machine in which the athlete's individuality was submerged."

The mid-century was, in fact, a pivot on which sport turned, leaving men like Bannister and Hillary as something of a rear guard for the past. Some of America, though, still shared their ideal. Sport here remained an activity at which one could excel as an avocation—and without being abnormal of dimension or temperament. Average-sized people could still play football and basketball; even the heavyweight champions weighed only 185 or so. If there was one American star most cherished at this time for representing the sturdy old values, it was Dick Kazmaier of Princeton, a slight, modest Midwesterner who won the Heisman Trophy in 1951, then chose Harvard Business School over the Chicago Bears. Yes, the debate over professionalism still simmered, the purists still firm in the diminishing belief that a man should play at games only for the joy of it. Really, the values in question were not substantively different from those that Walter Camp, the father of football, had championed back in the 19th century: "You don't want your boy 'hired' by anyone. If he plays . . . he plays for victory, not for money; and whatever bruises he may have in the flesh, his heart is right, and he can look you in the eye, as a gentleman should."

The '50s were the last gasp of that. While it is fashionable to write off that decade as an insipid time, one long pajama party, the '50s, in sport at least, were a revolutionary age. It wasn't just that amateurism was in retreat. Everything was changing. No major league baseball franchise had moved since 1903, and the pecking order of the most influential American sports had been set in stone for at least that long: 1) baseball, 2) college football, 3) horse racing, 4) boxing. Suddenly, National Pastime franchises were flying about the country. Pro football was rising to challenge college. Sweaty basketball became respectable. Something called NASCAR was catching on, and the popular shift to watching automobiles race—instead of horses or human beings—began. Moreover, the '50s institutionalized what Jackie Robinson had wrought in '47, as black athletes flowed into sports. Television entered the arena, then television *money*. This magazine [*Sports Illustrated*]—weekly and national, for goodness' sake, about sports!—was launched in August '54.

It is a cherished cultural truism of the century that rock and roll changed music in America at this time; what is usually overlooked is that while sport experienced as much of a sea change as music, it did more than just switch a beat. Sport was dramatically enlarged. And its impact was upon everybody, not just the giddy teen nation.

In 1946 Roger Bannister had started medical school in Oxford, where, every lunch hour, he would fork over threepence so that he might practice his running in Paddington Park, near the hospital in which he worked. Ed Hillary left his brother behind to manage the family bee farm in New Zealand, sailed to Sydney, where he picked up a larger ship, and, sleeping in a six-berth cabin, sailed for weeks to England, there to join his parents and drive them about on holiday. He hoped he also might break away and tramp the Alps.

But if we could not quite see then what was happening—that sport would become more about statistics than accomplishment, more about celebrities than heroes, more about gamesmanship than sportsmanship—there were still some bits of unfinished business from the olden times. Most prominent, there were left two of what were known as "barriers" or, more dramatically, "elusive barriers." The tallest mountain in the world was still unconquered by man, and the distance of ground that measured a mile had continued to resist all efforts to traverse it, on foot, in less than four minutes.

Of course, these were two very different challenges. Mount Everest was *there*; the mile could be anywhere. Mount Everest was the last in the geographical set that made up the goals of what had been known as the Heroic Age. The Poles had been reached, the mouth of the Nile found, the deepest oceans marked, the wildest jungles trekked. But no one had climbed the 29,000-some-odd feet of Mount Everest (29,002, it was thought then; 29,035, we have it now) to stand at the crest of the world. But neither had any human being run 5,280 feet in less than four minutes. The record had been reduced to 4:01.4, but there it had stood, unyielding, since 1945. A physical limit? A psychological hurdle? Whatever, 4:00.0 had become a symbolic figure, and the pursuit of it was essential to our mythology.

Oh, yes, it all might appear so quaint now, what with the mile record down to Hicham El Guerrouj's 3:43.13 and with tourist buses, it seems, stopping for Nieman-Marcus box lunches at the Everest summit. But in the early '50s these two romantic quests genuinely inspired the vision of good people who had fought wars and Depression for most of this century and who held to the faith that fine, intrepid men were still about, ready to astound us with their devotion to a noble goal. We had that on the best authority. Winston Churchill, who in 1951 had been returned to 10 Downing Street, had said of his people, "We have not journeyed all this way across the centuries, across the oceans, across the mountains, across the prairies, because we are made of sugar candy."

II. The Bugbear

It had helped Bannister that he was a good sort who would go over the Magdalen Bridge to the Iffley Road track at Oxford and help shovel off the snow. This was a factor in earning him a spot on the university's third team. Certainly, he was not a prepossessing physical specimen, and in fact, for a runner, he moved with an ungainly gait, rather prefiguring Monty Python's Ministry of Silly Walks. But then, out of the blue, on March 22, 1947, when Bannister was being used as a pacer for the first-team Oxford runners against Cambridge, something happened. Bannister simply did not stop; he won the mile by 20 yards in 4:30.8. "I knew from this day," he said, "that I could develop this newfound ability."

Still, however, he continued to view athletics primarily as something "fun," while his respect went to the well-rounded man. "We felt that we belonged to a tradition that was dying," he explains. "I don't mean the tradition of British privilege. In fact, I came from quite an ordinary background and attended Oxford only because I won a scholarship. No, the tradition was of running and working—and while you were studying, being part of a team."

Today, the esteemed Dr. Bannister and his wife, Moyra, have a flat in the city, to which he refers, like all English, irrespective of geography, as up in London." The Bannisters, in retirement, reside mostly in Oxford, which is itself north—up—from London. They returned there some years ago, when he was appointed Master of Pembroke, one of his alma mater's colleges. It is a position of honor and consequence, which he held until 1994. "It was a significant event in my life," he says, "to come back to Oxford, where I had been so very happy." Pointedly, he does not say, Where I came to fame as the first man to run the four-minute mile.

The Bannisters live barely a mile or so from the Iffley Road track, in a corner house with a perfect English garden, jammed with shrubbery and bright blooms—that familiar embroidery that lets us know precisely where we are. That assurance of place, of heritage, helps us understand why Bannister thinks back on the everyday at Oxford, rather than on his day of days.

In from the garden, though, the house is cluttered with the fine handiwork of Moyra—she paints and makes ceramic plates—played off against all manner of knockabout toy's for visiting grandchildren. However, virtually no trophies are on display, inasmuch as Bannister gave them to Pembroke, including the Greek amphora that *Sports Illustrated* presented to him in 1954 as its first Sportsman of the Year. In a dark hallway, beneath some apparently incidental family pictures, at about knee level, ignored and hanging askew, is the famous photograph of Bannister breasting the tape at Iffley Road.

Just turned 70, Bannister is exactly a decade younger than Hillary. In 1975 Bannister was almost killed in a head-on automobile collision. His injuries were so terrible that he never again could run. Today, however, no traces of his accident remain evident. Neither do his eyeglasses dim his bright blue-gray eyes, and at 6' 1-1/2" he remains lank and animated, downright antsy. He is more comfortable sitting atop a high swivel chair, in which he often spins himself around. If not twirling, he is wont to glance away, here and there, as he talks, always in sentences so complete that one all but hears the commas.

Sometimes, though, the doctor will throw himself off the chair and pace about.

Bannister is not irritated that his youthful feat follows him down through his years. For a long time, in fact, he presented commemorative neckties to those others who broke the barrier—till running ye olde four-minute mile became so commonplace that he would have needed to become a haberdasher to keep up with the demand. Still, Bannister has had to relive the memory so often that it bores him. So all of a sudden, "Can't we talk some about afterwards?" he cries out, springing off his chair, plunging about the room.

That somewhat mirrors the feeling he had at the time of his consummate achievement. "There was delight, yes," he says, "but also a feeling of liberation from the burden of being expected to do it." He might not have even competed after 1952 if he had won a medal at the Olympics that year. But he came up flat in the final of the 1,500, the metric mile, in Helsinki, and since he knew he would be practicing medicine by the time the next Olympics came around, he needed an alternative goal for the two serious years he would have left as a runner. "I regard the four-minute mile as a bugbear," Bannister said at the time, "but it is something that has captured the public imagination—and I suppose if it has got to be done, I would rather an Englishman do it."

He had no coach. He was too involved in his studies to run as much as he should have. He hadn't even managed a practice mile in the winter and spring of '54. Above all, he says, "there was the matter of desperation. I was about to start my residency. I wouldn't be able to properly prepare anymore. And I had no interest whatsoever in running badly."

Besides, Bannister knew that John Landy, the Australian miler, might finally best the elusive barrier once he got a couple of good warmup races and some nice weather. In England, Bannister didn't have that luxury. He decided to try for the record on May 6, in his first race of '54, at an otherwise run-of-the-mill meet. In the meantime he went off rock climbing in Scotland. It may have been, physically, the worst thing Bannister—or anyone—could do to prepare for a race. A coach today would go berserk at the thought. But it was a different time then. There was so much good whim about in those days.

Bannister figured he needed perfect conditions if he were to have any chance to do what no man had ever done. May 6, however, turned up raw and windy, with intermittent showers. So that morning in

London, as Bannister went about his usual hospital rounds at St. Mary's, he understood that his chance was lost. Maybe this thing is impossible here, he thought.

III. The Bastard

Jan Morris, the writer, remembers the young Hillary for "moving with an incongruous grace, rather like a giraffe," but now, just turned 80, Hillary has grown a bit stout and jowly, shambling. The lantern jaw is not quite so pronounced, but the eyes that Yousuf Karsh, the photographer, said held "infinity in them" are yet clear. He wears a tiny hearing aid but says he's in fine health; he is curly-haired and ruddy. Anyway, the best part of him was always what you couldn't see: his lungs. "I'm just a big hulk, but I knew I could perform," he says. "If there were far better-looking sorts, I was stronger and faster going uphill."

It seems such a puny word to attach to Everest: *uphill*. But more charming still is how accidental it all was. Today the best athletes appear almost ordained. Whether or not we have lost innocence in sport, we have, for sure, lost much of the haphazard, the spontaneous—and that may be the biggest deprivation. Hillary never even saw a mountain till he was 16, never ventured up one till that visit to the Hermitage; only four years before Hillary would stand at 29,035 feet, an older New Zealand climber, George Lowe, impressed by his talent, idly inquired, "Have you ever thought about going to the Himalayas, Ed?"

No, he had not.

The vision of his people was also limited then. At mid-century, the "pink bits" scattered about the map, which every British schoolchild knew signified the Empire, were still there on the classroom Mercators, but only in hue. It was becoming the Commonwealth now. However, a new ruler of the Empire-*cum*-Commonwealth would be crowned on Tuesday, June 2, 1953, and as heartbroken as the British were at the death of their admirable King George VI, young Queen Elizabeth II offered the promise of a new spirit. After all, England still struggled, so dispirited and disillusioned, all the worse as Germany and Japan—the defeated monsters—were rushing ahead and as Britain's special relative, the U.S., had become this vast duchy of luxury.

"Eight, nine years on, we still couldn't get over the war," Bannister recalls. "Even then, if you left the country, you had only a 25-pound allowance. The last of the rationing didn't end till '54, you know."

He finds a sports analogy to describe the huge chasm between England and America. Bob Mathias, an 18-year-old California schoolboy, had won the decathlon at the 1948 London Olympics. "An 18-year-old winning the decathlon would've been inconceivable here," Bannister says. "Not only [because of] the weather, but, all the more so, because of our lack of resources." Indeed, on the very morning of the day that Bannister ran his mile, an article in *The Times* of London lamented England's athletic plight. "In spite of our own standards," the paper groaned, "we are still hard put to keep up with the advances of other countries."

Ah, but despite such melancholy, the fond links forged by the Empire remained strong. Hillary declared, "Like most of my fellow citizens, I was British first and New Zealander second." New Zealand had been an independent nation since 1947, but still as the journalist Cohn James writes of his county, "It was British and white. It made lambs and butter and some of the most boring cheese imaginable, and it sent it Home [to England] in plain wrappings for a good price. . . . It was safe . . . a place of no choice and none needed. Small, rich and complete. Bland beyond boredom. The most comfortable place in the world to grow up in."

Nevertheless, the Kiwis have always been rugged sportsmen and the most courageous companions. John Keegan, the renowned military historian and author, calls New Zealanders indisputably the finest soldiers in the world in this century. So in 1951, when Eric Shipton, the pipe-smoking English leader of an Everest expedition, had the opportunity to add a few Kiwis, he invited them—the well-regarded George Lowe and the unknown Hillary included—to join him in Nepal if they could make it there on their own. Shipton knew the New Zealanders brought specifically useful talents, because their South Island Alps offered the same challenges of snow and ice (*ace*, in Hillary's Down Under accent) as were found in the Himalayas.

But there was a new problem. Everest rises out of two nations, Tibet and Nepal, and in 1951 the Chinese Communists had taken over Tibet and closed it off. Previously, Tibet had been open as the way up, while Nepal kept out foreigners. Around this same time, Nepal started to ease its restrictions and allow foreigners to travel there. So now the task was not only to get to the bloody top but also to discover a whole new route—which would obviously be even more challenging than the one that had already proved too difficult and had, in fact, taken at least 16 lives, including that of the legendary English climber George Mallory. Hillary finally caught up to the expedition, saw Everest and thought this: a white fang, thrusting into the sky.

Shipton quickly realized what a find he had in Hillary, and it was on their reconnaissance that they spotted the glacier pass that might make a southern route possible. It was at this point too that the competitor in Hillary emerged; it was, if you will, the Americanization of Edmund. Despite himself. In his heart, he wrote in a 1955 memoir, he knew Shipton had to abandon "the deep-seated British tradition of responsibility and fair play . . . to modify the old standards of safety and justifiable risk and to meet the dangers as they came. . . . The competitive standards of Alpine mountaineering were coming to the Himalayas, and we might as well compete or pull out." Nice guys finish last.

That expedition was a success, in Shipton's view, for his team had mapped a route he felt could be successfully followed to the summit, and they made plans accordingly for another trip the next year. However, when Hillary returned home, he learned that two Swiss teams had the only permits for an assault on Everest in 1952, and when he heard, incorrectly, that Raymond Lambert and the Sherpa guide Tenzing Norgay had made the summit, he was crestfallen.

For a mountaineer—all-for-one and all that—Hillary knew these jealousies were "unworthy thoughts." But the conceit of taking Everest had won out over his better British self. "Yes, we had to change the traditional attitude, accept the dangers and be prepared to take more risks than the older brigade," Hillary says. "But then, we're a bit that way in New Zealand—adventurers of sorts."

Still, on the 1953 British expedition led by John Hunt, Hillary knew he'd overstepped honor even more, because he had terribly mixed emotions about his "very good friends" Tom Bourdillon and Charles Evans when they made the team's first assault. He took small comfort that Norgay, whom he admired and who was now paired with him, felt even more conflicted with jealousy as Evans and Bourdillon closed on the peak. "Tenzing was very glum," Hillary says. He pauses as Big Red, his tabby, jumps up into his lap; then he goes on, remembering clearly, "I wasn't very proud of my feelings."

As it happened, Evans and Bourdillon had to turn back barely 300 feet below the summit. Upon returning to high camp, Evans told Hillary, "I don't think you're going to get to the top along that ridge." But, says Hillary, "I didn't take that seriously, because it reminded me of just another one of those good Alpine ridges I'd seen so often in New Zealand—demanding, yes, but climbable." So it was, to make a long story short, that at the top of the world Hillary and Norgay found a very daunting cornice and then, past that step, a. . . . well, a climbable South Island–style ridge. And they endured, confidently. "I suppose most people who find themselves in a dangerous spot pray to God," Hillary says. "But while maybe I have an arrogant view, I feel that I've gotten myself there, so it's my own responsibility."

So they pushed on together, the Kiwi and the Sherpa. At 11:30 on the morning of May 29, 1953, in the first year of the reign of Queen Elizabeth II, Hillary took one last stride up a gentle rise and found himself, first ever among humankind, standing and looking down at all the world beneath him.

He and Norgay shook hands, and then Hillary took photographs of the Sherpa. "It never crossed my mind to give Tenzing the camera to take my picture," he says. "That would never happen today. But I was just a naive country boy. Why did I need a photograph? I knew I'd been there, and that was good enough for me."

When he and Norgay came back down, they ran first into Lowe. "Well," crowed Hillary gaily, with the best extemporaneous victory line ever, "we knocked the bastard off."

Back in London, the news arrived, exclusively to *The Times*, late the night of June 1, just as the Coronation Day edition was being put to bed. In those days, *The Times* still ran only "notices" on the front page. There was otherwise only the paper's logo and, under it, LONDON, with the date and, over to the right, in the largest small type that would fit, *The Times*' editors added two little words: EVEREST CLIMBED.

So, with that gift from Edmund Hillary and Tenzing Norgay, did later that very day the Commonwealth crown its queen.

IV. Hip, Hip, Hooray

On the midday train to Oxford, Bannister chanced upon Franz Stampfl. He was the coach of his teammate Chris Brasher, who, along with Chris Chataway, was going to try and keep a minute-per-quarter-mile pace for him. Despite the nasty weather, Stampfl urged him to go for it. "He made the point," Bannister recalls, "that 'if you don't take this opportunity you may never forgive yourself.'" The thought stayed with him.

Bannister enjoyed a leisurely lunch with friends, but even when he took tea with Brasher later, he hadn't made up his mind. Only about 1,100 people were in the old wooden stands at the Iffley Road track, but Bannister's parents had been tipped off by a friend that "it could be worthwhile" for them to show up, so, unbeknownst to their son, they were among the small assemblage at the meet. It was Oxford versus Britain's Amateur Athletic Association. Down by the track, Bannister kept glancing up toward Iffley Road. There, on the far side of the street, flying above the steeple of St. John the Evangelist, was the flag of St. George, standing straight out in the brisk breeze.

Only shortly before the mile was called for 6:10 p.m. did Bannister note that the flag had begun to dip some, and so, just five minutes before the start, he decided that a man in England would never get anything done if he waited for good weather. He told Chataway and Brasher he'd go for it. Later, Bannister wrote a more beautiful description of what made him decide to try: "I felt at that moment that it was my chance to do one thing supremely well."

The six runners took off, the flag still drooping above St. John's, clouds but no rain, 54°, Bannister's seven-ounce spikes sinking into the damp cinders. Brasher took the lead and held it through the end of the third lap, when Chataway stepped up—primed, himself, to try for the 1,500-meter record. Chataway was on top at the bell in 3:00.5, but Bannister passed him on the backstretch and, lengthening his stride, moved farther and farther ahead. There was no pace but his own now, no one to push him. He must race into history on his own. He seemed on target too, until he came down the stretch, when the wind rose again, slapping him crosswise, slowing him, surely, precious hundredths—tenths?—of seconds. But Bannister kept churning, hitting the tape with his one last gasp, so that, yes, that final elusive barrier of the Heroic Age had been overcome in 3:59.4 by an Englishman in the second year of the reign of Queen Elizabeth II.

There was, then, as "Our Athletics Correspondent" from *The Times* reported, "a general swoop on to the centre of the field. . . . Bannister was encircled and disappeared from view, but somehow the news [of the record] leaked out. There was a scene of the wildest excitement—and what miserable spectators they would have been if they had not waved their programmes, shouted, even jumped in the air." There were also three cheers for Bannister and a kiss from Mum.

V. A Large Part of His Life

True to his intentions, Bannister quit competitive sport before the summer was out. He ran his last mile at the Empire Games in Vancouver on August 7. By then, John Landy had broken Bannister's record and was a 4–1 favorite. He led Bannister by 15 yards in the backstretch of the second lap too, but the Englishman came on to win in 3:58.8. It was a good finish for the new doctor and a good start for the new *Sports Illustrated*, which began publishing that week and made Bannister's victory its first lead story. Film of the race was on U.S. television too, watched hither and yon. If you want benchmarks, it is fair enough to say that one 20th-century era in sport ended on May 6, 1954, and another began on August 7.

Bannister became a neurologist. Why not a neurological surgeon? "The interesting thing for me was deciding where the tumor was—rather than taking it out," he explains. Then, typical of the man, after his terrible automobile accident Bannister took the recovery time to "rethink," and he went back to medical research, setting up a laboratory to study the part of the brain that controls blood pressure.

He has accomplished much beyond medicine, too. He's a fine writer who has produced scores of newspaper pieces and medical articles and has edited textbooks. He also was chairman of the national Sports Council that reinvigorated all manner of athletics in Britain in the 1970s. Bannister, too, foresaw the drug problem in international sport; he helped design the urine tests that would catch scoundrels like Ben Johnson. In this regard, he holds no brief for the Olympic and track and field pooh-bahs. "It's only gradually that they've accepted the responsibility that they must clean things up," he says. "They're all so rich now with television money that they can afford to provide constant and eternal vigilance."

It is also important to Sir Roger Bannister that when the queen knighted him in 1975, it was not for what a young student did one day in one May but for a man's whole measure of work. "Running was only a small part of my life," he says. "Even now, my friends and colleagues just accept the fact that in my life, I happened to do this one thing." Broke the four-minute mile? "Well, broke the four-minute mile as a student. I thought the ideal, if you like, was: the complete man, who had a career outside of sport. Obviously, that's gone out the window."

Nevertheless, he has mellowed in his attitude about the U.S. Perhaps that was inevitable. He studied neurology at Harvard in the 1960s, and three of his four children married Americans. "I had an absorbing passion about athletics, and I was very idealistic when I first came to America," Bannister says. "I have, unfortunately, had to modify some of my views. But America was responsible for the running revolution, when the middle class became conscious of health. That caused a monumental change in attitude."

England, too, has the vision and the wherewithal. When Bannister ran on the cinders of the Iffley Road track, green meadows were everywhere, over Magdalen Bridge, behind the poplars. Now, instead, the track is synthetic, and all around are artificial-turf fields and tennis courts. They rather resemble the facilities at a state university in, say, Ohio. The students hurry by, largely unaware that history was made here, rushing to their teams or their physical-education classes, looking, all of them, so very American, with jeans and backpacks and baseball caps. It is funny. When the century started, the sun didn't set on the British Empire, but now America is the sun and the moon that rise and fall everywhere upon this earth.

Off Iffley, down Jackdaw Lane, is Bannister Close, barely a block long. The only other recognition of his feat is a small plaque, hardly noticeable, set in the new concrete grandstand, declaring that, yes, ON THIS TRACK. . . . and so forth. Up and across the way, St. John the Evangelist still rises, and on the steeple on a bright English afternoon the flag snaps in the breeze, then suddenly goes limp, as it did that day 45 years ago, when a young man found that he could do one thing supremely well.

VI. Getting to the Bottom

In the symmetry of life Hillary, like Bannister, endured days as horrid as his earlier moments had been splendid. Another day that same awful year as Bannister's near-fatal car accident, Hillary suffered a far worse tragedy. In Katmandu, the gateway to Everest, a small plane took off and, stupidly, someone had neglected to free the ailerons. It crashed just after takeoff, killing Hillary's wife, Louise, and their youngest daughter, Belinda. "It took me several years to recover," he says, although, even now, a quarter century on, when he talks of it he must steady himself to keep from crying. "I had always thought that I would be the one to come to grief," he goes on, "but never once—never for a moment—did I think it would be my wife or one of my children."

Not long after that crash, Hillary was supposed to accompany a group of tourists on a flyover of the Antarctic. He could not go, so his good friend Peter Mulgrew went in his stead. "Peter was a great battler," Hillary says. "He lost his feet in the Himalayas from frostbite, so he took up yachting, and even with his artificial limbs, he became a competitive yachtsman." Mulgrew's plane flew flush into a mountain.

The widower Hillary and Mulgrew's widow, June, had known each other for two decades. After a while they moved in together, and eventually they married. They live today—along with the old tabby Big Red—in Auckland in the same house where Hillary raised his family with his first wife.

All you really must know about Sir Edmund Hillary is that while his face is on his country's five-dollar bill, his name is still in the Auckland phone book. Talking with him in his home seems a bit like chatting with George Washington at Mount Vernon.

The house is in Remuera, an affluent if not ostentatious suburb. You go down a hill to reach it, but it boasts a glorious vista, looking toward the harbor where the sleek America's Cup boats sail out to race. One huge tree soars over the house—a Himalayan deodar, a gift from Louise Hillary's father. Maybe that is proper. Symbolically, you see, something of Everest always rises above Edmund Hillary.

The reason that Hillary's wife and daughter were flying out of Katmandu when their plane went down was that Hillary returned there regularly. As Sir Roger would devote some of his later years to the sport that had brought him eminence, so has Sir Edmund dedicated much of his life to helping the indigent Sherpa people. Even now, Hillary goes back to Nepal every year, spending several other weeks in Europe and the U.S. to raise the funds to build hospitals and bridges and airfields and schools in the Himalayas.

Yet the irony that he has given so much love to helping Tenzing Norgay's land is heightened by the fact that when the two men came down off the bastard, Norgay's people let Hillary know they despised him. "Everyone in the crowd was pouring out hate toward me," he wrote in 1955. This was because those indigenous folk had lived in the lee of the mountain that they had called Chomolungma for eons before the British identified it as Peak 15 and then, in 1865, named it after Sir George Everest, a surveyor general of India. The Sherpas believed that Buddhist gods resided up there, in the clouds, and they did not want to accept that the first human afoot there had not been one of their own.

To Hillary the issue was meaningless. "I led all the way," he says, "but believe me, to us, to mountaineers, who's first is not important. We were a team. Who sets foot first bears no relationship to who makes the greatest contribution."

It was another example of Hillary's innocence that he would assume that no one—in Nepal or anywhere else—would be curious about primacy. But then, he also was astonished when the queen knighted him, and it did not trouble him that whenever he and other members of the expedition spoke about the conquest, his fee—a minuscule £25—was the same as theirs. "We thought all this reaction would quickly fade," he says. "I really didn't expect that the public would care much."

In any event, even before they came off the mountain, John Hunt, the expedition leader, met with Hillary and Norgay, and they agreed that they would say that somehow the two men had arrived at the top simultaneously. As soon as the expedition reached civilization, though, it found trouble. "In Nepal it became very important to believe that Tenzing was first," Hillary says. "That was proof that an Asian was as good as a Westerner. Norgay was quite frightened, actually, because politically he found himself in a very difficult situation."

The two men kept to the story, although in Norgay's final memoir, shortly before his death in 1986, he acknowledged that he'd been a couple of steps behind. That book didn't receive much attention in the West, so at last, as he entered his ninth decade, Hillary decided to set the record straight. "Finally, I just got a gutsful of it," he says. "I got tired of people saying that Tenzing had gotten to the top first."

That Hillary is such a munificent benefactor of Nepal mutes the issue. By now, the mountain people had learned that he was, if not a Sherpa himself, one of them in spirit who had first stood with their gods. "The Sherpas always impressed me with one element of their belief," Hillary says, "which is that you must choose your own path." As if on cue, Big Red jumps off his master's lap and strides away disdainfully, as cats do. Hillary goes on: "They don't preach at you if you choose a path that they wouldn't. No matter how strongly they may feel, they're unlikely to express judgment. The Hindu priests always welcomed me into their temples, and, you know, I adopted the attitude that anybody who wants to bless me—well, I'm quite willing to accept their blessing."

It is, perhaps, harder for Hillary to accept all the secular worship that has come his way. "I do not take it seriously," he says. "I have a wife who looks after me—bosses me around. I have both my children here in Auckland, my grandchildren. If someone wants to believe I'm a heroic figure, fine, but for me, I did a reasonable job at the time. I didn't get carried away then, and I never have."

He has—like Bannister—grown more forgiving of the U.S. and how it has helped shape the world in its image. "There is still too much hatred in the world—everywhere," he says, "and even though there's more awareness of what we're doing to the environment, it's still a shame what we are doing. We have a long way to go."

For years he kept up what he calls the "adventurous life"—most prominently leading a major expedition to Antarctica—but it still amazes him that Everest yet excites our imagination so. "Yes, of course there are challenges left," he says. "There was this Norwegian, for instance, a nice young man—skied across Antarctica, and believe me, that's quite a feat. He's been forgotten very quickly, though, whereas the Everest climb seems destined always to be remembered." He sighs in exasperation.

Sadly, the deaths of the inexperienced amateur climbers and their guides described in Jon Krakauer's book *Into Thin Air* has only heightened interest in Everest. Then, last May, the discovery of George Mallory's body, 75 years after he and his colleague, Andrew Irvine, disappeared into the mists, has only enhanced the peak's romance and mystique. Hillary minces no words on these subjects. Even before the ill-fated *Into Thin Air* expeditions, he had argued that it was disgraceful to let wealthy "no-hopers" pay for dangerous vanity trips up the mountain. He is even angrier—"horrified"—that genuine mountaineers took money for their unsparing photographs of Mallory's frozen bones. "He should have been left to lie in peace," Hillary says.

Yet he expresses equanimity in evaluating the possibility—which most experts think remote—that Mallory and Irvine made it to the top first. "For 45 years," Hillary says, "I've been regarded as the hero of Everest, so I really couldn't be upset now if it was someone else's turn." Then, wryly: "You know, to mountaineers, it's one thing getting to the top, but another getting back to the bottom. I'll settle for that."

VII. Precious New Times and Places

Who would ever have guessed, back in the '50s, that come the millennium, interest in the mountain would far exceed that in the mile? But even though the mile was once so glamorous, today, in a metric world, it is linearly incorrect and only occasionally run. Besides, whereas once the mile was valued as a beautifully strategic race, downright theatrical, with a beginning, middle and end, now, says Craig Masback, CEO of USA Track & Field, who is himself a sub-four-minute miler, "The appeal of shorter events has increased in a society that operates in short bursts." Three minutes and 43 seconds is too long nowadays?

There is hope. Over time Bannister expects the mile record to drop to where we will have the elusive 3-1/2-minute barrier to excite us. "The critical factor now," he says, "is racial selection—in the best possible way. If you have runners from Kenya or Morocco, whose line traces back there for thousands of years, then you are going to have runners who can deal better with oxygen deprivation—and ultimately, that determines speed."

It is, perhaps, poetic justice that just as the Asian Everest has become primarily the white man's challenge—even the rich white man's hazardous playground—the eternal mile, which was so long the property of Northern European stock (Bannister's own line is French, the Norman Banistre), now belongs to the darker peoples of Africa. Perhaps in this greater universality the mile will enjoy renewed popularity after the turn of the millennium. Someday, maybe even some boy from the U.S. will risk the effort and give us one thing in sport that not even Glenn Cunningham or Jim Ryun was able to give America in the American Century—the champion miler supreme. "It's so simple, really," Bannister says with a sigh. "You just run."

If not, well, a miss is as good as 1,500 meters. But what Bannister did on his day in May, no less than what Hillary had achieved 12 months before, can never be diminished by the history that followed. For the 20th century, these two modest men will always best represent the sportsman—the Anyman—who is bold enough to seize the main chance and make good on an improbable challenge. *To do one thing supremely well.*

Alas, though the queen yet lives and the U.S. still rules the roost, the world now is probably too technological and too packaged to allow anymore for much of that independent panache. Too bad. Not even victory can ever be as precious as venturing into a time or a place that has previously denied our intrusion. "Even if I hadn't climbed Everest," Hillary says with complete assurance, "still, I know I would've lived an adventurous life."

But will anyone be able to say that about a 21st-century life? Ironically, the new wonders we create in laboratories serve only to reduce the majesty of the natural world, so that the past's adventurer becomes the present's tourist; yesterday's milestones, today's "highlights."

But what Hillary and Bannister pioneered is forever secure in the history—and the legend, too—of our whole time and place. This is especially true because both of the men who achieved these feats when they were young went on to live examined lives, full of generosity and curiosity, so that what they became serves even more to ennoble what they did once, for us all, so many springtimes ago.